WHO WOULD WIN?

KOMODO DRAGON

VS.

KING COBRA

BY
JERRY PALLOTTA

ILLUSTRATED BY
ROB BOLSTER

Scholastic Inc.

New York   Toronto   London   Auckland
Sydney   Mexico City   New Delhi   Hong Kong

The publisher would like to thank the following for their
kind permission to use their photographs in this book:

Page 16: © Jonathan and Angela Scott / NHPA / Photoshot; page 17: Animals Animals / SuperStock;
page 18: Skulls Unlimited International, Inc.; page 19: Skulls Unlimited International, Inc.;
page 20: Michael Pitts / Nature Picture Library; page 21: Gary Graham / Newspix / News Ltd.;
page 24: Andy Paradise / Rex USA; page 25: Blaine Harrington III / Corbis

Thank you to Dr. Stephen Durant, rugby player supreme!
—J.P.

Thank you to Mr. Winslow Homer.
—R.B.

ISBN 978-0-545-30171-8

12 11 10 9 8 7 6 5 4   11 12 13 14 15 16/0

Printed in the U.S.A.   40
First printing, Novermber 2011

What would happen if a tough Komodo dragon came face-to-face with a deadly king cobra? What if they were both hungry? If they had a fight, who do you think would win?

SCIENTIFIC NAME OF
KOMODO DRAGON:
"Varanus komodoensis"

Meet the Komodo dragon. The Komodo dragon is the largest lizard in the world. It grows up to ten feet long and can weigh three hundred pounds.

DEFINITION
A reptile is a cold-blooded animal covered in scales. Turtles, snakes, lizards, crocodiles, and alligators are reptiles.

FACT
Komodo dragons live on four Indonesian islands: Komodo, Rinca, Flores, and Gili Motang.

SCIENTIFIC NAME OF KING COBRA: "Ophiophagus hannah"

Meet the king cobra. A king cobra can grow up to eighteen feet long. The king cobra is a venomous snake that can weigh up to twenty pounds.

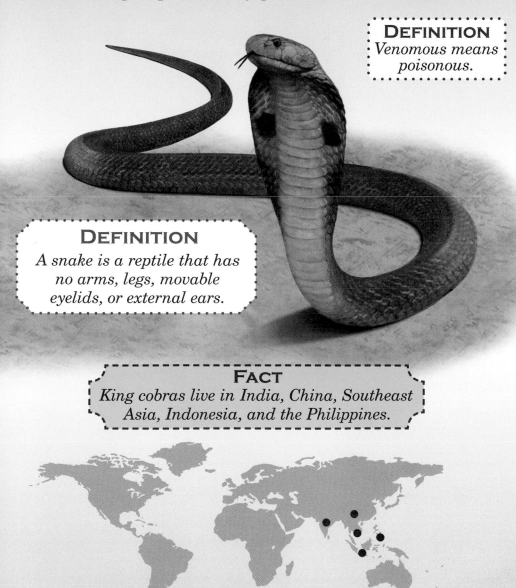

DEFINITION
Venomous means poisonous.

DEFINITION
A snake is a reptile that has no arms, legs, movable eyelids, or external ears.

FACT
King cobras live in India, China, Southeast Asia, Indonesia, and the Philippines.

TEETH

Komodo dragons have teeth. Their teeth are unusual for a land animal. They are serrated, like a shark's teeth.

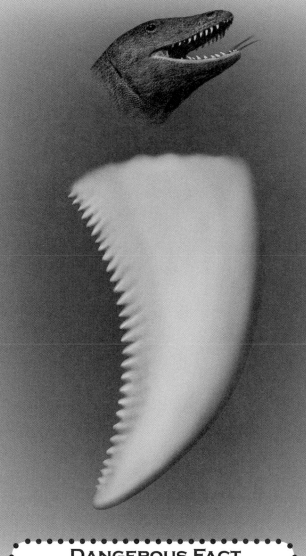

DANGEROUS FACT
Serrated means jagged, like a saw.

FANGS

King cobras have fangs. A fang is a long hollow tooth used to inject venom.

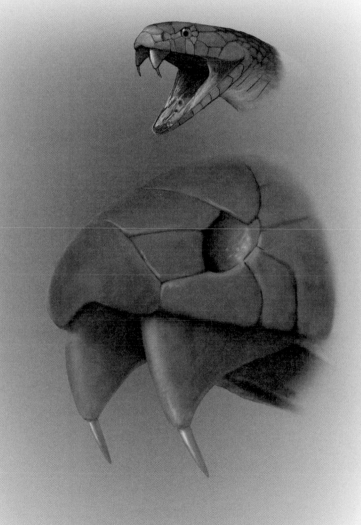

DEADLY

There are only three known poisonous lizards: the Gila monster, the Mexican beaded lizard, and the Komodo dragon. In addition to venom, the Komodo dragon has dangerous bacteria in its mouth.

DEFINITION

A lizard is a reptile with two pairs of legs and a tail.

GILA MONSTER

MEXICAN BEADED LIZARD

VENOM

A king cobra bite is deadly. A king cobra does not have the deadliest poison of all snakes. But it injects the most poison. Its poison is a neurotoxin. One king cobra bite has the strength to kill an elephant — or twenty people.

DANGEROUS DEFINITION

A neurotoxin is a poison that paralyzes its victim's nerves and muscles.

SNAKE TRIVIA

Some species of cobras can spit their venom, but a king cobra cannot.

FORKED

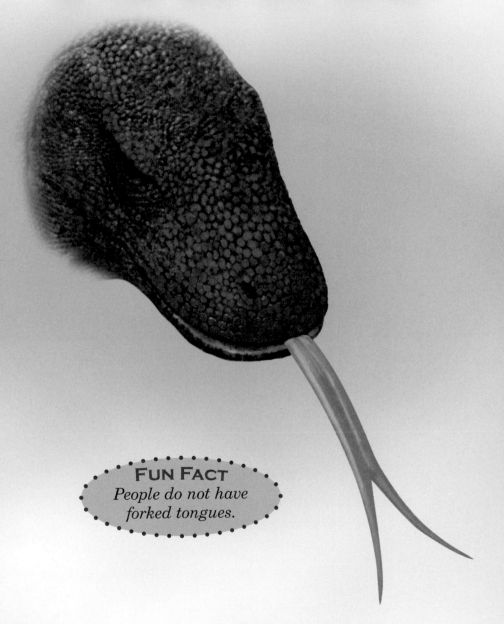

FUN FACT
*People do not have
forked tongues.*

The Komodo dragon has a forked tongue. It splits into two sides. A Komodo tongue is sensitive. When it flicks out its tongue, it can detect where a deer might be nearby.

10

TONGUES

The king cobra also has a forked tongue. It smells with its tongue. Its tongue can also sense motion and temperature.

ABSOLUTE FACT

You do not want to get bitten by a king cobra!

S C A

The skin of a Komodo dragon looks like this.

BONUS FACT
Reptiles have scales.

DID YOU KNOW?
Butterflies, moths, and most fish also have scales.

A king cobra is covered in scales. The scales are dry and not slimy. Most snakes' scales have a pattern.

The skin of a king cobra looks like this. The belly scales are the widest.

INTERESTING FACT

A group of cobras is called a quiver.

KOMODO DRAGON SKULL

This is the skull of a Komodo dragon. It looks a bit flat, like the skulls of crocodiles and alligators.

SHARP FACT

Anything that tries to escape it gets cut by the sharp side of its teeth.

WARNING!

You do NOT want to get bitten by a Komodo dragon.

OTHER KOMODO DRAGON NAMES

A Komodo dragon is also called an ora or a land crocodile.

KING COBRA SKULL

This is the skull of a king cobra. It does not have much of a skull. Its brain is mostly unprotected.

FUN FACT
The study of snakes is called ophiology or serpentology.

King cobras do not chew their food. In addition to fangs, they have small upper and lower teeth to pull food into their mouths. They swallow their prey whole.

QUESTION
Would you like to become a scientist and study snakes?

KOMODO DRAGON'S FAVORITE FOOD

Komodo dragons love to eat small mammals. They also eat lizards and snakes. They kill by tearing their prey to shreds.

GROSS FACT
Komodo dragons can easily eat half of their body weight.

DID YOU KNOW?
A Komodo dragon's venom prevents blood clotting. Its victims sometimes bleed to death.

DISGUSTING FACT
If a Komodo dragon eats too much hair, bones, nails, and scales, it coughs up a giant pellet.

KING COBRA'S FAVORITE FOOD

Snakes are the favorite food of king cobras. Their scientific name means "snake-eater."

JUST ATE		**FUN FACT**
ONE MONTH		*After eating a large meal, a king cobra might not eat again for one or two months.*
TWO MONTHS		

WITH LEGS

Look at the skeletons of the Komodo dragon and king cobra. What differences do you notice right away?

VALUABLE FACT
The government of Indonesia minted a gold coin in honor of the Komodo dragon.

The Komodo dragon has legs and toes. It also has a distinct tail.

WITHOUT LEGS

MONEY TRIVIA

This Russian cobra coin is worth ten rubles. Ten rubles are worth about thirty-five cents.

The king cobra has no legs, fingers, or toes. It has many ribs, making its body look like one long tail.

NEWLY

Mother Komodo dragons lay about twenty-five eggs per clutch. Komodo dragon babies live in trees. They eat bugs, small lizards, rodents, and eggs.

DEFINITION
A clutch is a group of eggs laid by birds or reptiles.

GROSS FACT
Young Komodo dragons roll in animal waste to protect themselves.

BORN

Here is a king cobra baby. A king cobra is the only snake that makes a nest. It looks like a bird's nest.

KING COBRA TRIVIA

After making a nest, mother king cobras lay between twenty and fifty eggs at a time.

STRANGE BEHAVIOR

DID YOU KNOW?
Baby Komodo dragons are born with stripes that disappear when they grow up.

A Komodo dragon sometimes eats its own children. Young Komodos are smart enough to escape up a tree.

MORE STRANGE BEHAVIOR

A king cobra can spread its rib bones and make itself appear larger. This behavior is called making a hood.

HOOD!

NO HOOD!

> ### FUN FACT
> *The design on the back of this king cobra's head are called spectacle markings.*

ZOO

You can see a Komodo dragon in some zoos. The experience can be disappointing, because reptiles spend many hours never moving.

INTERESTING FACT

The branch of zoology that studies reptiles is called herpetology.

QUESTION

Would you like to become a herpetologist?

PETS

If you travel to India or Thailand, you might see a street performer doing tricks with a cobra.

FUN FACT
Some people have king cobras and other snakes for pets.

The Komodo dragon walks around looking for food. If hungry, he would eat almost any animal. He doesn't notice the king cobra under nearby grass.

INTERESTING FACT
Of all the animals on Earth, the Komodo dragon probably most resembles the look and walk of a dinosaur.

The cobra has no interest in the Komodo dragon. Snakes like to eat things they can swallow whole. The Komodo dragon is way too big!

The Komodo dragon wanders a bit too close. The cobra raises its head, spreads its hood, and makes a growling sound. It is a warning to back off!

The cobra just wants to be left alone. The Komodo dragon circles around some more.

YIKES!
Not only can the king cobra slither on the ground, it can also swim and climb trees.

The clumsy Komodo dragon steps on the cobra's eggs by accident. The cobra strikes fast, biting the leg of the intruder! As soon as the cobra's fangs sink into the Komodo dragon's leg, they unload their venom.

The Komodo dragon walks a few steps, then starts to breathe heavily. Its legs get wobbly. It can't see, gets dizzy, and falls over.

The king cobra has killed the Komodo dragon with one deadly bite! Maybe next time, the Komodo dragon will bite first.

WHO HAS THE ADVANTAGE? CHECKLIST

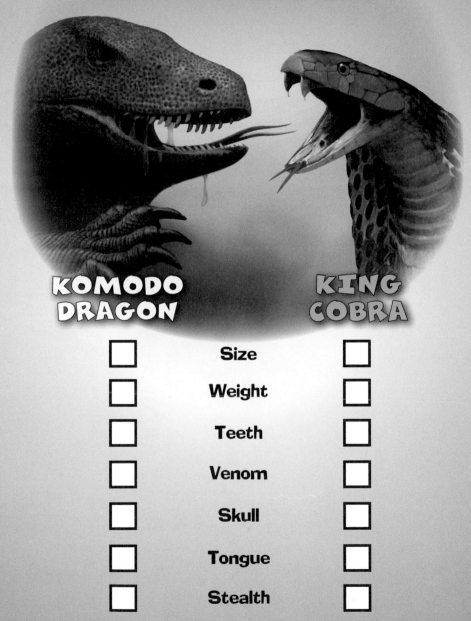

KOMODO DRAGON		KING COBRA
☐	Size	☐
☐	Weight	☐
☐	Teeth	☐
☐	Venom	☐
☐	Skull	☐
☐	Tongue	☐
☐	Stealth	☐

Author note: This is one way the fight might have ended.
How would you write the ending?

Gabriel P. Chang

JULIA MACDONNELL's fiction has been published in many literary magazines, and her story "Soy Paco" was nominated for a Pushcart Prize. Her journalism has been featured in *The Boston Globe*, the New York *Daily News*, and *The Columbia Journalism Review*, among other publications. A tenured professor at Rowan University, she is the nonfiction editor of *Philadelphia Stories*. This is her first novel in twenty years.

Also by
Julia MacDonnell

A YEAR OF FAVOR

Praise for
Mimi Malloy, At Last!

"Humorous and poignant . . . MacDonnell captures perfectly the family dynamics between sisters, mothers, and daughters, as if she were sitting in on their gab sessions, taking copious notes. For readers who enjoy Maeve Binchy and Rosamunde Pilcher, this is a highly engaging family chronicle, with a healthy dose of Irish history laced in as well." —*Booklist*

"Julia MacDonnell treats her characters with sympathy while never failing to show their flaws. . . . Highly recommended."
—*Blogcritics* (Editors' Choice)

"Lightened by her sharp wit, feisty Mimi's saga is a sometimes troubling but ultimately triumphant tale of aging, the Boston Irish immigrant experience, and redemption. . . . [*Mimi Malloy, At Last!*] will appeal to anyone who loves a good story with a strong heroine."
—*Library Journal*

"With every word, Julia MacDonnell carries us along as she tells an utterly engaging story of family, loss, heartache, love, and second chances. In *Mimi Malloy, At Last!*, we cheer Mimi on as she faces her later years with both fear and courage, confronting memories of her painful childhood and frayed relationships with her daughters and sisters. Full of healing, hope, and, yes, romance, this may be the book that convinces you that the best really is yet to come!"
—Susan Gregg Gilmore, author of *The Funeral Dress*
and *Looking for Salvation at the Dairy Queen*

"I love Mimi! . . . Julia MacDonnell's fluent writing beautifully observes the iniquities of old age and the complexities of family. But also the benefits of both. What a wonderful book."
—Hilary Boyd, author of *Thursdays in the Park*

"With sensitivity and humor, Julia MacDonnell paints a rich and engrossing family portrait in this delectable novel. Mimi Malloy—feisty, determined, and courageous—confronts her heart-wrenching past and opens herself up to an unexpected future. I loved falling into this story with a triumphant woman at its core."

—Katharine Davis, author of *Capturing Paris*
and *A Slender Thread*

"I gulped down Julia MacDonnell's juicy novel of revealed memories and startling characters. . . . Mimi proves that some revelations take living long enough to have. Extraordinary."

—Molly Peacock, author of *The Paper Garden*

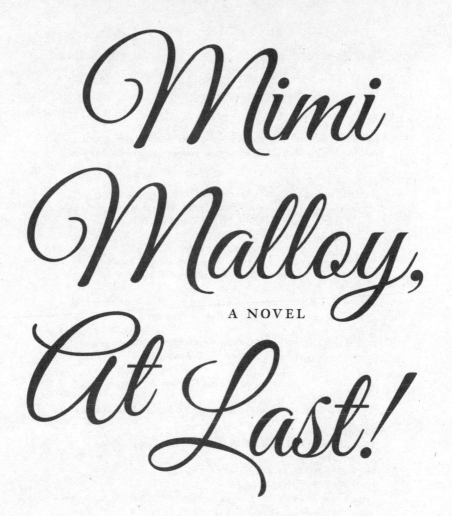

Mimi Malloy, At Last!

A NOVEL

Julia MacDonnell

PICADOR   NEW YORK

MIMI MALLOY, AT LAST! Copyright © 2014 by Julia MacDonnell. All rights reserved. Printed in the United States of America. For information, address Picador, 175 Fifth Avenue, New York, N.Y. 10010.

www.picadorusa.com
www.twitter.com/picadorusa • www.facebook.com/picadorusa
picadorbookroom.tumblr.com

Picador® is a U.S. registered trademark and is used by St. Martin's Press under license from Pan Books Limited.

For book club information, please visit www.facebook.com/picadorbookclub or e-mail marketing@picadorusa.com.

Designed by Anna Gorovoy

The Library of Congress has cataloged the hardcover edition as follows:

MacDonnell, Julia.
    Mimi Malloy, at last!: a novel / Julia MacDonnell. — First Edition.
        pages cm
    ISBN 978-1-250-04154-8 (hardcover)
    ISBN 978-1-250-04155-5 (e-book)
    1. Retirement—Fiction.   2. Life change events—Fiction.   3. Memories—
Fiction.   4. Family life—Fiction.   5. Domestic fiction.   I. Title.
    PS3563.A29142M56 2014
    813'.54—dc23

                                                                2013021147

Picador Paperback ISBN 978-1-250-06377-9

Picador books may be purchased for educational, business, or promotional use. For information on bulk purchases, please contact the Macmillan Corporate and Premium Sales Department at 1-800-221-7945, extension 5442, or write to specialmarkets@macmillan.com.

First published in the United States by Picador

First Picador Paperback Edition: April 2015

10   9   8   7   6   5   4   3   2   1

In memory of
Meg Felice, Veronica, Denise
Wondrous women who left too soon

Mimi Malloy, At Last!

One

TOO CLOSE FOR
COMFORT

I'm at my table by the window, watching, without wanting to, other tenants rush off to work, bundled up against the frigid morning—running to catch the T, or starting their cars, warming them up in the parking lot before they take off for offices, stores, banks, schools, hospitals, wherever, just the way I used to, not so long ago. The only work I'm doing now is on my first cup, Maxwell House Master Blend, and a True Blue, lit with the last match from a splint book picked up at Grab & Go. I'm enjoying the first drag, if not the scenery, when, like an alarm, my phone rings. I check the time. Just past eight. I let it ring a few more times. It's got to be Cassandra, my firstborn. This time of day, she works on her to-do list, at the top of which is my name, my life, her plans to make it better scribbled underneath.

"Mimi, there's an open house tomorrow at that new seniors' complex, Squantum River Living." She's breathing hard, like she's just won the Powerball, but me, I could spit fire.

"Squantum River Living," I echo. Just read about it in the *Patriot-Ledger*, in a special senior living section. Plus she already sent me a brochure.

"It's a great new place for seniors, subsidized too."

I swear, at times like this Cassandra's voice works on me like a dental drill.

"Let's go. It'll be fun."

"I already know all I want to know about that place."

Squantum River Living, an environmentally friendly low-rise development with three wings and solar panels on the roof. Three wings. What kind of creature has three wings? One wing is for the so-called active, independent living; the next is for transitional living, meaning one foot in the grave; and the last is an assisted living part, meaning they're only too happy to help you put the other foot in. After that, I figure, they can dump you into the river that runs through the property. Squantum River. No fuss, no muss. If you're lucky, you'll just float away.

"Squantum River Dying, that's what they ought to call it."

"You're so negative."

"Am not!"

Evicting Mimi from her home: a pot boiling on Cassandra's front burner ever since I lost my federal civil service position over at the VA Hospital in Jamaica Plain. Since I began living on a fixed income, fixed just above the poverty line—enough so you can survive, but not enough to have much fun—Cassandra's been trying to get me out of here.

"You're going to be broke in a couple of years."

"My money situation's not your problem."

"It will be when you don't have any."

"MYOB," I say, louder than I intended, but maybe the high volume will get through to her.

Instead, she starts sniffling. I made her cry. I'm so cruel to her, one of my many sins, my shortcomings. Not that my apartment is so great. Just three rooms—not enough space for many visitors and certainly not enough for a family party. But it's in a sweet garden apartment complex called Centennial Square, near downtown Quincy. I'm on the lower level—below grade, I think they call it—so the view isn't all that great, but the rent is cheaper. Plenty of windows, though. Those in the living room are level with my chest. Mostly what I see are my neighbors' feet when they're rushing off to work and home again. But it's mine. All mine. I don't have to share, and I don't have to take care of anyone else. The slightest little problem I have and Duffy, the super here, will come to fix it. A more reliable guy you couldn't find anywhere on the South Shore. I come and go as I please. No one criticizes me.

"Next question, baby." I'm nicer this time, certain Cassandra's got another item on her list or she'd have hung up by now.

"Did you get the questionnaire?" She's still breathing hard, as if the future of the planet depends upon my answer. "The questionnaire," she repeats, louder, like I'm deaf instead of only dumb.

"The questionnaire?"

"Oh, Mimi!" she wails in a way that tells me I've failed, yet again, to meet her standards of behavior and intelligence. "You've got a mind like a sieve."

"Do not." I picture one of those utensils, full of little holes, with a scalding liquid—soup, say—pouring through and the big chunks getting stuck. "It's just a senior moment. I'm entitled."

"Next thing you know, your senior moments will be stretching into days and you'll end up like Aunt Lillian. Anyway, you know darn well what I'm talking about, Aunt Patty's questionnaire. For the family history. The genealogy, a gift to our children. She sent it out last week."

Right, right. It comes back to me. My sister Patty, egged on by one of her grandsons, a gifted little prince—her words—came up with a plan to write our family history. Patty, of all people, who can't even write a postcard from Disney World.

"Oh, sure, the questionnaire," I say, though I haven't actually seen it. Most likely it's in the basket of mail on the table by my front door. With the ads for lube jobs and commemorative coins from the Franklin Mint, and solicitations from the Society for the Propagation of the Faith.

I've got a system: At about four each afternoon, I walk out to the foyer of my building and pick up my mail from its locked cubby. Back in my apartment, in my own little foyer, I drop it all into a basket, a pretty basket with apples printed on it. Unless I have an overwhelming urge to open something, which I rarely ever do, it goes into the trash bag on Monday night when I'm on my way out to the Dumpster. Cuts down on clutter and wasted time. The system works, as long as you remember to look for your rebates and Social Security check.

"Look in that pile by your front door." Cassie, bossy as always. She's like my ex, thinking that she, and she alone, can make the world run smoothly. "It's probably in there."

"OK, sure. If it's there, I'll call you back."

I hang up and finish my coffee and have another smoke before checking the mail. I'm in no hurry, in no mood to obey Cassandra's commands. I've got to take her in small doses, like bitter medicine for a chronic, low-grade pain. Besides, the last thing on my to-do list is Patty's genealogy. No interest in it whatsoever. I'm not the type to get all hot and bothered about the past. I look ahead, pride myself on it. Whatever might befall you, get over it, move on. That's how I've lived my life and raised my girls. Or, rather, how I've tried to raise them despite the constant undermining influence of John Francis Xavier Malloy, aka Jack, said ex.

The basket's on a table in the hallway with a mirror hanging over it, both the table and mirror left behind by the previous tenants when I moved in here fifteen years ago. I finger through the mail. A flyer for Senior Fun Day at a local wellness center, another for golden-age tai chi classes at the Y. *Lubricate your joints! Improve your balance! Find serenity!* Oh, and that damned brochure for Squantum River Warehouse for People Past Their Use-By Date. No questionnaire. Typical Patty—a day late, a dollar short.

That's when I catch sight of myself in the mirror. Is that woman really me? A fading brunette, well padded, and well past her prime. When I flip on the hallway light, it's worse. Mimi, all alone. Mimi Malloy by herself. Then, behind the old me, I see the shapely brunette I used to be, the one with the tiny waist and the dimpled smile, the one Jack Malloy fell in love with oh so long ago. Maire Sheehan, aka Mimi. *Little Mimi, I love you so.*

The mirror whispers something I've known for ages: I'm no longer the fairest of them all. Not a by long shot. Jowls around my chin line. Love handles, but no love. When I lean in closer, I find that one long hair, a whisker, growing out of my chin on the left side, white and thick as thread. I pluck it every couple of weeks, but it grows back every time. Sometimes I forget til one of my daughters sees it, screams, and goes running for the tweezers.

I flip the light back off.

Back when my daughters were growing up, I was the envy of all the other mothers. *Oh, Mimi, how do you do it?* they raved after every one of my pregnancies. *That shape with all those little girls.*

Chasing after children, all day, every day, I used to joke. *That's my diet plan.* The truth is I didn't dare gain an ounce. Gaining weight was not an option. A month after every birth, as soon as I stopped bleeding, Jack wanted me back in my straight skirts and high heels, my white maillot if it was summer. His fantasy was that I could be mistaken for Liz Taylor. I never dared to let myself go, which is exactly what my daughters have accused me of ever since I left him. *Oh, Mimi, you've really let yourself go.*

All women lose their looks. Sooner or later. It's inevitable, like sun in morning, moon at night. No female escapes, no matter how much time or money she's got to spend on herself. Most women, though, lose their looks in bits and pieces, a wrinkle here, an extra pound or two there, then the drooping boobs, the sagging bottom, the thinning hair and thickening waist. But me, I lost them all at once—here today, gone tomorrow—the same way I once lost a good watch and then a pair of rosary beads Jack had given me, no clue about their worth until I realized they were gone for good. I was forty-nine, hadn't even started the Change, when they cut me open and scooped me out like an old fruit. My female organs, turned into medical waste, carted off in a red plastic bucket to be incinerated who knows where. It was all those babies, six, Jack wanted me to have and then left me to care for— one of whom, Malvina, the nurses held inside me, squeezing my legs together until the doctor showed up twenty minutes later. The trouble with my girl parts started then. So they tell me.

But I didn't let myself go. Never, ever let myself go. If I let myself go, what would I be left with? Nada. Instead, I was erased. No more wolf whistles when I walked along the beach. No men making way so I could get into line ahead of them at the bank or the post office, or helping me put the groceries into the car. They didn't see me anymore. I'd disappeared.

The mirror's some type of fake filigree, with gold, curly things around the edges, not my taste at all. I reach for it, wonder why I haven't thought of this before: Take the damned thing down! Who needs reminders? I'll put up a pretty picture, say of children picking flowers in a meadow. I've seen some nice ones at Kmart. Or an arrangement of my grandkids' school pictures. That's it! Right here in the front hall. That would shut my daughters up, all their complaints about how I don't display the grandkids' pictures properly. That I don't show enough interest in the grandkids, don't love them enough.

I get my stepstool from the kitchen so I can grasp the mirror better. It weighs a ton. The wall behind it is pure white, the rest of the walls tinged yellow from my True Blues. "Imagine what they're doing to your lungs!" Cass would say if she were here, and then probably make a note of it to share with her sisters. I lug the mirror into my bedroom, stopping every couple of steps to catch my breath. I rest it against my bed while I look for a place to store it.

My bedroom has a big closet all along one wall. I use the closest half for my everyday things and the far half for storage, which is plenty for me. I'm not a saver or a keeper, not a pack rat like most of my sisters and my kids, who cannot bear to part with anything. I have a place for everything, and keep everything in its place. No skeletons in my closets, nor any dust bunnies, either, thank you very much. Crazy clean, my daughters say. I prefer to say I travel light.

I slide open the door on the far end of the closet. Click, the sensor light goes on. Love it! Plenty of room for the mirror. I'm sliding it in when a drop of water hits my head. I stand there for a minute, waiting for another, just to prove to myself that I'm not loony. Sure enough, another drop falls. This time, it hits the mirror. Splat! It slides down the glass, reflecting itself. Another hits my head, then another. *Rain-drops keep falling on my head.* . . . One of my ex's favorite songs. I look up and see a wet stain in the upper corner. I look down and see the carpet's sopping wet. Good lord, we've sprung a leak! Probably in the bathroom of the upstairs apartment.

I let go of the mirror, go into the kitchen. I keep the number of our super right by the phone. Dick Duffy, a World War II combat vet, a widower and one of the nicest guys you'll ever meet. I dial him up, get the answering machine. I give him my name and my apartment number, though no doubt he knows them both by heart. "I hope you'll get here soon," I say. "I don't want to be swept out in a flood in the middle of the night."

Two

FLY ME TO
THE MOON

This morning, I ran out to Kmart for some plastic sheeting to cover things in the closet. Otherwise, I hung around all day, listening to the drips and waiting for Dick Duffy's call. Last night, I hardly slept, hearing the water plunking—drip, drip, drip—into the saucepan I put in the closet, on top of a couple of folded-up towels to absorb the puddle. Every couple of hours, I had to empty the pot. The leak kept getting worse. And the entire time I listened to it, I heard my daughters, one after the other, accusing me of letting myself go. I thought about broken pipes, falling plaster; about deterioration—a word my daughters have used to describe my mind, and one I've used myself when I think about my own body, full of parts that are wearing out and breaking down.

But I will not breathe a word about this leaking pipe. If I tell Cassandra, she'll declare the entire complex substandard and ramp up her campaign to get me out of here. She'll gather the others—Celestine, Ruth Ann, Siobhan, and Delilah—and incite them to riot against me. My own daughters.

Usually Duffy calls right back, though I've rarely had a problem in this place. I go outside to check his parking spot, but it's empty. It's almost dusk, so cold I can hardly catch my breath, an early dark New England night a moment or two away. Maybe he's abandoned us for good, Duffy. If so, the whole complex, the pride of our neighborhood, Callahan's Corner, would go down the tubes in a heartbeat. Complete deterioration! Inside, the drip, drip, drip continues, pushing me closer to the edge. I'll sleep out on the couch tonight.

On my way back inside, I check my mailbox, and, sure enough, it's stuffed with a big fat envelope with extra postage. The questionnaire. I squelch the urge to trash it. Cassandra would hand my head to me on a platter. Instead, I place it on the table next to the basket, beneath the empty white rectangle on my wall where the mirror used to be.

Around suppertime, I mix myself a Manhattan, straight up, and put on my favorite CD, *The Very Good Years*. My Friday routine. My boy Frankie croons to me from the overpriced Bose Wave thingy my grandkids gave me last Christmas, all of them chipping in. Oh, but I've got to admit Frankie sounds divine, like he's right here in the room with me!

I settle onto my sofa and turn on the news, but without the sound. I like to watch it while listening to Sinatra. Nobody knows, so I don't have to explain. Though I can't help reading some of the headlines crawling along the bottom of the screen. Tonight, pedophiles were arrested in a kiddy-porn ring just north of Beantown. They're everywhere these days, those child molesters. I shut the TV off—too depressing. I try calling a couple of my daughters, first Ruth Ann in New Hampshire, then Delilah in Andover. I even think about calling Malvina, my lost child in the Bronx, but I don't have her number. We haven't spoken for years.

Then I try calling my sisters, but they, too, are out or not answering. Only four of us left, the remainders of the glorious Sheehan girls. That's what they used to call us when we were growing up, *those glorious Sheehan girls*. The way the old folks said it, their Irish accents thick as clotted cream, it sounded like a prayer.

So I'm stuck by myself with my Manhattan, the leak in my closet, and my thoughts about deterioration; Ol' Blue Eyes singing to me and the bad news shut inside the TV. I light up, enjoying the cigarette even more because it's forbidden fruit, my daughters and surviving sisters unified in their determination to get me to quit. Next thing you know, there's a knock of my door and, sure enough, Dick Duffy's calling through it, "Mrs. Malloy, oh, Mrs. Malloy."

I snuff out my cigarette and hide what's left of my Manhattan in the sink. Don't want Duffy to think I'm a lush, drinking alone on a Friday night. I open the door, and there he is, Dick Duffy with his nice smile and his bum leg—an old war wound, they say. He's wearing one of those jumpsuits with snaps up the front, his name stitched over the pocket on his chest. He's got a metal toolbox in one hand and a small stepladder in the other. His silver hair is slicked back nicely, and when the smell of his Old Spice gets me where I live, I realize that the Manhattan has gone straight to my head.

"Sorry I couldn't get here sooner, Mrs. Malloy," he says, his voice just above a whisper, his South Boston accent thick as chowder. "Family business. Now, let me see that leak. We'll get it fixed for you right away. If I'm not mistaken, it's the cold-water pipe in the bathroom upstairs. That's what goes through your bedroom closet."

I like Duffy's manners, the way he's always so respectful.

"Come on in," I say, sounding like a game-show host, proud of how I keep my place picture-perfect, even when I'm not expecting company. I take him into the bedroom, to the storage end of the closet. Right away, he opens his toolbox, takes out a big flashlight, and shines it up into the corner.

"Hmm, yup, there she is," he mutters.

I lean in close to him to see the big wet spot in the corner, more of a seepage than a leak, with the wall and ceiling looking as soggy as a sponge. The little drips spill down into the saucepan.

Duffy grunts and hums and hmms, then says he'll do some first aid until he can get a plumber. He climbs up on the ladder to get to work and I sit on my bed to watch. A man in my bedroom. More excitement than I've had in years. Duffy's mostly hidden, standing on the ladder with his head stuck up in the corner, while Frankie says he gets a kick out of me, then begs to be flown to the moon where we can play among the stars.

"You like Sinatra?" Duffy asks from far away.

"Oh, he's the best. He's my boy." Like Frankie's an old friend, living just around the corner, not all the way across the continent.

"Saw him once, out in Vegas."

"No kidding? Lucky devil."

"At the old Desert Inn, before they tore it down." He twists this way and that, his head and shoulders missing. "Great show. My wife, Virginia, she was already sick, but it was what she wanted more than anything. To see Sinatra in concert. So I took her. Worth every penny."

Next thing I know, the top shelf collapses, snaps in two. Cheap fiberboard. Knocks Duffy off the ladder. He stumbles backward, landing on his bottom on my floor. The shelf and its contents explode above him. I grab a big piece of shelf before it lands on his head, lose my own balance, and almost fall on top of him. I use the shelf to keep myself upright and burst out laughing. Duffy laughs too, thank God.

"You OK?" I put down the shelf and try to help him up. He doesn't need it, but he doesn't push my hands away when I grab one of his arms and pull.

"My pride, Mrs. M, that's all that's hurt."

"Who needs pride anyway?"

"It's an occupational hazard. I'm used to it."

We stand looking at each other for a moment. He's grinning, but his smile doesn't quite make it all the way through his eyes. Standing closer to him than I ever have before, I see a dark layer there, an unlighted place.

"Hey, you better sit down," I say. "You really took a spill. Let me get you something to drink. How about a cup of coffee?"

"I'd love a cup."

"I could use some myself."

I lead him back into the living room, gesture to a seat at the table by my window. I go brew us up some Maxwell House and put on another Sinatra CD, *Songs for Swingin' Lovers!* Once I'm seated at the table, the two of us take out our butts. Duffy lights my True Blue with his Zippo. With Duffy, unlike when I'm with my kids, I don't feel like I'm committing a mortal sin by lighting up.

"Great coffee," he says, sipping from a yellow mug.

"It's the percolator," I say. "Takes longer than those electric drips, but it really brings out the flavor."

We drink our coffee and smoke and gab a little, listening to Sinatra. *I've got you under my skin.* For the past few years, whenever we run into each other outside and the weather's nice enough, Duffy and I'll sit together on one of the benches in the courtyard and share a smoke and small talk. Duffy, with his bum leg and his big heart. That's how I've always thought of him. Sometimes, though, when I see him drag that leg around, I think he's also dragging sadness—that same sadness I glimpsed just a moment ago in his eyes, an unending sadness he can't do anything about.

"How long ago did you lose your wife?" I'm thinking he might like to talk about it, since he brought it up.

"Almost twenty-five years. But sometimes it still feels like yesterday."

"You never got over it," I say, and he looks up at me, that extra layer even darker.

"No, I never did. Had a couple of boys to raise. Me, a combat vet, but it was still rough. Two boys. Give me war any day."

"I'm the mother of six. Six girls. So I hear ya."

"Six? Mrs. Malloy's the mother of six? Wow." He shakes his head, smiling his nice smile, this time his eyes bright and twinkling.

I'm a sucker for a compliment. I can't help preening a little. "One of them, Cassandra, comes by a lot. She's always trying to run my life."

"The one who drives the Bimmer? Well put-together?"

"The very same."

"I've got one of those too," he says. "The run-your-life type. My oldest. Always coming up with a better way for me to live. Wants me to move up to Vermont, near him, but I figure it's cold enough here. Besides, we're near the water."

"Yes, the water." One of the big attractions of the South Shore: the Atlantic, just a couple of blocks away, plus countless bays and inlets here and there, the Fore River, the Back River. When the wind's right, you can smell the nice fresh salt air. I'm out there walking every sunny day in the summer.

"And the other one, where does he live?"

"Bridgewater. Over in Bridgewater."

"A state college and a state prison," I say, but he doesn't add anything. "Hey, how about a sandwich, grilled ham and cheese?"

"Sure, Mrs. Malloy, thanks."

His smile is so sweet. I get right to work. While I'm cooking, he goes back into the bedroom closet and does something to the leaky pipe. *You make me feel so young*, Sinatra croons, and I laugh to myself. All the years I've lived here, and all the favors Duffy's done me, and I've never had him in for a bite to eat. The sandwiches turn out great—he eats two, while I settle for one.

"Now, how about that front-hall mirror?" he asks while we're chowing down. "I'll put it back up for you?"

My turn for a funny look. "Oh, that." I feel like he's held his Zippo to my cheeks. "I'm going to put up a display of my grandkids' pictures instead. My daughters are always nagging me."

A convincing fib, I think, but the way Duffy looks at me, I can tell he's found me out. My cheeks burn hotter. "That's how I found the leak, when I was putting the mirror away."

"Well, thank God for small favors," he says, which seems to me to have at least two meanings.

Just to change the subject, I tell him about Patty's nutty plan to write our family's history. I show him the unopened envelope. "You know, a genealogy," I say, "going back to before we even came here. My sisters and my kids are all excited about it, but me, I'm not one to dwell on the past. Water under the dam."

"The bridge, Mrs. Malloy."

He looks at me like maybe he hasn't seen me before or is seeing something new about me—good or bad, I cannot tell. I wonder, can't help it, if I've ever really looked at him. "Water goes over the dam, under the bridge."

He moves his hands to demonstrate.

"Whatever. What's done is done, in my opinion."

"Can't argue with that," he says. "One of my sons is a Civil War nut, a reenactor. Gettysburg. For the life of me, I can't understand getting all dressed up in wool uniforms and going back there every July. Risking heat stroke to reenact a bloodbath."

"It happened, what, over a hundred and thirty years ago? The North won. Yippee. Get over it."

Duffy cracks up.

"Of course," I add, "you can't live in Quincy, the City of Presidents—"

"Or anywhere else in the Boston area," he interrupts.

"—without running into history on a daily basis. You run out to fill a script for your arthritis medication, and you pass the Josiah Quincy House, with all those plaques and such."

"The City of Presidents," Duffy repeats. "The Adamses and John Hancock born and raised here. A battle in the Revolutionary War fought where the CVS now stands. Oh, and don't forget this place. Built in 1976, and called Centennial Square." He laughs and lights up. "Every building named for a Revolutionary War hero."

"To think, I've been living in Paul Revere for better than a decade."

"Patrick Henry for me. Since the complex opened."

"And don't forget Dunks," I throw in. "The City of Presidents is also the birthplace of Dunkin' Donuts."

"And Howard Johnson's."

"Wow, that's right. How could I forget Ho-Jo's? But that's honest-to-goodness history." I light up too. "Not the kind my sisters love gabbing about, the goings-on in some long-gone branch of the family. The Sheehan sisters, with the exception of yours truly, are charter members of what I call the Yik Yak Club. Whenever they call it into session, they get all hot and bothered. And now they plan to write it all down, preserve it for posterity."

Duffy grins.

"I kid you not," I tell him. "And a couple of my daughters can't wait to join."

Duffy's chuckles, then grinds out his cigarette.

"That was swell, Mrs. Malloy," he says. Maybe it's my imagination, but there seems to be a little extra sparkle in his eyes. I see him to the door.

Once I've opened it, he steps right through, like he's in a rush. He makes his way down the hall, with his ladder and his toolbox, listing to the right due to that old war wound.

"I'm sure glad you weren't swept out on a flood in the middle of the night, Mrs. Malloy," he calls, not looking back.

My bedroom's a disaster, stuff from the broken shelf scattered everywhere. Gotta clean up right away, that's just how I am. Won't sleep a wink unless it's done. Going through the mess, I come across photo albums of family events from years and years ago. I'll pass them on to my girls, since I never look at them. Stacks of summer clothes and purses. You'd think I'd recognize everything, but I don't. Everything looks different, out of place. A golf visor decorated with pink flowers in puff paint, though I've never golfed, and I've got no plans to do so. A school craft project from one of my grandkids. I toss it into the trash. A lacy Victoria's Secret thong, XL, given to me by Delilah when I lost my job, like I'd retired by choice. "You're a free woman now," she said. "Go have some fun." Ha-ha-ha. I wouldn't be caught dead in that thing, with the string between your cheeks, your girl parts barely covered. The price tag's still on, $15.99 for a tiny scrap of silk. That, too, goes in the trash. I'd be too embarrassed to send it to Goodwill. Most puzzling of all is a little velvet pouch near the closet door. I pick it up, open it. Inside is a pendant, a large and clear blue pendant set in filigreed silver. You could pin it on a collar, or hang it from a chain. It looks really old, just the type of thing I wouldn't save, and it knocks me onto my butt—I follow Duffy's route straight down. A beautiful blue pendant. No idea where it came from. When I go to bed, I set it on top of its pouch and place it on my bedside table.

Three

I GOTTA RIGHT TO
SING THE BLUES

They say birth, death, and taxes are the only certain things in life, but in my case, you can add one more thing to the list: Cassandra, calling up and butting in; I'm shocked that she hasn't called already. It's gotten worse since I was "riffed." Yes, the federal civil service came up with this new word to use when they started firing people, a euphemism for the massive "reduction in (labor) force" that happened when the president was on his way out the door—his promise to create a kinder, gentler nation out the door with him, a lame duck if ever there was one.

"Enjoy your retirement," the HR supervisor told me with her anchorwoman smile, her blond bob all neat and shiny, and her Volvo in a reserved spot just outside the door. "You've earned it."

Yeah, right, I thought. What would you know about my life and what I have or haven't earned?

"Do some volunteer work," she suggested, volunteer work being so good for the soul. "You could be one of the president's thousands of points of light, shining out there in the darkness," she said.

"I prefer a paycheck," I told her.

I never missed work. I was never late. I was promoted five times in fifteen years and earned many federal civil service citations for my diligence. I took pride in my work. Then, all of a sudden, I was out—knowing that if I were young and built, I'd still have a paycheck. But I didn't have the means to fight it. You've got to pick and choose your battles. Learned that long ago.

For the first time in my life, I had time on my hands, and I hated it. I couldn't wrap my mind around the concept of not working anymore, me, a divorcée and an empty-nester, with no more kids at home to worry about 24/7. How would I fill up my days? I filled out an application for Kmart and another to work at the Hallmark card store down the street. God knows I could use the income, not to mention the employee discounts for all the gifts I have to buy. I've heard it's even better than my senior discount.

But when Kmart called me to work the Christmas season, I turned them down. Decided it wasn't worth the aggravation, not for minimum wage at my age. I don't like driving on the highways anymore, or facing so many people every day. Quincy's surrounded now, Routes 128, 3, 3A, 93, and I-95 all twisting and looping around one another, merging and splitting away, clogged with SUVs and tractor trailers and nobody yielding. Terrible traffic, all hours of the day and night. Too many cars and too many people driving them too fast, many of them with these car phones stuck to their ears, blabbering away, paying no attention to the road, and then there's me, a nervous nanny in a Dodge Shadow. I couldn't keep up and I knew it. So I said thanks but no thanks to Kmart, and now I'm stuck here without enough to do, Cassie and her sidekicks forever scheming and butting in.

Sure enough, I'm no sooner settled into my La-Z-Boy recliner with another cup of coffee, holding that mysterious blue pendant I found last night, when she calls.

"Such a nice day," she says. "What are you up to?" Nosy, as always. And I can guess what's coming next—she's trying to set me up with a fitness routine.

"Same old."

"You ought to get out, go for a walk," she says. "Get your exercise."

"You know my exercise, honey, getting up out of bed; heaving myself off the sofa to go get a snack."

"Very funny, Mimi. You know what the doctor said. Have you been taking your blood-pressure medication?"

"Check." I hate being at the top of her to-do list, and also, at times, the victim of her mood swings, up one day and down the next.

"Let's go for a walk by the water. Maybe Wollaston?"

"OK, sure, why not," I say, because I can't figure out how to say no fast enough. And I do enjoy walking by the water.

Waiting for Cass to come get me, I recall bits and pieces of a dream from the night before, that two of my late sisters, Eden and Alberta—the top of the line, they used to joke—sneaked into my bedroom and left that sapphire pendant on the floor, right where they knew I'd find it. My old sweethearts. It was crazy, the day I moved in here—my sisters and my daughters, at least half a dozen of them, helping. Mass confusion with everyone running around, shoving stuff here and there. No doubt some things slipped through without me seeing them, like the little pouch holding the blue pendant. That part's a no-brainer. And I know that my dearly departeds, Eden and Alberta, didn't leave it in the middle of the night. I'm not that far gone yet. But how did I get the thing in the first place? That's the real question. As I sit there looking at it, I get this feeling that it must be part of me, a deep part, though I don't have a clue about it. And when I realize I don't have a clue, and wouldn't know where to find one, I want to cry, a feeling I haven't had for years. Not since Malvina said good-bye and really meant it. Not since Dr. Jack F. X. Malloy flew down to Santo Domingo and divorced me, then married the bookkeeper in his office, the blonde I call Miss Piggy, and the two of them honeymooned in Punta Cana on some all-inclusive deal at an oceanside resort. Not since I found out my two youngest, Siobhan and Delilah, had forged my signature on several legal documents, helping Jack hide our assets during the divorce so I wouldn't get my fair share. The urge to cry, something on the inside pushing to get out, but not a single tear.

Mimi with her heart of stone. That's what my sisters and my kids call me because of all the weddings, graduations, baptisms, and First Communions I've been to without shedding a tear, as well as my generally even temperament throughout the rest of life's ups and downs. Mimi with her iron constitution, her heart of stone. But sometimes I'd like nothing better than a good cry. Maybe I cried myself out when I was growing up, no more tears left inside.

Cass shows up in two-hundred-dollar sneakers and some kind of jogging suit that shines and rustles when she moves. Her blond hair shines too, but not as brightly as the diamond studs on her earlobes, swag from her ex before she kicked him out.

"Mimi!" she yells when I open my apartment door, like my presence here is a big surprise. She takes in my workout uniform: mail-order pull-on pants; Rockport walkers; a sweatshirt from Middlebury, one of the grandkids' colleges; and a baseball cap from Georgetown, where another one of them goes. I watch her looking at me with her sharp, appraising eyes and wonder if she's willing to be seen with me. I wait for a crack she does not make.

"Well, OK, let's hit it," she says, and we're off to the beach on a cold and sunny winter day. We take her BMW, which beats my Shadow any day, on any highway, and I'm just about asleep in the heated seat when Cassie pulls into the Wollaston beach parking lot—empty now, the water stretching out before us, blending into the sky at the horizon, with flocks of seagulls wheeling and gliding and squawking overhead.

"Daddy's in San Diego with Miss Piggy, at the Del Coronado," Cassie says as we head down the stairs to the sand and the water's edge. Her words cut neat and clean, like a Swiss Army knife. Then I see the two of them, Jack and Miss Piggy, eating breakfast in an oceanfront dining room set with linen and real silver. He's feeding her a bit of cantaloupe on a silver fork, his hair slicked back neat and shiny like the big bandleader he's always longed to be.

"Doing what?" Like I care.

"A conference of some kind. They're staying a couple of extra days, then going up to Santa Barbara."

"Santa Barbara," I repeat, but she doesn't hear me. The nicest place Jack ever took me to was a cottage on Craigville Beach with all six of our girls in tow, a place with an outdoor shower where I got to cook in a kitchen even smaller than my own. While he swam and built sand-castles with the girls.

Cassandra's up ahead, trying to set the pace. Santa Barbara. Good for them! Jack showing off the young blonde on his arm—young enough so that by the time she loses her looks, he'll be long gone. He won't have to trade her in for a new one.

The tide's low, and the sand along its edge is firm, so that's where Cassie leads me. Wouldn't you know she's got one of those pedometer thingies strapped to her ankle to measure just how far we've gone, and she keeps dragging me farther, while I keep pointing out that however far we go, we're only halfway done because we've got to turn around and get back to the Bimmer. At one point she stops, and insists I take my heart rate, my fingers pressing on the pulse point at my throat. She counts ten seconds with her watch.

"Time's up. What's your pulse? I'm seventeen, which is just about my target."

"Zero. No pulse. Guess I'm a goner."

"Oh, Mimi," she says, dripping irritation along with sweat, "you're pressing the wrong spot."

Mimi, what Cassandra's always called me, her first word. I tried to teach her Mammy like our Irish forebears used to say, then Mommy, but she refused to learn it. Instead, she imitated Jack, Mimi this and Mimi that. Our other daughters copied her. Not Mammy or Mommy, Ma, Mom, but Mimi. After a while, I figured, close enough. One vowel sound just wasn't worth a fight.

We walk some more, picking up the pace, and when we check our pulse again, she presses my neck for me. Feels like she wants to wring it. "Your pulse is racing," she says. "We better slow down. Your heart rate's, like, twenty-three or twenty-four. Way too fast, even for a woman your age."

"Let's go back, baby," I say after a few. I'm not feeling so great. Out of breath, but also something underneath that, something I can't explain. She set the pace too fast, but I can't tell her, or she'll recite her litany of concerns about my health and haul me off to the doctor's. Or to that warehouse for oldies. This time, she agrees without a word.

We turn around and when we do, I see in the distance the Fore River Shipyard where my father, my sisters and I, and my ex-husband worked. Not to mention countless other relatives and friends. Owned first by Bethlehem Steel and afterward by General Dynamics, but always called Fore River—one of the world's busiest and most versatile shipyards beginning in 1883, and lasting for a century. It's why the ancestors left Belfast and headed here. When I was a kid, I thought Bethlehem meant the town where Jesus had been born. I loved the sound of it. Bethlehem Steel.

The shipyard, shuttered and abandoned since 1986, and struggling for years before that; its Goliath crane, the second largest in the world, still punctuating the skyline, eye-catching but useless. Its vast structures—the building bays, that useless crane, the enormous brick building where I met Jack—are rusted and forlorn, but still in place, like they might come back to life at any moment. So many types of vessels built here: battleships, aircraft carriers, landing ships, heavy cruisers, light cruisers, destroyer escorts, ammunition ships, supply ships, high-speed transports, antiaircraft cruisers—each with its own complex specifications. The first nuclear subs were built here too. And just beyond the shipyard, across the water—out of sight, but present nonetheless—is the little house we lived in when we first got married, the house Jack built for me. I feel a stabbing pain, but one that isn't physical, despite my shortness of breath. A Weymouth cop lives there now.

"You OK?" Cass asks.

"Of course," I lie. She takes my arm and we slow down.

"We used to live there," I say, pointing into the distance. "Your father built that house for me. For us." She nods. No big deal for Cass, just a stepping stone on life's journey.

"I pass it most every day," she says. "Can't believe how small it is. I can't believe we really lived there." She laughs her typical ha-ha-ha.

We trudge back to the Bimmer, beneath the beautiful empty sky, the wintry sun. Even now, after all this time, it hurts to say my marriage was a failure. I'm the one who left. After thirty years. I'd had enough after finding out about the third or fourth or fifth young girlfriend—which Jack insisted were not girlfriends, but mentees. What on earth is a mentee? I asked. Some type of bird that can balance on one leg? Or a marine mammal? Mentees. Whatever. Lipstick on your collar isn't just a song. So I left him in a fit and went to stay with Patty, thinking he'd come after me and beg me to return. But while I waited at Patty's, he flew to Santo Domingo and divorced me. On the grounds that I'd abandoned him. Right after that, he married the new one. It was like we'd been playing bridge and he trumped me. I'd walked out on him, after all, and our two teenage daughters, Siobhan and Delilah, who were still at home.

Of course they—my ex and my youngest daughters—said that I was crazy, leaving behind a beautiful home and all inside it; a late-model luxury sedan; the security of Jack's income and his pension; my only job seeing to it that his life went smoothly. What could have possessed me? I was nutty; I'd lost it. That's the excuse Jack used during our divorce when he recruited Siobhan and Delilah to help him hide our assets. He sneaked stuff into various new accounts that the two of them had authorized, forging my name. Convinced them I couldn't handle money, stocks, bonds, mutual funds, whatever. Said I'd squander them in a heartbeat, and they, my babies, they went along with him. *You won't inherit a thing*, Jack told them, and they believed him. Even now, they gather evidence against me about my instability, and, lately, my memory lapses. Sometimes, though, I just don't feel like paying close attention anymore.

Jack believed I was so dimwitted that I wouldn't notice that our assets had suddenly disappeared. Against the advice of my lawyer and my sisters, I settled for twenty grand and my walking papers. Less than a thousand bucks a year for all that aggravation. I was too worn out to fight. But the truth is, I didn't care. And I still wouldn't give a rat's ass for Jack F. X. Malloy's money. They can have it. And may they spend it well. I only wanted peace. Serenity, like it says on the flyer for golden-age tai chi. The betrayal by my daughters, however, remains a deep, unhealing wound.

We reach the car and Cassie helps me in. Unlike yours truly, Cassie took care of herself and her son before she dumped her husband, a CPA. She'd been miserable for years but waited until he made partner before she cut him loose. Hired a killer lawyer. Got child support and alimony and the house, a Georgian colonial, in one of the South Shore's richest towns. She works because she wants to, for Hallmark, going around to malls and shopping strips to set up and maintain their displays. Cassandra loves greeting cards and is always sending them, even when there's no occasion. *Hang in there*, said one she sent to me last month. A scared kitten clung to the high branch of a tree. The Gay Divorcée is what I call Cassandra, although, unlike Ginger Rogers in that movie, her gaiety is less evident with each passing year.

"Working out gets easier after a while," Cassie says, offering me a quick, encouraging smile, then pulling out and heading back to Paul Revere. "You've just got to keep at it."

As usual, the traffic's awful, but it doesn't matter. I'm stuck on Memory Lane with Jack. All those years we were together, my husband was a holy roller, R.C.-style: God forbid you should miss Mass on Sunday, eat meat on Friday, or forget to fast before Communion. He knew the Catholic rulebook by heart, and felt it was his moral obligation to enforce it. Even after Vatican II, Jack stuck to the old ways, attending outlawed Latin Masses. He fooled me for ages. Until I realized he was a card-carrying hypocrite who beat his breast in the confessional on Saturday afternoons, then went out and screwed anyone he could.

After he got back from the Dominican Republic, he tried to have our marriage annulled, too—this time on the grounds that I was crazy. So that he and the bimbo could be officially married in the Church and still go to Communion. He wrote an affidavit, listing all of my many failings, in order to demonstrate that I had been a nut job back when we got married, thus the marriage was invalid, and our daughters were illegitimate. Bastard daughters, all six of them. He expected me to sign it. Who's the wacko here? I wondered. Despite pressure from several of my daughters, I refused to cooperate.

But leave it to Jack Malloy. He went and found a long-haired, sandal-wearing priest to perform the marriage, a priest who has also been giving them Communion and Absolution ever since. After supper every night, Jack and Miss Piggy say novenas together, kneeling on the living-room floor. Hardwood, no carpet. That's what I hear through the grapevine, anyway. The grapevine being Ruth Ann, Del, and Cassandra. Maybe it's a form of foreplay.

Once in a while, I'll pluck a real juicy one from the grapevine. Like that Jack has to send his shirts out if he wants a clean one anytime soon. Or that if he wants a balanced meal, he's got to order it from Boston Chicken. Or that the house is filthy. Dust and scum; trash piled everywhere. They say Miss Piggy's a shopaholic with more shoes than Imelda. Del's old bedroom, I hear, is now stacked floor-to-ceiling with the unused bargains—watches, bed linens, sweaters, umbrellas, underwear—that Miss Piggy couldn't leave behind. Hah! It tickles me, I can't help it, to think of the two of them, wallowing in squalor, and Jack blowing a gasket every time she walks in the front door with another loaded shopping bag. I'd love it if just once, just a single time during his marriage to the young blonde, while he's peeing into a scummy toilet or trying to balance his checkbook, that he realizes all I did for him, and thanks me in his heart. Fat chance.

"Women who exercise vigorously three or more times a week substantially cut their risk of breast cancer and heart failure. Not to mention osteoporosis."

I turn to look at Cass, whose unasked-for opinion shoves me back into Quincy traffic. We're stopped at a light and she's drumming her manicured nails on the steering wheel.

"I'll be your support," she says. "I'll support you."

"You'll support me? You mean like an undergarment? A panty girdle? I used to hate those things. Never needed one." I look out at the landscape of banks, bars, and triple-decker houses, the sidewalks thronged with people.

"Oh, Mimi," she says, accelerating with the changing light. "I mean the people who love you and want to help you achieve your weight-loss goals."

I don't answer, don't even look at her.

"Want to drive by the old place?" she asks, like this might make me happy.

I shake my head no, and she shuts up. Every time I think about our homes—we moved every few years, following Jack's whims, always to a bigger house in a better neighborhood—a clot fills up my throat and I have trouble seeing clearly. What I wanted, all I ever longed for, really, was to stay put in that first house, that little Cape Cod cottage on the bluff above the Fore River. The house Jack built for me, for us, a cottage with big windows on all sides where no one else had ever lived. Where, on sunny days, the light shined like sequins on the water.

"We can add on. We can push up and out," I kept telling him. I went so far as to make drawings of the plans, crude drawings that he, a naval architect, squashed in his fist and dropped into the nearest wastebasket. He kept wanting to buy up. And up and up. He couldn't stop. He had to show the world what a big shot he was. And I kept getting what I didn't want: gloomy old Tudors and Victorians, full of nooks and crannies, gables, stained glass, closets, attics, cellars, shadows. More space for me to clean. More dark places for me to get scared in.

"Like it or lump it," Jack told me once when I complained. I guess I lumped it. I was his handmaiden. Yes, me, Maire. Behold, a handmaiden of the Lord! Until that last place, where I finally went on strike. The washer and dryer were in the cellar, a creepy place with cobwebs, dirt, no light, no windows, and an old coal bin to one side. I refused to go down there by myself—I couldn't, which is the part he didn't get. At last he broke down and built a new laundry room right off the kitchen. Too little, too late.

"You should feel really good about this, Mimi," says Cassie when we pull up to my apartment. Then, God bless her, she blows me a kiss out her open window and promises to take me for another walk on the next nice day.

Four

I'M GONNA LIVE
TILL I DIE

At last, some peace and quiet. Time to think, which I've had more than enough of since I got laid off. Thinking, my new hobby. Cheap and easy. I get the blue pendant from my bedroom, sit with it in my recliner. I stare hard at the beautiful blue stone, like it's trying to tell me something, but in a voice so faraway, I can't quite make out the words. A piece of jewelry talking to me. If my daughters only knew. I call Patty, the great historian.

"What's doing?" she asks, and I tell her all about the leaky pipe and Duffy's spill, and then finding the velvet pouch on the floor with the blue pendant inside.

"It was Mam's." Patty laughs like I'm kidding her. "It was Mam's aquamarine. I've always wondered what happened to it. A big blue pendant, set in silver."

"That's it, but what's it doing in my closet?"

"Daddy gave it to her when they got married. I know that much. You do too, Mimi. You've just forgotten. Maybe Daddy gave it to you. I didn't know any of us still had it."

"Me neither."

Patty laughs again. "Can't wait to see it. Show us next time we go to brunch. Oh, and I mailed out the questionnaires. You should be getting yours any day now."

"Got it yesterday."

"Great," she says. "It's going to be a gift to our children, something they'll always treasure." Then she gabs on and on about her kids and her kids' kids until I just about can't stand it anymore.

Five

ME AND MY
SHADOW

I'm about to nuke a Lean Cuisine, eggplant rollatini, whatever that is, when Cassie shows up. "Mimi!" she hollers when I open the door. Her usual greeting, like it's been ages, and a big surprise that I'm still here. She's wearing a lime green suit and matching pumps. "I brought you something really good."

What? I'm wondering as she puts the goodies on my counter, cold cooked lobster out of the shell, some kind of fancy salad with asparagus and sundried tomatoes, bakery rolls, and a couple of bottles of Chardonnay. I can read her like a book: she wants something from me. She plans to ply me with wine, and the kind of food I can't afford, and then get me to do something against my better judgment.

"Hope you have a corkscrew." A little wail. "You're always drinking wine from those screw-top bottles."

"Am not. I buy my wine in boxes now. Stays fresher that way."

She gives me a look.

"You keep it in the fridge and just hold your glass up to the spigot." I hand her my corkscrew. "Only trouble is, you can't see when you're running out. You have to shake the box."

I pull out a couple of wineglasses, Lenox crystal she gave me one

Christmas, and watch her work the corkscrew on the dark-green bottle. Her manicured fingernails, recently done, make me think of small, sweet fruit—the kind with a hard shell you can't ever break.

"Well, this is really good stuff." She pours each of us a healthy measure.

"I could get two or three boxes of blush for what you paid for that."

"Wait til you taste." We clink glasses and I swallow. OK, the pricey corked wine, whatever it was, some name in a language I couldn't read, beats Wine in a Box hands-down. Still, as we sit feasting at my table by the window, watching the sun set outside, I know she's up to something.

I'm swallowing my last yummy bit of lobster when she says, "Tell me a story." Her cheeks are flushed and she's breathing fast, like my sisters do when the Yik Yak Club's in session. Or maybe it's the sulfites in the wine.

"A story?" I think of *The Runaway Bunny* or *The Poky Little Puppy*, books I read to my girls when they were kids. I recall the gist but not the exact details.

"Tell me something about your family, about what it was like when you were growing up. You never talk about it."

She taps her shiny fingernails on my table. In my mind's eye, I try to see a story from my childhood, from happy times back in the day, but all I see are lines and shadows, like I do on TV when the cable's out.

"Everybody remembers something about growing up. Unless they're mentally defective." Sometimes her tone reminds me of my ex's.

"Thanks a lot." I take another swallow of wine, trying to cool down the hot buttons she keeps pressing.

Cassie has, to hear her tell it, done a lot of work on her inner child, and it makes her feel superior to the rest of us when it comes to family matters. She's spent years in therapy and insists on sharing every grim detail with me, blabbing about her dysfunctional family, and I always wondered, was it the same one I'd been living in all those years? "You just don't get it," she's told me a million times or more, and she's right, I don't get it. Not even for a hot second have I ever understood

Cassandra's anger, her mood swings, her loneliness, her lapses into despair.

She had a great childhood, one most kids would envy. Jack and I saw to that. She had a real mother, an honest-to-goodness mother on call 24/7. She grew up with every possible advantage, three square meals a day and endless snacks in between, a closet full of pretty dresses, and new shoes for every holiday. Not to mention the fine homes, and me, always there to make sure things ran smoothly. She got dancing lessons and violin lessons and a new gown for the prom. No hand-me-downs for my girls. Jack wouldn't allow it. She even had her own room with a pink canopy bed. I sewed the damned canopy myself, out of dotted Swiss.

During all those years of what Cassie called her recovery, she carried around this little white stuffed teddy bear that she would cuddle. The bear held a plastic ice-cream cone—chocolate—between his paws. Cassie called him Sweet Stuff.

Sweet Stuff got dumped for good soon after Cassie's "rebirth," and not long after that, her husband got dumped too. Cassandra found some nut called a rebirther and paid her damned good money so she could be born again—in the actual, not the Christian, sense. She spent a day on the floor of a dark room—lit with scented candles—wriggling through a tunnel made up of the arms of the rebirther and her pals. This was supposed to wipe out any lingering effects of the trauma she went through when she was wriggling out of me. I didn't get it, but didn't ask. Pretended it didn't bother me, my firstborn feeling the need to be rebirthed.

Now that we're full of lobster and loopy from the Chardonnay, Cass takes a copy of the questionnaire out of her Coach bag and smooths it out on my table. She holds a pen, Cross, gold-plated, or maybe the real thing. That's what she's after: answers for the genealogy.

"What was your mother like? Start there." She holds her pen over the paper.

"Hmmm, stump the stars," I joke, stalling for time because Cassie's question draws a blank. I have no memories of Mother, not a one and, hence, no stories, either.

"Come on, Mimi. She was your own mother."

"What do you want from me? She died when I was a kid, a little kid." I count back to myself. "I was seven when she passed." A fact I've lived with all my life. "She died before I had any memories." Cassandra looks at me, cheeks pink, eyes bright blue. She doesn't believe me, but it's true.

"I don't remember anything about her. Right before I left your father, I went to a shrink," I hear myself tell Cassandra, against my better judgment. I was stuck, deep down in the dumps, and everything I looked at seemed to be filmed over with murky water or layered in smoke. "He said I had to make my way back through my childhood, step by step, like Hansel and Gretel in the forest, in order to feel whole again. Whole. Like I'd ever felt complete, or even expected to. The shrink kept asking me about my childhood and I kept telling him I couldn't remember." I see him now, plain as day. "I couldn't stand that guy, Dr. Nobody, with his black-rimmed glasses, his three chins and creepy smile."

"'Come on, Mimi,' he said again and again. 'Everybody remembers something. You remember. You're just not telling.'" His pen and notebook at the ready.

"I got so upset, the way he kept badgering me, I got up and left and never went back. But even after I got home and tried and tried, I still couldn't remember. Then your father hollered about all the money he'd wasted, three hundred something dollars on a worthless psych evaluation. 'Take it out of my allowance,' I told him."

"Well, try again now," Cass prods, just like the shrink. I light a butt, which I usually try not to do when she's around because of her snotty attitude. But this time she seems not to notice. I crack the window on my side and exhale in that direction.

"No point. After that shrink experience, I said the hell with it. The past, I mean. What's done is done. Be grateful." And eventually, the smoke and murky water went away on their own. One day I woke up and felt like my old self again.

"That wasn't the first time you got depressed." I look at my daughter.

I can't tell if this is an accusation or a question. "Right after Malvina was born."

She might as well have slapped me.

"How do you know that? You were what, five or six years old?"

"So you're not denying it," she says, her face scrunched up in a way that makes me sad, not angry. One of the deepest shames of my life, how I could not take care of Malvina after she was born. Me, still in my twenties, and she, Malvina, my fourth in six years, with a miscarriage wedged somewhere in between. I can hardly bear to think about it, even now. Patty took Malvina in for two, maybe three, months before I got myself together. And after that, nobody ever spoke of it again.

"Your aunt told you," I say, and she nods ever so slightly. "Patty, the blabbermouth."

"Aunt Patty said you could have died. Malvina, too."

"But we didn't."

"Obviously," she says, again in that snotty tone. "But I was thinking of how history repeats itself. Or almost repeats itself. Didn't your mother die in childbirth?"

"History does not repeat itself. Not in this family, anyway." I'm as certain of this as I am of my name. "History will not repeat itself."

"Well, how old was your mother when she died?"

"Thirty-four. She started her family late for those days. She'd been a teacher before she married and had us kids. She graduated from Bridgewater Normal School."

"And she died in childbirth."

"Not exactly. She gave birth just fine, but then experienced toxemia. And eclampsia."

"Toxemia? Eclampsia?"

"It happens right after you give birth, something poisons the blood. Your blood pressure spikes sky-high. You have convulsions, go blind, and then you die. Never happens anymore. At least not here, in the United States."

"With Auntie Keeley?"

I nod yes, but I feel queer.

"What was it like when she died?"

The wine and lobster bubble in my gut. My mother, Mam, gone for good, before I could even remember her. And we didn't get to say good-bye.

"You girls don't know how good you've got it nowadays." I grin, pretending I feel great. "With all the prenatal care you get, the steak and Champagne after—"

"Answer my question." Her eyes blaze the way they used to when she was about fourteen and beginning to feel her oats.

"I told you I don't remember anything about it."

"Can't or won't? You and all your secrets."

"Secrets? I don't have any secrets." Well, maybe one, not counting the blue pendant. For many years, I bowled in a church league on a team called the Angel Babies. We wore satin jackets with our names embroidered on the back, and on our ball bags. I never said a word about this to my daughters. Didn't want them gossiping about one of the most enjoyable things I'd ever done. All too soon, though, slipped disks, arthritis, high blood pressure, and macular degeneration—the other girls' problems, not mine—broke up the Angel Babies. I donated my jacket and the ball bag to St. Vincent de Paul, though I doubt there are many other bowling Mimis out there. That's my only secret.

"Your whole life is a secret, Mimi." Cass polishes off the last of the wine. "You never tell us any stories. You never have."

"Be glad," I say, though I'm not sure why, and I get up to bring our dirty dishes to the sink. Cassie follows, her high heels clicking on the tile.

"I don't even know her name."

"Mary." This word pops out by itself, four letters stuck together, no pictures attached. "I was named for her."

"Why?" She scrapes the plates and rinses them and puts them neatly into the dishwasher. In a minute, my kitchenette will be spic-and-span and she'll have a pot of coffee brewing.

"No clue," I answer, and for the first time in more than fifty years, I begin to wonder about it myself. "Nobody ever told me." All my other sisters were named for the sons my parents hoped for, even Patty, whose real name is Padraic. And Eden, whose name was Aidan.

Cassie wants the grim details, when everybody was born and when they married, how many kids they had, and when they died, all the stuff I've never cared a whit about. Leave it to Cassandra to take over the genealogy like she's the one who thought of it.

"I promised Auntie Patty," she says.

"Promised her what?"

"That I'd make you do this. She knew you'd procrastinate. Blow it off."

"Would not," I protest, but Patty's got my number. She knows exactly how I feel about ancient history.

I wrack my brain and come up with a few answers, like my mother's and my father's names. Mary and Joe. Like Jesus's parents, Cassie says, and I nod yes though I'd never thought of it before. I can more or less figure out their dates of death, though I'm not sure where my mother's buried. After she died, her parents—loathing my father—reclaimed her. At least according to the myths and legends of the Yik Yak Club.

Cassie picks and probes with her gold pen and twinkly fingernails. It's odd to see the details of my life being written out like that, names I haven't spoken or even thought about for maybe half a century. I watch the words form on the page in my daughter's lovely handwriting, all loops and curlicues—that at ten I was an orphan, though I never thought about myself that way. She writes down a true fact, that my mother died the day Keeley was born. But my sisters and I didn't even see Keeley until she was a toddler, two or three years old. After Mam died, she was sent to live with a wet nurse, but we didn't know this until she was delivered to our doorstep, already talking and walking like a Chatty Cathy doll.

"Aidan's drawing a big tree in his computer class," says Cass.

Patty's grandson. Aidan Shmaidan, I think.

"It'll have lots of little branches. We'll handwrite all this information, then scan it onto them."

"What about the broken ones?" Our family tree as I see it: an old maple suffering from blight, a tree with broken branches, some dangling from the trunk, and others, having fallen, rotting on the ground beneath it. "What's he going to do about those?"

"Oh, Mimi," says Cassandra. "There are no broken branches."

"Of course there are."

"You can't get broken off a family tree. Family's family, no matter what they do or what happens to them."

That's when I realize what's coming next. I look at pretty blond Cassandra, who has it all under control, and I see it coming, head-on. Realize, too, that I've known it from the first time this genealogy was mentioned. Knew exactly where we'd end up with our ancient family history.

"Even your sister Fagan."

"Fagan?" My other baby sister, gone now for almost sixty years.

"Fagan's got her own little branch on the family tree."

"Fagan?" The name burns my lips, a name never spoken, not even by the members of the Yik Yak Club. Now Cass declares it, right here in my kitchen. Fagan. After all this time.

"That's right, Fagan."

"What about her?" I can't repeat her name again. Pronouns will have to do.

"Patty and Jo told me about her, Miss Mimi Who Has No Secrets." I look away. "Somebody I never knew existed. My own aunt."

I spy a hangnail on my pinkie. I bite it off, wince from the pain.

"We can't have a family tree without including our poor little Fagan." Cassandra's voice wobbles, somewhere between rage and sorrow.

"'Our' poor little? . . ." Fagan. The name swells inside my mouth, a lump, a malignancy. I look at Cass, my perfect eldest daughter, so smug sitting there, in her Talbots suit, clueless. "Our poor little? Our? First-person plural, like you've got some claim to her when you don't even have the right to even bring her up." My blood rises like steam in a pressure cooker just before it starts to hiss and squeal.

"She was my aunt. Or would have been if she'd lived."

"But she didn't." Hot steam shoots out my ears. My other baby sister, sent away at five years old, back to the old country, never to be heard from again. I'd like to call Patty to read her the riot act. She ought to mind her own business; let bygones be bygones.

"You should have told me, told us, all of your children. You should have told us long ago."

"Let her rest in peace, wherever she may be." It comes out soft as a prayer, and I mean it that way, I really do. *Fagan, rest in peace. Wherever you may be.* That's what we—Eden, Alberta, and I—decided way back when.

Cassandra's quiet for a minute, and for a second I believe she might actually drop the subject. Fat chance, though.

"Patty says you're the one who knows the most because you were the oldest when she got sent away. The oldest one still living now." She scribbles something in her notebook.

The oldest one still living now. That's right; that's me, Mimi, the survivor. Because we also lost Eden and Alberta along the way. The dearest friends of my youth, both gone before their time. "I don't know anything."

"When Auntie Patty told me that you girls had this other baby sister before Keeley showed up, it blew me away. And that she got sent away because your stepmother couldn't handle her. Your stepmother. I didn't know about her, either. Then you found out that Fagan had died of a wasting disease."

"You want to talk about our stepmother?" My voice is cold and quiet. I look at Cass with pity. She nods yes, all excited. She, who's so eager to march into the past, where she thinks she'll find what she's been looking for, some kind of treasure, when what's there is more along the lines of a Bouncing Betty, guaranteed to devastate.

"OK. Yes, my father did remarry. He remarried right away, another source of shock and shame for all of us. Because we thought he loved our mam as much as we did; that she couldn't ever be replaced. But no. He remarried so fast, brought home our stepmother. Her name was Flanna Flanagan. Be sure to write that down." She does.

Flanna Flanagan, my stepmother. Da's second wife. Who sent away my baby sister Fagan before the other baby, Keeley, the one we weren't even sure existed, came back to live with us. She's here now, Flanna. I see her, hovering outside over the parking lot, like Christ above the tomb on Easter morning. Flanna, resurrected, only she's charred and blackened, like she'd gone down instead of up.

"So what happened with Fagan?" Cass prods again, cold as could be. I take a few slow breaths, light another butt.

"One morning we get up and Fagan isn't there, OK? My father with the new wife gather us together and tell us they've sent her back to Cullyhanna in County Armagh, up north where we came from. My father was crying when he told us, and the new wife sat there weeping too. Fagan was going to live with somebody else's family, because our new mother couldn't handle her. 'We'll get her back, as soon as everything's under control here, girls, I promise,' my father told us. Then he raved about the beauty of the countryside in Cullyhanna, and the new wife clung to him, nodding and weeping." Cassie stops writing. She looks up at me, her eyes so familiar, so much like her father's, but now there's a different look in them, sadness maybe. "That's the last we ever heard of her."

Because nothing was ever under control again, and before we even knew where to go to look for her, Da himself passed on, and the wicked stepmother flew away on her broom. And whatever Daddy knew, he took that knowledge to his grave.

"Mimi, poor Mimi," Cassandra says. A big tear rolls down her cheek, making a track in her Mary Kay foundation.

"Here today, gone tomorrow," I tell her. "No big deal, honey. That was the world we lived in. It's how we grew up. Lots of other kids did too, back then. Our troubles were like everybody else's, common as potatoes. Nobody used the word 'trauma.' Nobody thought of things that way."

Cassandra sobs. Again I feel sad for her. Poor Cassie, almost always just off balance, and grabbing on to whatever's in reach to try to stay upright. I reach across the little table to pat her shoulder. "Ancient history," I say.

"So after Fagan was sent off, Keeley showed up?"

I nod yes. "Keeley took her place, and that was that. Whatever else had happened up til then, we cremated. Scattered the ashes. We all loved Keeley, still do, right? She's the best of the bunch."

So much happiness the day Keeley appeared on our doorstep, which is how I always think of it, even though I have no actual memory of that day, nor any idea of where she'd been or why she joined our family when she did.

"What did you do after Fagan got sent away?"

"Nothing. What could we have done?" My daughter's face falls, the way it used to when I closed a book before the story ended. "We didn't do anything at all. We were kids. We were still waiting, no, hoping, I think, that our real mother would come back."

Then, maybe as the result of Cassie's disappointment, or all that pricey wine, I go get the blue pendant. I bring it back, the velvet pouch on my palm, the shiny blue stone on top. Cassandra snatches it, examines it as if it might hold the answers to all her questions.

"Where did you get this?"

"In my closet." I leave out the details about the leak, the collapsing shelf. "I was organizing things, and there it was."

"No, I mean where did you get it? Whose was it?"

"It was my mother's. My father gave it to her when they got married."

"You never told me you had this. You never told me, Mimi, and you know how I love old things."

I shrug.

"Let me bring it to my jeweler," Cassie says, and the next thing you know, she's dropping the pouch into her purse. "He can appraise it. Maybe tell us its provenance and what it's worth."

"Its provenance?"

"Where it comes from . . . who knows . . ." The sparkle is back in my daughter's eyes, she's got something to hold on to. Then she's gone, and so is the blue pendant.

Six

THANKS FOR THE
MEMORY

Flanna Flanagan. Just off the boat is what our grandmother, our father's mother, Nana Sheehan, said about her. She didn't mean it as a compliment. Whenever Nana said this, I saw Flanna climbing off a big boat in Quincy Harbor, one with flapping sails, and she the only passenger. She walked across the water, the last few steps to shore, her bright hair spilling from under her hat, her eyes shining like the sea beneath her feet. Da was there to meet her, the brand-new wife he called his secret rose, like in that poem by W. B. Yeats, whose words Da preferred to prayers.

Enchanting Flanna. With her flaming hair, her pink cheeks, her deep brown eyes. *She does not have to labor to be beautiful*, Da said the day he brought her home. We girls were so excited. We were getting a new mother, a beautiful new Mammy. An angel or a queen, we couldn't pick between the two.

So long ago. During the worst part of the Depression. But even so, Daddy still worked as a riveter at the shipyard, one of the few they'd kept on. Spent his days working with a welder's torch, and bore the scars to prove it. Angry red ones and pearly white ones, hieroglyphics on his fingers and forearms. No pattern, yet a complex topography, over which my sisters and I loved to run our fingers. Daddy's scars, the visible ones. Never complained, not once, no matter how much they might have hurt. So proud of the work he did, building ships.

He took the trolley there, we didn't own a car. We used to love to wait for him outside, especially on paydays, when he brought us treats—bubble gum, cookies, hair ribbons, pretty buttons. We weren't allowed to leave the yard, so we took turns running to the edge of it, trying to spot Daddy as soon as he reached the crest of the hill. Da. How he loved to tease. Like a magician, he pulled our treasures from his pockets, then hid them up his sleeve or in his hat or collar. He made the goodies disappear, then reappear, while the bunch of us squealed and hollered. *My little bouquet of beauties.* That's what he called us until Mam died and Flanna became our new mother.

I'm on my way downstairs to meet my sisters outside, it's almost time for Da to get home from work. I pass their open bedroom door. Mam's come back, I think for a split second. No, not Mam, but Flanna in one of our mother's best dresses, a brown silk with white pin dots. She's so beautiful. I love her, want her to love me back. She fixes herself in the big mirror, turning her head this way and that. She does not have to labor to be beautiful, that's what our father said about her. Flanna, with her dimpled smile, wearing my dead mother's dress.

In the mirror, Flanna sees me. "What're you lookin' at?" she asks, her voice as sweet as syrup but her accent so hard to understand. I try to smile but can't. "Come in, Miss Maire, Quite Contrary," she says, stabbing words. Da told her his special name for me, Contrary Maire. Flanna smiles, holding out her arms. I go, slowly, ever so slowly, my feet sinking ankle-deep into slush and ice. When I'm close enough, she smacks me. Right on my face, hard enough to snap my neck. "That'll teach you not to spy," she says.

I joined my sisters and waited for Da outside on the steps. I didn't say a word. Didn't tell my sisters anything. Pretended to myself it didn't happen, Flanna smacking me in the face. She stood in the doorway at the top, her hair swept up but with curls falling all around her face, in our mother's best silk dress. Payday, but Da forgot our treats.

Still, we surrounded him as Flanna sang in her sweetest voice, *"Leave him be, girls. Give the poor man some peace."* Da pushed past us, rushed up the steps to his secret rose. The two of them embraced, and then they were gone. We knew where they were going, upstairs to their room, to the bed where our mother died. They'd stay up there for ages while we girls hung around in the kitchen.

Fagan, the youngest, Keeley not yet known to us, got fussy and I soothed her, the only one who could. I held her on my lap and whispered nursery rhymes. *"Do you know the muffin man? . . ."* Fagan drifted off to sleep, but Eden, Alberta, and I could still hear them upstairs. Grunts. Cries. Laughter. We didn't get the particulars, but we knew what was going on.

Bad memories flood out the good. Destroy the good so you wonder if you ever had any, flooding in like a red tide and overwhelming the beautiful clear water that was there before. Back in the early 1970s, we had a real red tide in New England. It stretched from Cape Cod all the way up to Casco Bay in Maine, five hundred miles or more. The blue water turned red as if the earth underneath were bleeding. A stunning thing to see, terrifying until you understood what it was. Lucky for us, it happened in September, after the girls went back to school, not during summer when we went swimming every day and could have gotten poisoned by this toxic tide before it was even visible. Some type of algae, phyto-somethings, blooming like a rose garden in the salty water all along the coast, hundreds of miles, and out as far as we could see. An overgrowth of algae. That's all it really was. But it killed an entire harvest of fish and bivalves—clams, mussels, oysters, scallops. A vast destruction, the dead ones heaved onto the beaches by the tide, the stench impossible to describe. An ecological catastrophe, but also an economic one for the clammers and fishermen who earned a living off this bounty.

" 'All the waters in the river turned to blood,' " declared Jack, quoting from the Bible, the first time we saw it. All the waters have turned to blood. For those of us who lived so close it did seem biblical, the enormity of it. The red tide gave off light, and once, after dark, Jack drove me and the girls over to Nantasket to see the waves in the moonlight, glowing with this bioluminescence. A wonder in our world, beautiful if you didn't know what was really going on.

Flanna. A red tide who flooded into our lives when we were too young, too weak to hold her back, or to even understand why or how she poisoned everything. After my father died, I promised myself I'd never think of her again. I cut her from my mind the way surgeons, a few years ago, cut a melanoma out of Patty's arm. They sliced away fat and muscle all around it, leaving a crater on the upper backside of her arm. All because of a mole no bigger than a tick. Ugly as sin, but it did the trick. Destroyed the cancer. Saved Patty's life. No longer any evidence of disease. My surgery worked just as well. I cut Flanna out, along with the surrounding tissue. Didn't think of her once in almost sixty years. But now, thanks to Patty's all-important genealogy and my daughter's chronic nosiness, the red tide is coming back.

Seven

IF YOU ARE BUT
A DREAM

The next time Cassandra calls, before I've even recovered from all that overpriced Chardonnay, she's bounced off in another direction. Still, she's got me in her cross-hairs.

"Maybe you've got Alzheimer's," she bleats into the phone, her voice high-pitched and edgy.

"OK, so I forgot to meet you at the mall. Big deal." Thankfully, when I heard the phone ring, I remembered that she'd planned for us to do a power walk, then catch a movie—something starring Kevin Costner. Cass has the hots for him.

"It's not the first time, Mother." Mother, not Mimi. Now I'm really in it. "And Aunt Patty told me you didn't know what she was talking about when she called about the genealogy."

"Did too. She just caught me by surprise."

"You ought to get a physical and talk about your memory lapses with your doctor."

"My 'memory lapses'? You ought to mind your own damned business."

"It is my business," she says, snotty as could be, but the phone's stuck between my hand and ear. I can't hang up. "You could end up like Aunt Lillian."

"That's not fair. I'm not anything like Lillian." Poor Lillian, my aunt. She used to be a paralegal for a big law firm in Boston, a real stickler for details. Lillian, the nitpicker, and proud of it. That's what everybody said about her. But in her later years, she forgot entirely who she was, and even who her children were. Lillian lost track of the most basic things, like what happens in winter and summer and where you sleep and where you pee. The last straw was when her kids—their own kids in tow—went to take her out to Denny's for a patty melt, her favorite meal. They found her in a neighbor's yard, naked in the snow, insisting that she was going to take a bath. Turned out to be her final expedition. Her kids had her locked up in one of those special places for "Old Timers" patients where they strap you to your wheelchair so you can't strip and go wandering around. Lillian died within the year. Not a minute too soon. My sisters and I had a Mass said for her. And may perpetual light shine upon her.

"I want to plan ahead if I'm going to be changing your diapers this time next year."

"You'll never change my diapers, you brat."

"Oh, Mimi," she says, softer this time. "I don't want to fight. I only want to help. You know you need it."

Just to prove her wrong, I let her make the appointment. I'll show you, I'm thinking to myself. I'll show you who's losing her mind.

"I'll pull some strings," she says. "We'll get you in to see somebody really good, the best brain guy on the South Shore."

Much as I hate it when Cassie picks on me, she's not entirely mistaken about my memory. For some time now, it's been springing leaks, just like the pipes in Paul Revere. I've forgotten her phone number, and the Mass schedule at Our Lady Queen of Peace, both of which I know by heart. When I was playing Scrabble with my grandkids, I forgot how to spell a couple of simple words, "apple" and "pear." I got away with "pare," but not with "appel." "You're letting us win," the kids accused me, but I wasn't. "It's called a memory lapse," I told them, but they didn't understand. And the last time I tried to knit a sweater, which neither my kids nor their kids wanted anyway—not stylish enough, no corporate logo embroidered on the front—I had trouble following the pattern. I kept screwing up the knits and purls. Out of frustration, I shoved the half-finished sweater into the trash and gave up this hobby, one that I'd kept busy with for more than thirty years.

A couple of times lately I've gone to the Plaza, and when I finished shopping, I walked out to the parking lot but couldn't remember where I'd parked. Couldn't find my little white Shadow, but I couldn't tell anyone either. If I did, they'd realize I was losing it, and maybe tell my kids. So I strolled up and down the rows of cars—casually, in case anybody saw me, so that they wouldn't know I was looking for my car. I walked with my head held high, as if I knew exactly where it was, as if I were wearing the high heels I always used to love instead of Rockport Walkers.

And I knew my memory couldn't be that bad because, while I was searching, I kept thinking about all the awful things they do to old people when they can't remember anymore. I also thought about how I've always had nice legs, with thin ankles and pretty feet; how I figured these were good for life, that I'd get a lifetime guarantee on something. My ex is a confirmed leg man and he always told me that my sexy ankles drove him crazy. "Great gams," he whispered to me every now and then, in a way that turned them into Jell-O. He always wanted me in pumps, three- or four-inch heels.

All those years I was home raising our daughters, I'd bathe and change into heels by the time he came home from work and meet him at the door with a highball, as if I had nothing else to do all day except make myself sexy for him. Even after he turned me in for the newer model, I kept wearing the high heels, thinking, Ankles, don't fail me now. Maybe I'd attract a rich old man. Then the falling arches and the bunions got me. Some mornings I could hardly haul myself out of bed. Lose the heels, then some weight, the podiatrist told me, and he suggested the Rockport Walkers, genuine old-lady shoes.

Then, a week or so ago, I went to Grab & Go for my groceries, the little that I need, cranberry juice and English muffins and some

Stouffer's Lean Cuisines. When I was done, I went outside, happy to see my Dodge exactly where I'd parked it. Ta-da. But when I got inside, I couldn't remember what to do with the keys. For a split second, a terrible one, I looked at the dashboard not knowing what it was, and holding this sharp metal object in my hand. I might as well have been in the cockpit of a DC-10. Then it came back to me: the key goes into the hole on the steering column. It's called the ignition. Phew! Once that motor rumbled, sweetheart, I was fine. Found my way home in record time. Not that I shared this little victory with my sisters or my kids. It's strictly between me, myself, and I. So, no, my mental faculties might not exactly be in tip-top shape, but I haven't yet lost anything I can't live without.

All too soon, Cassandra calls to tell me we've got an appointment with the best brain guy on the South Shore. Again, first-person plural.

"Lucky me."

"You are lucky," she says, "darned lucky to have somebody like me looking out for your best interests."

My best interests.

Cassie calls the night before, and again the morning of, to remind me. Like I could forget an appointment with the best brain guy on the South Shore. When she picks me up, she gives my comfy sweats the evil eye, and I give her one right back, though her crisp slacks and blouse and blazer would pass muster even in the highest levels of the government. Her foot heavy on the pedal, she drives me to South Shore Neurologic and Radiologic in Braintree, a name that gives me the heebie-jeebies. It's in a new brick medical arts building just past the Plaza.

After we wait for what feels like forever, a nurse takes us to an examining room where the best brain guy, whose name I don't recall—minor lapse—asks me a million questions. He looks into my eyes and taps me here and there with a funny little hammer. Then he says he's sending us downstairs to a radiologist who'll make maps of my brain. Maps. To the tune of several thousand dollars, which Medicare will in fact cover—Cassie already checked. Just so they can find out more about what's going on inside my head than any sane person would ever want to know.

"It's totally noninvasive," the brain guy says, not looking at me, but riffling through my file, full of the notes he's been taking. "All you have to do is lie there and relax." I'd heard that advice before.

We find our way through a maze of hallways, lots of doors—all shut—until we reach Radiology, a windowless little room where, again, we wait and wait. Then a technician comes for us and brings us into a dark room. There, they make me strip and put on this thing that's misnamed a gown. Then the tech tells Cassie to stay where she is and he brings me to an even darker room and makes me lie on a narrow table. My heart's revving up, moving toward overdrive, when he leaves and presses a button from wherever he is and the table slides backward into this metal tube.

That's when I know I've bitten off way more than I could chew. This MRI device is an airless tube, steel wrapped all around you, just inches from your face, and it echoes every sound, even your own breathing. They tell me not to move a muscle, but the moment they slide me in there, I don't believe it's possible to get back out alive.

The noise is terrible—a pounding like a jackhammer wedged into my ear—and I lose it. I try to sit up and I bump my head. Can't find my way out. "Cassie, honey, get me out of here!" I holler and my voice echoes back at me, vibrating inside my skull. "Cassie, honey, I'm suffocating."

"Hold on," says the tech, even though there's nothing to hold on to. Next thing you know, I'm sliding back out of the tube and Cassie and the tech rush in while I lie there, twitching like a victim of electric shock.

They pull me out, and Cass pats my back until a nurse shows up with a small blue pill. The tech says he'll do someone else while we wait for the pill to take effect. Sometime later, I've settled down and when they slide me back in, it's like I'm drifting on a cloud. This time they make me choose from a rack of CDs, and they give me headphones, so I go back into the tube listening to Sinatra, "Zing! Went the Strings of My Heart." They let Cassie stay with me. She sits at the end of the table and holds my ankles, the same ones that drove Jack crazy oh so long ago. Inside, I feel like I could float away, right through the metal tube, right up through the clouds. But I also feel Cassie holding on, like she's keeping me on Earth.

Cass sits there while the technician talks above the racket and Sinatra, promising me we're almost done. Just a couple of minutes more. *I still recall the thrill.* Yup, almost done. I can hear the technician breathing, his voice or maybe it's Sinatra's echoing from very far away. *I guess I always will.* "How are you doing in there, Mrs. Malloy?" he asks, and I wonder who she is.

Cassie takes me to lunch, salads at a local grill where the smell of broiling burgers drives me crazy. "No way," she says, reading the menu as if reading my thoughts. "No burgers." Due to the effects of the pill, everything happens through a gauzy curtain. My daughter orders for me, a big bowl of bitter greens, fit for a small rodent, not even a roll or cracker. "Arugula," she says, tapping her fork into my bowl, pointing out a piece. "It's loaded with micronutrients." I can hardly taste it, which is probably just as well. Next thing I know, Cassie and I are back at the brain guy's. She wouldn't miss this for the world. I want a smoke more than anything, but the signs are everywhere, the smoldering butt with the red slash through it. The brain guy's got these pictures up on a lighted board, human brains in strange bright colors. Maps. He points to the map of my brain, comparing it to the other one. That other brain's the normal one, he says. It's all swirls of greens and reds and purples inside the outline of a skull. My brain has those same colors, but they're splattered with black spots, like someone's cut it full of holes.

"Atrophy?" asks Cassie.

"Degeneration," says the brain guy, who is young enough to be my son. Degeneration. Oh, great.

"The good news," he says, "is that you don't have Alzheimer's or a brain tumor."

I turn to Cassie with a big smile, but she's staring at the maps.

"The bad news," he says, "is that you've suffered something called transient ischemic attacks, TIAs."

"Small strokes?" says Cassandra. The brain guy nods.

"You probably didn't even know they were happening," he says, a smarty-pants, just like my daughter.

I nod, but he's wrong there. A couple of times, during the past year, I'd feel my body start to tremble—nothing painful, just a queer buzz from deep inside. If I tried to write, or light a cigarette, my hand wouldn't work. Or maybe I'd try to talk but my mouth and tongue would be stiff, and I'd slur my words so people would think I'd been drinking. Once or twice, one of my legs gave way. Luckily, it happened when I was home alone so nobody saw me fall. I'd rest, and eventually the peculiar sensations would pass.

"You mean those black spots are dead?" Cassie points.

"In my estimation, it wouldn't be inaccurate to say that," the brain guy answers.

I'm pretty sure he means yes. He makes a humming sound. He won't look me in the eye.

"And you have to stop smoking." He stares at the file, all shiny surfaces like Cassie, his skin and scalp and starched white coat. "Nicotine constricts the flow of blood and oxygen to the brain. And with your particular biology, that's very damaging." He seems to have mistaken that file for my face. Some brain guy. "You should also lose some weight and start exercising. With a change in lifestyle, you could have a long and healthy life."

"Will the black spots change color?" Cassie asks.

"What's gone is gone."

We leave the brain guy's office, but I don't think he told me everything, and I didn't know how to ask. At the same time, all of a sudden and very strongly, I feel that my brain belongs to me and what's happening inside it is nobody else's business.

As for my lifestyle, I figure, what I do or don't do is none of their business either, though I'm much too polite to say so. Butt out, pun intended. On the drive home, my daughter is silent, but I feel her gloating, a breeze rippling the still surface of the water, as she speeds me back to Centennial Square. After all, she's right, she's been proven right: I'm losing bits and pieces of my mind.

"Mimi, don't—" she starts to say when she lets me out, but I cut her off.

"Enough's enough for today," I say, and slam the door, grateful to be home and alone. At this point in my life, pushing hard on seventy, I figure I've earned the right to have a highball, a smoke, and a bowl of salted nuts whenever I want them. Give them up for what? To live a few more years? Ridiculous. So that's exactly what I do. Four Roses and ginger ale, with lots of ice. Plus a little bowl of roasted cashews, shiny with salt and oil.

Eight

YOU CAN'T TAKE THAT
AWAY FROM ME

few days later, after finishing up her greeting-card displays, Cassie stops by my apartment. This time, she shows up in a blue suit, empty-handed—no lobster or white wine. It's just about suppertime so, who knows, maybe she's in the mood for some home-cooked Lean Cuisine. I'm sipping a straight-up Manhattan, a rare treat, and having a smoke, and right away she's ticked.

"What do you think you're doing?" Her pretty face is scrunched up like a fist.

"Stay for dinner." I look at her. I can't remember ever being so young or so pretty, but that must be a normal type of forgetting. Otherwise, how could you go on?

She shakes her head no, tosses something onto my counter, like she can't wait to get it off her hands. The velvet pouch. I should've known. The pendant inside makes a soft clunk.

"It's worthless," she says, louder than necessary. My hearing's perfect. "Water and paste." She flicks the pouch toward me with her pretty fingertips. I grab it, take out the pendant. A scratch runs sideways across the stone, little fissures cut deep into it. Feels like I've been cut myself.

"It wouldn't scratch if it were real."

I look at Cassandra.

"My pendant."

"It has no value." Her eyes are harder than the stone. "So it really doesn't matter if it's scratched."

"Its value—"

She cuts me off. "Have you made your will yet?" She grabs the pendant from my hand, shakes it like a pair of dice. Her eyes bore through me, like Jack's whenever he moved in for the kill.

"What kind of question is that?"

"Have you?"

"That's for me to know and you to find out."

Her jaw drops and hangs there. "At the very least, you should consider giving me power of attorney."

"Power of attorney?"

"Over your affairs. In case you become incompetent."

"Incompetent?" I take a big swallow of my Manhattan. It spills onto my fingers, my hand's shaking so much.

"You have the brain of an eighty-five-year-old woman." She speaks quietly and slowly. "You have an eighty-five-year-old brain and your body's only sixty-eight. That's what the doctor told me. He couldn't get over it, the way your brain looked, like the brain of a very elderly woman."

I hear her but can't say a word, not even to correct her. I'm not even sixty-eight. Not by several months, last time I checked.

"You could stroke out any day." Cassie stands there in her blue suit, and the fluorescent light in my kitchenette makes her look green and old. "The doctor said those little strokes are probably warnings that the big one is coming. You know, like those earthquakes in California. If you're lucky, he said, the big one will take you all the way instead of leaving you here paralyzed and speechless."

"I take my BP meds. My blood pressure is under control." Except when my kids and ex attack me.

"It's not your blood pressure." She shakes her head, not quite believing the imbecile she's dealing with. "It's those heart flutters, the atrial fibrillation. The doctor explained it to me. The A-fib throws off clots, and the clots can move up or down. If one moves up . . ." She snaps her fingers to signify the Big One and stares at me.

She points to my cigarette and I take a good, deep drag. "You know every time you do that, you're destroying more brain cells. And I, for one, don't think you can afford to lose any more."

Then Cassandra turns and walks out, high heels clicking, and I'm stuck, alone with my Manhattan, feeling like I've just been rabbit punched and robbed of fifteen years.

Nine

IN THE SHADOW
OF THE MOON

The next morning, I'm still stewing. I take my coffee and the pendant and go sit in my La-Z-Boy. I look hard at the pendant, scratched now and declared worthless by Cass and her jeweler. Worthless, maybe, but still part of me—me with all the black spots in my brain. I hold the stone and rub the scratch, rub and rub, like maybe I can smooth it out.

The blue pendant warms in my hand. I look down at it, and the color reminds me of Daddy's eyes. Like watching a movie, I see myself one Sunday falling down the front stairs of our house. I couldn't have been more than five or so. I was sliding down the banister, roughhousing, disobeying, when I slipped and fell onto the front hall floor. I landed on my left hand. Snap. A bone cracked. It hurt so badly I retched and pain danced at the edges of my eyes. It felt like I was going blind. The rest of them, Mam, Da, and my sisters, gathered 'round, looking at me crumpled at the bottom of the stairs.

Snapped it like a dry stick, said Daddy, examining the damage. Then he lifted me as if I were a scarf or dress that had fallen to the floor. Ran with me, cradled in his arms, all the way to the doctor's house across the railroad tracks on the far side of town, his chest heaving like a bellows. *Da*, I cried into his neck. *Oh, Da*. He squeezed me harder.

The doctor was in his garden in the backyard, kneeling, pulling weeds with his gloved hands. He looked holy, like the statue of the Blessed Virgin stepping on a snake, rising from the flowers in my nana's garden. The doctor stood up out of the tulips, peeled off his gloves, and brought us inside the house to his office, where it was dim and cool. His wife brought us lemonade in blue glasses. The doctor set my wrist, fussing for ages over the plaster cast. The pain kept dancing at the edges of my eyes but Da held me, his arms wrapped tight around me, not once letting go.

I get up from my recliner and turn on the TV, just for company. More news, all of it bad. A house fire in Roxbury, sweeping down the block, an entire family killed. Started by a cigarette smoldering in a couch. The body of a child found in a freezer in a basement, dead for years, and nobody ever noticed she was gone. Corruption in the mayor's office. The attorney general bragging that the Commonwealth of Massachusetts has the highest conviction rate for child molesters in the United States, and the world's best facility to lock them up in, the Bridgewater Correctional Complex. I switch it off. Who needs that kind of company? I go back to my La-Z-Boy, pick up the blue pendant, hold it close. Black spots. My brain is full of them. Maybe that's where I, neatnik that I am, stashed all of my bad memories.

Fagan Sent Away. A chapter I hardly remember, though my surviving sisters insist I know more than anyone. Fagan Sent Away. These words come to me with side effects, the kind they yammer about on TV ads: cardiovascular risks, ulcers, nausea, diarrhea, tremors, and delirium. And sometime after Fagan Sent Away, the rest of us, Keeley included, went to live with our grandmother—Nana, Annie Sheehan, Daddy's mother. Life started over once we moved in with her. The past melted away, making us certain that, from then on, life would be good again. I was just ten at the time.

I look closely at the blue pendant, try to see past the scratch, but my vision wavers, shot through with shiny lines, like a migraine's coming on. Again the six of us, my sisters and me, are sitting on the front steps of our old house in Quincy, waiting for our father. Today he carries a white bag from the bakery, Hanrahan's, a cookie for each of us and an éclair for Mam. My sisters jump and dance when they see the bag, but my stomach clenches. I know what's inside: chocolate chip for Eden, Alberta, and Keeley; sugar cookies for Patty and Josephine, and caraway seed for me. Yes, I got the cookie full of bitter seeds. I only had myself to blame, but knowing that didn't make them any easier to swallow.

The first time Daddy brought those awful cookies home, he was so excited. *A real Irish treat,* he declared in his soft brogue. *The genuine article.*

Daddy loved anything to do with the old country. But when Alberta took her first bite, she spit it out and made a throw-up noise. Then Eden and the rest of them carried on, spitting out the seeds and making vomit noises. Daddy looked so sad. That's why I kept chewing mine and smiling, taking more little bites.

Look at Maire, here, he said, fluffing my hair and tickling my neck. *She knows a good thing when she tastes it.*

After that, Daddy brought my sisters their favorites, whatever they wanted, and he brought me the cookies full of bitter seeds. He did it with such love that I'd gobble them down, smiling and trying not to gag. What I would've given for a ginger snap! But I could not bring myself to tell him.

After he handed out our cookies, Mam, our real mother, called from inside the house, *Joe, you're ruining their appetites for supper, and me, slaving here, over the hot stove.* Daddy swept Keeley up onto his hip and kissed her freckled cheek. No, wait. Keeley didn't have freckles. Not a one, vain as could be about her perfect skin. Besides, Keeley was never with us when our mother was alive. Mam died giving birth to her. The memory breaks up, like pictures torn into little pieces. I struggle hard to put them back together, and I realize it's Fagan, my original baby sister. She's the one on Daddy's hip, eating a chocolate-chip cookie, ruining her appetite for dinner.

She shows up in this memory like she's been waiting for her chance, popping out from behind Keeley in a game of hide and seek. She, not

Keeley, is the one who used to wait with us for Daddy. Not a shadow or a ghost, but a little girl I haven't seen since she got sent away before we had a chance to say good-bye. The sister I buried along with all the other things I didn't want to remember.

I grab Daddy's sleeve. I tug and tug. Jump up and down, tugging, begging. I want him to put Fagan down and pick me up instead. Me, a little snot-nosed kid in hand-me-downs, raggedy, just like the others, and jealous as could be. Fagan giggles from her perch on Daddy's hip. She kisses his whiskery cheek. She owns him, and she knows it. *Fay*, he calls her, *Baby Fay, my wee love.* She not only gets the chocolate chip, she gets held in Daddy's arms.

I open my eyes and look at the pendant. This time, the sky shrinks up inside it. Again, I see myself, but I'm old enough to walk down the hill to meet my father. After our mother passed, I often did this, especially if my sisters weren't around. I'd wait for Daddy and walk back up the hill with him, holding his hand. Sometimes, while I was waiting, I'd imagine him in the distance, coming toward me but not yet seeing me. My father. Daddy. Da. Thin but strong. Wiry. Tired from a long day at the shipyard, crouched in hot darkness, on the scaffolding inside the hull of a tanker or destroyer, fastening the red hot rivets that were shoved through the holes by a worker on the outside.

Nana used to complain that he—*Joey, my Joey*—didn't eat enough. *Looks like a strong wind could knock him over,* she said, a theory my sisters and I were always testing, running at him, leaping up on him. Daddy swore that whatever he ate melted off him while he worked, welding together layers of steel with rivets the size of a big man's thumb. When I was really small, that's what I imagined—fried eggs and bacon, lamb stews and mashed potatoes, melting off him and puddling on the scaffolding beneath him in the dark hull of a ship.

Today I'll run to him, slam into him, going fast as I can, but my father will not fall. No, he'll grab me, laughing. *Contrary Maire*, he'll say. *Think you're stronger than your old man, huh?* His face will be smudged with sweat and smoke and grime, and the visor of his cap will make a half-moon shadow on his face. I'll tilt back my head to see the sky spread out all around him, the exact same color as his eyes.

I wait and wait, walking down the block, way past where I'm allowed to go. I walk past all the other houses out to the corner store and the newsstand and the drugstore. Back and forth, back and forth. A million trolleys come and go. Neighbors watch me through their windows. I almost hear their whispers, *There's one of those Sheehan girls, out looking for her father.* Doesn't stop me. I couldn't care less what they think. I walk back and forth, back and forth, until long after dark, but Daddy, Da, my father, never shows.

From far, far away, I hear knocking. Who else is in trouble? "Mrs. Malloy, oh, Mrs. Malloy." The sound of Duffy's voice brings me back to my apartment; he's calling through the door. Well, dammit. Dammit all to hell. Reluctantly, I get up and open it.

Duffy's standing there with a big smile and the new shelf.

"Sorry I didn't call ahead." He's so sweet, apologetic.

"No problem," I lie through my teeth.

"Everything OK?" he asks as I lead him into the bedroom. "You look a little pale."

"I'm fine, just a little headache coming on."

"Won't be long," he says. Once he's set up, I go back to my chair and the pendant, hoping Da's showed up. Duffy drills and hammers, making a racket to wake the dead, but my dead will not awaken. No. Da has disappeared again, like before.

Ten

I'M BEGINNING TO
SEE THE LIGHT

I suffer through the migraine, a day and night of darkness, blurred vision, zigzags, like lightning bolts flashing behind my eyelids. But when, in the morning, it departs, the world is beautiful, bright, and sparkling. Right away I want to call Cassie, and the snotty brain guy too. I want to call them both and tell them those black spots aren't dead. Because one just broke open and inside it was my father, Joe Sheehan, the real deal, with his spiky cowlicked hair, his laughing eyes, his dimpled smile. Joe Sheehan, Daddy, Da, and stuck to him like the sticky notes I used to love at work were memories of my sisters and me, back when we were little. Even if at first I confused Keeley and Fagan, a simple mistake anyone could make.

I speed-dial Cassandra—her son Mikey set it up for me. Wouldn't you know, she's in Orlando for a greeting-card convention. I'd forgotten until I heard the message on her machine. But as soon as I put the phone down, it rings. It's Ruth Ann, calling to remind me about her son Jared's concert tonight at the middle school. Forgot about that, too.

"I hate that drive, honey," I tell her. "I'm not up to it anymore." I think about Routes 3 and 93 and 101, and how they all merge and you've got to get yourself into the correct lane at fifty-five miles an hour or more or it's sayonara. Fighting eighteen-wheelers for every inch of highway.

"Oh, Mimi, for heaven's sake, you're what? Sixty-eight? You can handle it."

"Sixty-six."

"Sixty-seven. You're sixty-seven. Last November. You were born in 1927."

"Don't remind me." I try to make a joke of it, but I can't help but think about my ancient brain. Ruthie's getting in on Cassie's act. No mercy for Mom.

"Take the train to Nashua," Ruthie says, "and I'll drive you back to Quincy in the morning, after the kids are in school."

I can't think up an excuse fast enough. Plus, Ruthie's a good girl, and I don't want to hurt her feelings, even though she's always hurting mine. So I call Duffy and he's only too happy to drive me to the train station. Duffy's Car Service. He's got a big blue station wagon, a Caprice Classic, which he keeps in mint condition and neat as a pin, just as you'd expect from an old soldier, but with that nice tobacco smell from his Marlboros.

In the past, when I've called upon him for this favor, which he'll do for anyone who asks and a nice tip at Christmas, he's let me out at the entrance to the station. But this time he shows up at my door smelling of Old Spice, his cheeks pink and his silver hair combed wet. He walks me out to his car and then he parks and waits with me on the platform until the train pulls in. Takes my bag, even though it's one of those little ones on wheels with a handle like a telescope. A real gentleman. I keep the pendant in my pants pocket where I can feel it. I might show Ruthie, depending upon how things go, although that scratch has marred it, like a beautiful woman with a scar along her cheek.

The blood of folks living north of Boston must run thick as syrup, or maybe it's hot-fudge sauce, which we gorged on after Jared's concert. The thermostat at Ruthie's is set at fifty-five degrees when we hit the sack, Jared bunking with his brother for the night so I can sleep in his room. I crawl under layers of down that Ruthie promises will keep me toasty even if the temperature drops below zero and the boiler blows. "You'll sleep like a baby," she says. Maybe I do, but before I nod off, I think about my grandson's concert, Jared on the trumpet in the jazz ensemble. My kind of music, "Sing Sing Sing," "In the Mood," "Begin the Beguine," "Straight, No Chaser." But the truth is, I can hardly stand the sound of horns. They're painful to hear, like fingernails down a blackboard. Not that I'd dream of telling Ruthie, let alone my grandson. Like some type of parasite, the high notes crawl under my skin, linger too long. A sax, or a woodwind, is much more pleasing to my ear. Although, truth be told, Jack ruined me for clarinets.

When we got to the middle school, Ruthie wanted to sit right down in front. We'd get to see the whites of their eyes, wouldn't miss a note. We had a great view of all the darling girls and boys, all dressed in khaki pants and white polo shirts, giggling and poking at one another and trying, but failing, to act grown-up. Finally Jared was standing in the middle of the stage alone, blowing that horn, a solo part. But when he started playing, something sharp and hard stabbed me from the inside. I cringed and shivered. Ruthie grabbed my hand and squeezed.

"He's improvising," she whispered, her eyes soft and full of love. But me, I got a killer hot flash, the type I haven't had for years, where your face and neck turn scarlet and your underwear gets wet, and then you're shivering from the wet underwear. We stood up to applaud. Everyone else did too. Ruthie smiled, her cheeks shiny with tears, so proud.

Afterward, we went to Friendly's for ice-cream sundaes, my treat, with Jared still floating on Cloud Nine from the standing ovation.

"I got a standing O, Mom," he kept saying. "Didja see it? A big standing O!"

"He got his musical gift from Daddy," said Ruthie, digging into her sundae. "It must have skipped a generation, since I'm tone deaf."

"Daddy?" I echoed, my voice sharp. She was referring to Jack F. X. Malloy. My girls think that every good thing they and their kids got came by way of him. "Since when does your father have a musical gift?"

She turned to me, a fleck of hot fudge on her chin, her eyes as big as saucers, a pretty girl like all my daughters, but the only brunette. No makeup. Ruthie goes for that plain Yankee look, buys all her clothes from the L.L.Bean catalogue. It works for her.

"Oh, Mimi, did you forget he played the clarinet? Professionally? He could've had a musical career. . . ."

"Oh, honey, if he coulda, he woulda, believe me."

Jared watched us, a big spoonful of ice cream halted near his mouth. I scooped up some whipped cream and sauce. Delicious.

"You're always putting him down," she wailed, another sound that goes right through me.

"Am not." I gave Jared a big grin. "Hey, so how much do you practice every day?"

"Don't," he said, grinning back, but far more interested in our dispute than my question. "Mom's always nagging, but I hate to practice."

"No point discussing this with you, Mimi," said Ruthie, her heart shutting down. I watched it through her big blue eyes. But she was right. Because, in my opinion, Jack Malloy could play the notes, but he couldn't make the music, an opinion that enrages my daughters and results in bitter arguments.

In the morning, I wake up in the cold room surrounded by posters of soccer players and rock stars, and a band called Rage Against the Machine. What machine? I wonder. The washer? Or maybe it's the garbage disposal. Ruthie was having trouble with hers the night before. I can see my breath when I exhale, and I shut my eyes and snuggle deeper, not wanting to get out of bed, knowing that, in the cold, these old bones will creak and groan. I reach under my pillow for the pendant. I close my eyes and think about Jared's trumpet solo, the stabbing pain, and that thing inside me pushing to get out. Then it's my father I see, not my grandson, blowing on the horn. Da, standing tall, holding a shiny brass instrument. A cornet, not a trumpet, but with almost the exact same shape and sound. A hymn, "Amazing Grace." Sad notes glide and soar. I listen hard.

The sad music calls to me and my sisters, and all of us gather in the hall outside the parlor. Da's behind the closed French doors, the glass panes covered with lace curtains. We watch Da through the lace, stand-ing, his hands around his horn, his head lifted to the ceiling. The notes slide and swirl, tickling my belly, raising goose bumps on my arms.

"Mimi!" Ruthie hollers. She bangs on my door. "Want to say good-bye to the boys?" I pretend I'm still asleep. Not my idea of fun, getting children up and dressed and fed and off to the school bus on time. Been there, done that, too many times to count.

Instead I see Da, stippled with lace shadows. His fingers press the valves of his golden horn and the notes fly up, birds we hear but cannot see. He played in an Army band in World War I; went to Europe, not for combat, but to play music for the troops. Nana always bragged about him. Told anyone who'd listen, mostly us, how good he was, playing this wonderful American instrument that nobody in Ireland had ever laid their hands on. American music on an American instru-ment, it didn't get any better for her. "Last call!" Ruthie shouts through the door. "Your grandsons would like to say good-bye."

Da's uniform, with its shiny buttons, its epaulettes, its embroidered patch—PFC Joseph D. Sheehan—was kept in mothballs in a chest upstairs. Once in a while, my sisters and I sneaked up to look at it, our eyes and noses stinging from the naphthalene. Now his great-grandson Jared plays first trumpet in his junior high jazz band.

When I get up, I'll show Ruthie the pendant, let her in on the mys-tery, how it showed up on my closet floor, and how it's helping me to remember. It's filling the black spots back in. How Jared got his musi-cal gift from my father, not hers.

But when I walk into the kitchen, all showered and dressed and good to go, Ruthie's in a mood.

"I'm meeting Daddy for lunch. I'm going to be late."

"I'm ready, I'm all set, but I could use a cup of coffee."

"Fine. We'll go to Dunks."

Next thing we're in her minivan, making a quick stop at Dunkin' Donuts for coffee and bagels to go before heading south to Quincy. What I really want is a French cruller, or a vanilla crème in powdered sugar, but I don't have the nerve to ask. If I do, that news flash—Mimi Eating Doughnuts—will be flying through the wires all over the northeast where my daughters live. While Ruthie orders, I light up in the parking lot, thinking I'll grab a couple of puffs to hold me til I get home.

When Ruthie comes out, she gives me one of those looks to kill.

"Don't worry, I'll put it out," I tell her. "I wouldn't dream of polluting the air in your minivan."

"You were smoking in my driveway last night." She shoves the coffee into my hand. "I counted the butts, six of them."

"Well, excuse me. Didn't know you were the smoking police."

She gives me another look.

"You really shouldn't be smoking at all," she says. "It says right on the pack, 'Hazardous to Your Health.' But to yours more than others. That's what I hear, anyway."

She's looking at my lighted cigarette, not at me.

"You've been talking to Cassandra."

"What do you expect? If you won't tell me anything important, Cassandra has to."

"She's a blabbermouth. She ought to mind her own business."

"She says you've got black spots in your brain, Mimi. Black spots. You've got an eighty-five-year-old brain, for heaven's sake."

I take my time on one last drag, then grind the butt under my Rockport Walker. Blood, thin and cold, rushes to my head.

"Cass says you could stroke out any day. She says you're not supposed to light another cigarette."

Ruthie climbs into the van and starts the ignition. I'm so mad, I'm seeing stars. "And you don't even care enough to get up and say goodbye to your own grandsons." We take our seats in the minivan, which is all nice and warm because Ruthie left it running while she ordered. She's a good, fast driver, and traffic isn't bad, but my fun is ruined. It'll be a cold day in hell before I show her the pendant, or tell her about Da's music—how Jared's following in his footsteps, not those of Jack Malloy. The highways stretch out before us, six lanes, eight lanes, where once there was only forest. Ruthie negotiates the merges like a pro, without the slightest hesitation.

Again, I see my father with his horn. When we were really young, Da played all the time. He let us in to sit with him in the front parlor, a room we hardly ever used. The same place we gathered years later, when he told us Fagan had been sent away. Way back before then, my sisters and I, including Fagan, would lounge around him on the slippery brocade couch, or sometimes on the floor. Listening, not recognizing any melodies, but loving them just the same. When Da finished, we watched him put away his instrument. He let the spit drip out into a little can, then he cleaned the inside with an old diaper and a long, thin brush. He'd take apart the valves to clean and oil them. Once he was satisfied that his cornet was spotless and dry and perfect, he wrapped it in a white linen cloth and put it inside its leather case. The outside of this case was plain black cowhide, with brass clasps. But the inside was lined with the most beautiful red velvet, and shaped exactly like his cornet. He put the cornet inside just so, smoothing out the linen covering before closing the lid. He kept it on a closet shelf where none of us could reach it.

"Cassie says you've already had some little strokes."

We've hit the long straight stretch on I-93, the subdivisions and shopping strips of Pepperell and Leominster on either side. Ruthie's tone's a little gentler now. "Those TIA things, whatever they call them. She says they left areas of atrophy in your brain."

Her sweet voice doesn't soften me.

"Is that why you had me up for a sleepover? Did Cassie put you up to it? So you could get on my case?"

"Cassie didn't put me up to it," she cries in a way that convinces me otherwise. "It was my own idea." She turns to me. "I'm really worried about you, Mimi."

"Look, Ruth Ann, you're a great girl and I love you." She turns her attention back to the highway. "Your son's a wonderful musician. I'm glad I came to visit. But we won't be talking about what's going on inside my brain. Have you got that? And you can tell your other sisters in case any of them ask."

We go the rest of the way in a loud, aching silence.

Eleven

THE CURSE OF AN
ACHING HEART

hat happened to Daddy's music? That's the burning question after Ruthie leaves me off with an air kiss that's even colder than the temperature in her house at night and a promise that she'll call me soon. Not that my hug was any warmer. On her way back to the Granite State, she's stopping north of Boston for lunch with Jack F. X. Malloy. No doubt he'll take her out in his Grand Marquis, which he trades in for a new one every third year. He'll wine her and dine her at a place with linen tablecloths, servers instead of waitresses. Jack still can't resist a chance to show his daughters that he's got more money, more class, more style than their mother, the raggedy-ass orphan he lifted out of poverty.

We had some hard years, many hard years, Jack and me, but the beginning of the end didn't come until my hysterectomy, when the doctors cut me open and scooped me out. They went into that place way down below, where I'd been cut open and sewn up so many times from all those babies, it's no wonder I had trouble keeping what was inside me in, and what was outside out. And he, my husband, didn't visit because hospitals depress him.

For six weeks after that surgery, I was laid up at home, unable to cook or clean, a terrible inconvenience to him. I couldn't steam press his shirts and starch the collars, organize his socks into perfect little balls in his bureau drawers, or give him the occasional piece of tail—all out of the question in my condition.

Once I tried to tell him how I felt. "You and the girls, you take whatever you want of me, whenever you feel like it. I can't keep anything to myself, or do anything for myself. Sometimes I don't even know who I am, or who I'm supposed to be." Words deeper than the deepest prayer I'd ever prayed.

"You've never had it so good, and you know it," Jack answered, fixing me with those gorgeous blue bedroom eyes of his, eyes that had once made my heart go pitter-pat. "You've got a beautiful home, a new Ford Fairlane of your own, and six smart, healthy daughters. Whoever would have expected that from one of you Sheehan girls?" Then he walked away and my face burned as if he'd slapped me. I heard the other words he didn't say: *You Sheehan girls, raggedy-ass orphans, with the no-good drunk for a father.* Like my sisters and I were damaged goods, something from Filene's Basement after two or three markdowns.

I'm glad to be home. Glad to be alone. I love my little place. It's all mine. When I moved in, neutered by the hysterectomy, wiped out by the divorce, stung a thousand times by my daughters' swarming attitudes, the rooms were empty and I loved their emptiness. Those rooms seemed somehow holy, like the kind nuns have in a cloister. I might have left them that way, except I was too old to sleep on the floor, and my daughters would've taken it as further evidence of my craziness. So I bought some furniture, not Ethan Allen, not what Jack's house was full of—a lower grade, but good enough for me.

For the first time in my life, I had a room of my own. I could take long baths with the bathroom door open, then wander from room to room wrapped in just a towel. I had a bed all to myself. I could watch *The Late Show* whenever I felt like it. Johnny Carson cracked me up, especially Carnac the Magnificent. What a hoot. God, I miss him, wish he hadn't retired. Leno can't hold a candle to him, and I've never warmed up to that other one, the geeky one with glasses. I'd rather sleep.

My bed is covered with the loveliest wedding-ring quilt, one that Ruthie sewed for me, in shades of yellow, pink, and green. I've got one of my own crocheted afghans, in coordinating colors, stretched out over the foot. Feather pillows, Laura Ashley sheets with little flowers, 400-thread-count cotton, found by yours truly in a clearance bin at Marshalls—a real steal. I hurried to the checkout with them, thinking they'd made a mistake and wouldn't find out if I got out of there fast enough.

I spend a couple of hours reorganizing my closet and its nice new shelf with scented shelf paper. Soon, everything's in its place, just so. I get some laundry going in the coin machines down the hall. Then I settle into the La-Z-Boy, holding the blue pendant, still wondering about Da's music. How I wish I had a photo album of our family way back when—one I could open at my leisure, lingering over the pictures. But we don't have any photos, we surviving Sheehan girls.

I think about how my father, unlike my ex, didn't just play an instrument. No, he made music, the most beautiful music. But he played less and less as the years went by, and one day he just stopped. Was it before or after Mammy died? Before or after he remarried? Before or after Fagan Sent Away? I can't remember. Not that I've thought much about it.

Then, out of nowhere, I see myself with my sisters, and we're gathered by the old black stove in the kitchen, the house around us cold and dark. My heart thumps when I see Da, sitting in a straight-backed chair, my sisters and I wrapped around him like vines, hanging off him every which way, every one of us determined to get a piece of him. I rub my cheek along his arm, the soft cotton of his shirt. He pats my hair, absentmindedly, perhaps, but I'll take what I can get. I'm Daddy's girl, I know it, a conviction each of the others shared. Every one of us believed we were Da's special girl. We'd been wheedling, the bunch of us, begging him for music. *Da, Da, please. Pretty please with butter and sugar on it.* But he did not give in. Then I asked him, *Da, why don't you play your music anymore?*

Can't, he answered, making funny faces.

Why not?

I lost my lip. Which struck me and my sisters as the biggest joke, Da losing his lip. My sisters laughed.

You did not, I cried. *It's right there on your face.* And I grabbed his lip to prove my point.

Then Da laughed too, tugging on his lips, pulling them every which way, because they weren't lost at all but were still there, glued to his face, exactly where they were supposed to be.

But in the middle of our laughter, Da stopped; looked up as something stopped him cold. I felt it in his body, but would not turn around to look. It was Flanna. We all knew, every one of us, that it was Flanna, who could not bear to let him love us. She had to keep every last bit of him for herself. Again Da disappears before my eyes, the worst of his magic tricks.

I get up from my chair and go into the kitchen for a glass of cold water from the tap. I wipe down the counter and the stovetop even though they're already clean. I go out and move the laundry from the washer to the dryer. Things I don't quite recognize fly around me, like clothes when they're on the fluff cycle. Fear and maybe longing, stuck together, static cling. Beyond them, I see the maps of my mind up on the screen in the brain guy's office. Black spots among swirls of color. *Areas of atrophy,* he said.

I go into my bedroom looking for a project. I need something to do, gotta keep busy. I learned that from Nana, who never rested. But everything's already in its place. I open my bureau drawers and see the neat rows of bras and panties, lined up as perfectly as cars in a dealer's lot.

Of course, longing takes many forms. Even I know that. Longing to be young and thin and beautiful again. Longing for a straight-up Manhattan, so you can forget you're not. Or the sound of Sinatra singing so it doesn't matter quite as much. Longing for a bit more money so you won't have to pinch pennies, worrying every minute about how to make ends meet. Longing to take a cruise to the Caribbean, to bake half-dressed in the sun all day, and dress up every night for dinner, a dinner you haven't cooked and won't have to clean up from. With somebody who doesn't mind a little extra padding around your hips and thighs. Who loves you anyway.

Longing to be that special someone to somebody, like it always says on Cassie's greeting cards, the way it never was with Jack. Longing for a photo album of my family back when we were kids. Longing to make it right with Malvina, my lost kid in the Bronx. A woman now, with children of her own. Longing. Longing to be loved.

Fear, on the other hand, well, it pulls tight like a fabric winding, stretching, binding even though you can't see it, can't touch it, can't wrap your mind around it. Fear of what the test results will say. Fear of what will happen when your car won't start and you don't have anyone to call. Fear of being stuck in an elevator, or locked in a dark closet. Fear of falling in the shower, breaking a hip, with nobody there to pull you out. Fear of living too long and running out of money, of becoming a burden to your children. Fear of being old, alone, and feeble. Forgotten. Fear. You can't see it; can't get a handle on it; can't contain it, but there it is: One size fits all.

It's almost dark now, so I switch on a light but don't pull down the shades. That way, if Duffy wants a cup of coffee, he'll know he can stop by. I go back to my recliner and pick up the pendant. How I wish I had Da's picture; that I could see him, handsome Joey Sheehan, just once more in his prime, with his dimples and those dreamy eyes with the thick eyelashes he hated, because the fellas at the shipyard teased that they were pretty as a girl's. Da. He had a bunch of brothers, and people used to call them those good-looking Sheehan boys. Sam, Teddy, Leo, and Joe. It was the same way, in the next generation, with me and my sisters. *Those glorious Sheehan girls.*

One of them must have an old photo of him, and I make a mental note to ask the next time we're together, though even I'll admit my mental notes are nowhere near as effective as they used to be. Not that we had any kind of family album growing up. We were too poor to have many pictures. And the ones we did own, the very few photographs of my parents and my sisters and me as babies, Flanna Flanagan tore up and burned.

Flanna, with her enchanting face for Da, another one for us—exactly alike, but not at all the same. Switched so fast you couldn't predict when it would happen. She sang and prayed in ways we didn't understand, had a garden where she grew forbidden things. There was hell to pay if we dared step into it. I never did. She would harvest those forbidden things and boil them up on the stove, stinking up the house. Old folks in the neighborhood would line up to buy them. Flanna, a Lucky Strike between her fingers, a glass of whiskey by her side. Whispering to herself, making us eat and drink the awful stuff she made when our father wasn't there.

Flanna Flanagan. *How blessed Da was to catch her, himself a widower with all those little girls to raise!* That's what everybody said. A godsend was Flanna Flanagan. But we wondered, right from the start, my sisters and me, what type of god would send someone like her our way. Somebody who was always present even when you couldn't see her.

Da said he lost his lip that night when we begged him to play music, but he didn't lose it. Flanna stole it off his face. I slip and slide into the tunnel of memory, Flanna standing over the burn can in the backyard. Smoke and flame shoot out of it. Flanna, with her face as pretty as an angel's painted on the ceiling of a church. The wind lifts bits and pieces of what she's burning, scatters the ashes like snow. Pictures of my mother, and of my mother and father together, the only photographs we owned. *No no, no,* I say. She shoves me away. I grab her arm; she grabs my neck and shakes me. I topple, taste dirt and ash. Hear her scrape another match down the side of the can and toss it in. All the scraps of pictures are in flames. *I'm your mammy now,* she says.

I heave myself up out of the chair. Suffering a sudden palsy, I am like one of those decrepit patients at the old folks' home. Jittering from head to foot. A side effect of memory, of shaking loose the promise I made to myself long ago, to erase Flanna from my life. And now she's back again, tagging along with Da, hanging on to him for dear life, refusing to ever let him go.

The pendant flies out of my hand, bounces across the floor, and lands on the far side of the coffee table. It sparkles on the carpet. Worthless. No value whatsoever. That's what Cassie's jeweler said. Water and paste. Nobody ought to have to go through this, I decide. I'm going to get rid of the damned thing. Throw it away. Good riddance to bad rubbish. I snatch it off the floor and head out back to the Dumpster.

Twelve

ARE YOU LONESOME
TONIGHT?

The Dumpster's just outside the back door, in an alcove near the parking lot, the area lit by a motion-sensor floodlight. As I head out to it, my pumper settles down and the palsy eases, and who do I see on the other side of the glass back door but Duffy. He's sweeping up, or trying to sweep up, a mess of Styrofoam peanuts scattered like drifts of snow around the Dumpster. A careless tenant must've thrown in a carton, and the peanuts have blown back out. So here's Duffy, chasing them down, which is like trying to catch air. He holds a broom in one hand, and in the other one of those nifty dustpans janitors use, with the long handle so you don't have to bend over and the flap in front to hold the dirt inside.

But every time Duffy tries to sweep in the peanuts, only a few go in and the rest blow back out, even farther away, and he chases after them, looking awkward, with the bum leg. He tries really hard, but the harder he sweeps, the more the peanuts fly around, like they're doing it on purpose, just to get his goat. The poor guy bends this way and that, trying different sweeping strokes, like he thinks he can outsmart them. I crack up, can't help it. He turns and sees me, and, if it's possible, his face gets even redder. I push open the door.

"Mrs. Malloy, oh Mrs. Malloy, what brings you out here on such a chilly evening?" His question makes me laugh even harder.

"Stalking. I'm stalking you."

"I should be so lucky," he answers without missing a beat, and I laugh harder still.

"Well, I'm glad to be so entertaining. For the second time in recent memory, I'm putting on a show for you." I picture him on his butt on my bedroom floor and laugh some more.

"No way to outsmart those little devils," I say, pointing to the peanuts between snorts and giggles, and at last he's smiling too. Then I get an idea.

"Where's the box they came in?"

Sure enough, it's right there on top of the Dumpster.

"Fold back the flaps," I tell him, getting myself back together. "Then I'll hold it, and you sweep."

Works like a charm. I bend over to hold the box steady on the ground while Duffy sweeps. In minutes, we scoop up every last one. Then we redo the flaps so the peanuts can't escape and Duffy tosses the box back into the Dumpster while I stand over to the side, breathing hard from laughter and exertion.

"Good thing you came along when you did. I'd be out here all night, still chasing them."

"Don't hate me because I'm efficient," I say in a teasing way, and he grins.

"What brings you out here?" he repeats.

"I was only kidding about the stalking thing."

"I wasn't," he answers. My turn to blush.

"Doing a little trashing of my own," I say, to switch the track of our conversation. I take the pendant out of my pocket. In the floodlight by the door, it's so lovely, my heart aches. You can hardly see the scratch. He gasps.

"You mean to tell me, Mrs. Malloy, that you're going to put that beautiful piece in the Dumpster? Have you lost your senses?"

I nod yes, feeling ridiculous, knowing now I could never toss it.

"If you don't want it, hock it. At least get a few bucks for it."

I nod.

"Good thing I was out here."

"One good turn deserves another, right?" I grin and look up into his nice eyes.

"That's right. But why toss it?" he persists.

I don't have much of an answer. "It brings back bad memories. Every time I look at it. Memories I don't want to have."

He wraps his big old hand around my small one holding the pendant and presses my hand around it.

"Out of sight, out of mind," he says, like he's some kind of expert on bad memories. "Solves the problem, doesn't it?"

I'm turning to go back inside when I hear him call out again. "I don't suppose, Mrs. Malloy, that you'd want to walk up to Clancy's with me in a bit? It's ladies' night. I'll buy you a beer."

For all the complaining my kids do about this apartment, they fail to see one of its best points: location. Just two blocks from the Square, within easy walking distance of just about anything I'd ever want or need. A pharmacy, a deli, a butcher's, a baker's, a package store, a diner, several Irish pubs, and an underwear place called Fanny's Foundations—not to mention my parish, Our Lady Queen of Peace, an honest-to-God old cathedral. We could be snowed in for weeks and I could still take care of both my corporal and my spiritual needs. You've got to think about such things when you're old and on your own and living in a cold climate.

Duffy and I agree on a time to meet by the front door, leaving plenty of time for the two of us to shower and change, and before you know it, we're sitting at a barside booth at Clancy's, and we're lighting up with a couple of frosty ones in front of us. I'm not crazy about beer—too gassy—but when Duffy said he'd buy me one, it seemed pushy to say I'd prefer a highball.

"It's all your fault," I tell him once the beers are placed before us.

"My fault? What's my fault, Mrs. Malloy?" I've told him at least a million times to call me Mimi, or even Maire, but he insists on Mrs. Malloy. Which I now realize seems to be a little tease, because the way he says it, it has a sexy sound to it. *Mrs. Malloy.*

"When you came to check that leak and the closet shelf fell down. That's when I found the pendant—on the floor, like someone had just dropped it there. It was my mother's, but I have no idea how it ended up in my closet."

He nods like he wants me to go on.

"Well, we lost her when I was six, no seven, my mother. She died when my baby sister was born."

"Not so unusual back then, not like now. Still, forgetting isn't always such a bad thing," he says. "Sometimes you've got to in order to go on." I look at him, grateful that he seems to understand. "Forget too much, though, and you risk forgetting who you are." He takes a swallow of his beer.

"Perish the thought," I say, and we both laugh.

"So you decided to throw it away, the pendant?"

"Well, I was looking at it, and all of a sudden, I saw my stepmother, who was worse than the worst one in a fairy tale. I mean, she was right there with me, in my living room. Like she'd come back to finish the job she started when we were kids. Scared the hell out of me."

"Finish the job?"

"Ruin us all, all over again. That's why I decided to throw the pendant away."

"She doesn't live inside the pendant."

"No, it was an irrational fear. I know that."

"But you survived." He smiles, like he's glad about this fact. Before I can answer, the waitress appears. She's an old gal like me, but with dangly earrings. She's got red hair, with a quarter inch of pure-white new growth like an outline around her skull. Asks if we want another, and Duffy tells her yes, then asks me am I hungry? It's Friday, fish-and-chips night, and everybody knows Clancy's fish and chips are the best on the South Shore. Chunks of boneless haddock, batter-dipped and deep-fried. The chips hand cut and shining with hot oil when they bring them to the table. A nightmare of saturated fat, but truly scrumptious, especially with the tartar sauce and coleslaw. How can I say no? But thinking of the havoc the coleslaw will wreak on my stomach, I decline the second beer.

"What about something else? Whatever you want."

"A highball," I tell the waitress. "A nice rye and ginger, with lots of ice."

When she's gone I tell Duffy, "Thanks so much." He's the kind of man who treats you right. I can't remember the last time I sat across a table from a man who wanted to hear what I have to say. "This is lovely. But I'll spare you the grim details of my childhood."

"I'm interested. I mean, if you want to talk."

I shrug, not sure I believe him. I think about Cassie and her healing therapies.

"You've seen my oldest, right? Cassandra?" He nods. "Well, she's been in therapy for ages, every time I turn around, a different type of therapy, names I can't even remember, with Twelve Steps this and Twelve Steps that. Behavioral, cognitive, whatever. She's made a career of it." I catch my breath. "All because of the quote-unquote dysfunction in our family."

Duffy grins. It's familiar to him, this aggravation from the kids, so I play it up a bit.

"She goes to seminars 'on the family' and to expensive retreats about codependency. Whatever that means. Codependency. She's never been able to explain it in a way that makes sense."

Now Duffy's chuckling. "Adult children," he says, shaking his head.

"Adult children. Perfect," I repeat, and it tickles me that he gets it. We're on the same page.

"Once, when Cassie was in the middle of one of these therapies, she tells me I must've suffered child abuse when I was growing up. That I'm emotionally absent because of this child abuse. Emotionally absent. Me." We laugh as the waitress shows up with our drinks. We touch glasses, say cheers, and have a swallow.

"I told her that we didn't have child abuse when I was growing up. 'You mean you didn't have a word for it,' she says, correcting me in this high-and-mighty tone she has. 'No,' I tell her, 'I mean we didn't have it. People raised their kids however they saw fit and everybody else minded their own business. Nobody had anything to say about it. The kids were expected to carry on.' Isn't that right?" I ask Duffy.

"You bet," he says. "Not like now. Nowadays you bring your kid into the emergency room after he falls off a bike, and they give you the third degree, suspect you've committed child abuse, or something worse."

"What's worse?"

He shakes his head no. His cheeks turn pinker.

"Well, Cass won't leave it alone. She can't leave anything alone. Tells me maybe my problems—I have problems just because I'm not perfect—my so-called problems stem from post traumatic stress disorder. That I show symptoms of PTSD. That's what she called it. PTSD. 'Alphabet soup,' I answered."

The waitress shows up with our food, a golden display, except for the coleslaw and tartar sauce in little cups on the side. Steam rises from our platters and Duffy says, "Dig in." And that's exactly what we do.

The fish and chips don't disappoint, and while we eat, I think about how we've known each other for the almost fifteen years I've lived in Centennial Square. Knew he was a widower, a disabled World War II vet, but our friendship never went beyond that. Of course, until recently, I worked full-time. Always rushing off to work, and too pooped to pop after I got home. Weekends were taken up with housework, and socializing with my kids and sisters. And me, the walking wounded, I wasn't close to being ready to take a chance on another guy. Jack did me in. But in the past year, since my retirement, we keep running into each other, and when we sit and share a smoke, I feel a warmth—not the hot-flash type—but something softer and deeper.

Now, between bites and swallows, he tells me about his two sons, the married one in Vermont, but not far too from Ruthie in New Hampshire, and the other in Bridgewater. Three grandchildren. Grew up in Southie, married a girl from Dedham, then went off to war, like all the other good Irish boys. Served in the Navy on a destroyer, the *Quincy II*, built right here at the yard. Took part in D-Day. He processed the bodies of the American dead, a job guaranteed to send most people over the edge, but Duffy apparently kept his act together, even after he took a piece of shrapnel in the thigh. Won a Purple Heart; was permanently disabled. His wife, Virginia, a junior high school teacher, died of breast cancer at forty-three, when the boys were in their teens. That's when he moved into Centennial Square, where, between his disability benefits and his free rent and salary as a super, he was able to make ends meet.

"Well, up until a few months ago, I worked at the VA Hospital over in Jamaica Plain. Medical records."

"Then you know it's real, PTSD."

"Sure, but that's for combat vets, not a little girl growing up on the South Shore."

"Maybe you shuffled some of my papers."

I look up at him, and it feels a whole lot more personal than it ought to, this shuffling of his papers. Odd that among the thousands of files I handled every week, some might've belonged to Himself: Mr. Richard J. Duffy, the silver-haired super of my apartment complex. Not a dead ringer for Paul Newman, Paul being Jewish, after all, but close enough to give me those zings and ring-a-ding dings that Frankie sings about, especially when I look deep into his eyes. They're hazel, Duffy's eyes—like the color of the sea, but in a darker shade, instead of Paul's sapphire blue.

"Forgetting's not always such a bad thing," he says again. I nod in agreement but close my eyes, shutting myself off from his sympathy, or maybe it's my shame. Even after all this time, I still feel it.

"Getcha anything else, hon?" I hear the waitress say, and I turn to her, pretending I was only blinking. We order coffee and agree, without saying a word, to leave the dark place of ancient history, and instead talk about the rising cost of gasoline and how much snow we figure we'll get this winter. Duffy pays in cash, and leaves a generous tip in the middle of the table. He helps me with my coat.

Outside the air's still but very cold, cold enough to suck away our breath. The sky is clear and full of stars. About halfway home, he takes my hand, but both of us are wearing gloves, Gore-Tex lined with

Thinsulate, the kind you need to protect yourself from frostbite during a Boston winter. I'm still wondering what his hand would feel like when we get to the front entrance of Paul Revere. I punch in my code. Next thing I know, he touches my cheek with his bare hand, kisses the spot he touched, and then disappears into the night.

Thirteen

IN THE WEE SMALL HOURS
OF THE MORNING

My head is spinning after I climb into bed, but not from the beer and the highball. I had a date with Duffy. A date with Duffy. He bought me dinner, walked me home, and kissed me at my door. That part keeps replaying, Duffy touching my cheek with his sandpapery hand, then kissing me on the cheekbone, just below my eye. A sweet kiss, and him gone by the time I realize what he's done. Just as well. I might've grabbed him and kissed him back, assuming I can remember how to kiss a man. But maybe it's like riding a bike: once you've got it, you never lose it.

I toss and turn. Can't quiet my mind. Lots of uninvited guests stopping by, my kids, my sisters, my ex. A regular family reunion, chaotic like always. So many people blabbering at once I can't understand a word. Then Fagan emerges out of the chaos, as if she'd been there all this time—almost sixty years. Fagan. I loved her so, but I forgot what it was like to feel that love after she got sent away. Da called her his squeaky wheel, his fire engine. *Cute as the devil*, Da said. With her red hair, bright and shiny, like a new penny. *A holy terror.* That's what everybody called her. Pale white skin with freckles, cinnamon sprinkles, across her nose and cheeks. Da's bright eyes.

Back when we were little, we girls could never keep our fingers off a scab, and my own daughters, I'm sorry to say, repeated this disgusting habit. Mostly skinned knees and elbows, nothing serious. No matter how often we were warned about infection, told that the scab was a good thing, allowing healing underneath. Did my sisters and I listen? Not on your life. We'd pick away at the brown crust—sneakily, enjoying the pricks of pain—until we saw the shiny pink new skin underneath. Left behind worse scars than if we'd done what we were supposed to and left the scabs alone. Alone now, in the wee small hours, I can't help picking at the scab, the unhealed place where the memories of my first baby sister wait. Why did she get sent away? And why didn't anyone in our family say one word about it?

Thinking hard, hard, hard about her, I get a dark feeling, then a hot flash. Fagan was a whiner and a pest. After Mam died, she never stopped. Pressed my buttons more times than I could count, and wouldn't stop even when I warned her off. Fagan, the Olympic gold-medal champion of button-pushing. Knew how to get everyone's goat without even trying, causing trouble was her special gift. *She deserves to be sent away.* That's what I thought when it happened, that Fagan was the source of all the trouble in our family. *She deserved to be sent back to Ireland, to Cullyhanna, County Armagh, where she would learn how to be good.*

Well, it worked. What a relief! Because after Fagan Sent Away, everything was peaceful. For a little while, at least.

You're a brat, a baby.

Am not!

You are too. Fusspot! Tattletale!

What could we have been fighting about, Fagan and me? Back then, everything was life and death, a piece of candy, a doll, a soft place in the bed, all the things we wanted in a world of Not Enough. I remember when she scribbled on every single page of my coloring book. I could have killed her. And I might have tried, knocking her to the floor, twisting her arms behind her back. Another time, she ripped my favorite paper dolls. Not on purpose, by accident, but what difference did that make? She destroyed them. Talk about the pain of loss! My

Shirley Temple paper dolls! Still, I loved Fagan, I really did, in spite of all of that. Fussy little Fagan, Da's holy terror. She couldn't help herself.

All of us, except maybe Eden, wore hand-me-downs. That's how it worked, not just for us, but for all the other kids we knew. Anything usable was passed down to the next one. In our family, by the time a dress or sweater got to Fagan, it had already been worn by three or four others.

Once Fagan got passed an old pair of my Mary Janes, blue, with T-straps and pretty perforations on the toe. My favorite shoes. Granted, they'd been Alberta's before they got to me, but they were still in pretty good shape, and Da brought them to the cobbler for new buckles and new heels.

Me, I'd know enough to be grateful. I'd have kissed Da like he'd given me a gift of finest gold. But those shoes weren't good enough for Fagan. She blew a gasket when Da gave them to her. She hollered and threw herself onto the floor, kicking, flailing her arms, turning herself purple. Then she opened the door of the old black stove and tossed them in. Da tried to get them out with an iron poker, but they were already burning, stinking up the house.

I'll put you over my knee and warm your little bottom for you, Da threatened, but all of us, including Fagan, knew he wouldn't. Da never laid a finger on any of us in anger. Next thing we knew, Fagan had new Mary Janes, red ones, that turned me green with envy. She never took them off, never missed a chance to make me jealous, tap-dancing around the house in them. She even tried to sleep with them on her feet. I know because I saw her.

Fagan must have burned the old Mary Janes between the time Mam died and Flanna Flanagan showed up. Because everything changed once Flanna arrived. Well, Fagan didn't change. She was her same old self, a squeaky wheel, and nobody could oil her into silence.

One Sunday morning not too long after Flanna became our new mother, all of us were getting ready to go to church, a big deal in those days. Everybody dressed up in their best, all the girls with a hat or scarf or veil to cover their heads. Fasting from suppertime the night before, and then there were all the preparations, shoe polishing, hair curling, dress ironing. Well, Fagan was supposed to wear a pink ruffled dress that Flanna had starched and pressed for her, a pretty dress that had already made its way from the top of the line on down to her. But the starch and ruffles scratched her delicate skin and, again, she threw a fit, a Fagan fit.

Over my dead body you'll take off that dress, said Flanna, who kept going about her business, getting herself ready for church—wearing, I might add, another of my mother's dresses. Next thing we knew, Fagan had cut the skirt of her dress into ribbons. Somehow, she found Flanna's sewing shears and went to work. While she was still wearing it. Hilarious, so funny, my sisters and I thought, but we knew enough not to laugh.

At Flanna's insistence, Daddy took the rest of us to Mass. Flanna and Fagan stayed home. When we got back, with a box of pastries from Hanrahan's, Daddy's way of smoothing troubled waters, Fagan was nowhere to be found. Flanna refused to let her have a pastry, and the next time we saw her, her beautiful red hair was cut off into spiky little tufts and she was wearing only underpants. She had to stay in just her underpants for a week or more.

That'll teach you, you devil, Flanna kept repeating, her accent so thick we made fun of her behind her back. Alberta, a hot ticket, was the best. She could do a perfect Flanna until the rest of us were paralyzed with laughter. That Sunday, we three oldest saved Fagan pieces of our pastries, crushed and stale by the time we got them to her. Fagan gobbled them down.

Lick your mouth and fingers, I warned her, *so Flanna doesn't know.*

Fagan Sent Away, an ancient injury that hasn't healed at all. My pistol of a sister. A piece of work they'd call her nowadays. Yes, Fagan was a piece of work. Then she was gone. Just like that.

I sit up in bed with the light still on. The pressure of the black spots hurts, places where the stories end before they're over. I pick up the blue pendant, run my fingertip around its edges. I'm glad Duffy made me keep it, yet I'm still afraid of what it holds.

Queer light shines at the edges of my vision. Flanna Flanagan, Da's secret rose, my stepmother. At the sight of her, my heart kicks into overdrive and a lump swells in my throat. Got to get around her, past her, no matter how much it hurts; no matter how afraid I am. Wade into the red tide, even if it poisons me. I have to remember how things were before she came, and everything that happened afterward.

A searing pain flashes behind my eyes. A black spot bursting open. Mam's gone, but Da is with us. He takes us, one by one, my sisters and me, to the neighbor's to wait while the midwife birthed the baby. That's how it was done in those days, not like now, in the hospitals, where parents-to-be, my daughters tell me, take lessons on how to breathe during labor, then get Champagne and filet mignon to celebrate after the baby's born. Learning how to breathe. It's all I can do to keep a straight face when my girls show me how they huff and puff. Oh, and their husbands have to huff and puff along with them because, somehow or other, they tell me, it doesn't hurt so bad that way.

Da walks me down the street to the Callahans'. "Let's Have Another Cup of Coffee," he sings, and he makes me sing too, to mimic him, in his silly voices so I won't cry about leaving Mam. *Just around the corner, there's a rainbow in the sky, so let's have another cup of coffee and another piece of pie.* I laugh and laugh, and Da laughs, too. *There's a rainbow in the sky, let's eat another slice of pie.*

I played hopscotch on the sidewalk with the Callahan kids, but it was February, too cold to play outside for long. Afterward, we colored in the kitchen where Mrs. Callahan was cooking. We ate mayonnaise sandwiches for lunch. Finally I stood by myself, by the storm door down the back stairs. Suppertime, because the Callahan children were squabbling at the table, and I smelled their stew. But I wasn't hungry. Knew, though I could not tell time, that I'd waited long past the time Da ought to have come back for me. Waiting and waiting. Finally, I walked downstairs to the back door and pressed my face against the glass so I could see up the street in the direction Da would come from.

Mrs. Callahan let me go. Didn't say a word. Let me stand in the shadows by the back door while she fed her family. By then she must have known, even without a telephone, that something had gone wrong, that too much time had passed. It felt like forever before I heard Da whistling, saw him stepping out of the shadows. He had a loping walk, scarecrow-skinny Da. That's how I knew him in the dark.

He comes toward me, but I do not run out to him. Still he whistles, such a sad song, no more cup of coffee, no more rainbow in the sky. When he sees me, he breaks into a run. *My sweet little contrary Maire.* He opens the door, gathers me up, tosses me into the air so the dark sky spins around. He catches me, hugs me tight, so that his whiskers scratch my face. *You have another little sister, a real beauty*, he whispers. The sharp smell of whiskey stings my eyes.

I get up out of bed. It's three thirty A.M., too late to call anyone. They'd have me put away for sure. I get up and get Patty's questionnaire and a pen, and bring them back to bed with me. I look at the questions, and the lines where you fill in the answers. All it asks for are facts, no spaces for the blood, sweat, and tears attached to them; my mother, Maire Margaret Ahearn Sheehan, a green-eyed brunette, black Irish, who played piano and loved to sing; who had, despite her family's poverty, graduated from teachers college and worked as an elementary school teacher before becoming a mother. She died at thirty-four, leaving behind a husband and seven daughters, most of us Irish twins, and one set of real ones.

Maybe the grown-ups thought we girls were too young to notice Mam was gone. Looking back, that's the only explanation I can come up with—they thought we wouldn't notice our mother had disappeared. Wanting to make them happy, I suppose, we pretended that we didn't. We girls ranged in age from eleven to three, not counting the new baby we didn't see for a couple of years, but we weren't allowed to cry. I don't remember that we did, except maybe into our pillows, scrunched up in the beds we shared, swallowing the hiccups so no one else would hear.

Irish wakes, I've heard, are the best parties in the world. They last for days, with singing, dancing, and drinking; the old women keening. But you can't prove this by me. When Mammy died, my father, my grandparents, my aunts and uncles acted like it hadn't happened.

Mammy, who got to live less than half her life—who didn't get to raise her own kids—didn't get any kind of royal send-off.

If there was a funeral, we girls didn't go to it. We didn't even know our mother had been buried, let alone where. Afterward, it was as if she had never been. No one ever spoke her name. Then one day, who knows how long after that, Da came home with Flanna and said she was our new mother.

I fill in the spaces with these facts, the ones my sisters will repeat on their questionnaires. I lost my mother young. A fact of my life. When I was too young to know what losing a mother meant. I've already lived so much longer, but I've never once thought about it, how Mam got cheated out of living most of her life, and we got cheated out of having her in ours. How nobody I know of, not even her own daughters, ever keened for her.

I wake up with the pen still in my hand, the light still on. It's after nine A.M., but I feel like I haven't slept. I get up, get dressed, drink a cup of coffee. Looking through the blinds, I see it's gloomy outside, the parking lot smeared with ice and dirty snow. I put on a warm coat, hat, and gloves, and go out to warm up my little Shadow because she gets balky in the cold. On the far side of the parking lot, Duffy's sprinkling salt along the walkways. I wave to him as I drive by. He stops to watch me go.

Turns out to be one of the coldest days of the year and the roads are terrible, ice everywhere. Metro Boston during a deep freeze, last week's snow not yet melted. I skid a couple of times. Can't remember if you turn into or away from the skid, if you tap the brakes or take your foot off. I'm scared, but I figure what the hell. Half a century has gone by now, and I am going to visit Da. I have some questions for him; don't know why I haven't thought of them before. At least I know where he's buried.

Gate of Heaven Cemetery. Yes, Da was buried there, way back when, more than half a century ago. I have trouble finding it. I make a couple of wrong turns, and when I finally get there, the whole cemetery is covered under a blanket of snow.

What could I have been thinking? I drive slowly along the cemetery's curved and hilly lanes, through a garden of granite stones, but only the biggest stick out of the snow, and Da, I'm certain, doesn't have one of the biggest. I park near where I think Da might be, get out, and trudge ahead, but I can't remember if Da's buried to the right side or the left. Can't even remember the last time I was here. I step through the snow, colder and deeper than I'd figured. It spills into my Rockports. I get a terrible feeling of being lost.

I stumble across a stone with a familiar name—Jimmy Callahan, our paperboy, the grandson of the neighbor who watched me the day Mam died. Brown-eyed and freckle-faced, full of the Dickens. Jimmy used to babysit my girls, playing and roughhousing with them so every one of them had the biggest crush on him. He was walking home from school late one day when a drunk driver struck him, crushed him against a utility pole, just a few steps from his home.

Later I'll feel sad for Jimmy Callahan, but at the moment I'm too cold. I see the white cottage where the cemetery's caretaker works. Smoke is coming from its chimney. I go over and knock. After a few minutes, a middle-aged man opens the door, gestures for me to enter. Fire spits and crackles in a wood-burning stove. He's listening to an oldies station out of Boston. A *Globe* is folded neatly by his rocking chair.

"I'm looking for my father," I say. "Joe Sheehan. Can you tell me where he's buried?"

"Joe Sheehan?" His voice is high-pitched, whiny. "Which one?"

"Which one?" I'm still shivering, and he gestures for me to warm myself by the fire. I step closer to it, holding out my hands, feeling like a lost child in a fairy tale, Gretel without Hansel.

"We got a half dozen. At least."

"Joseph Daniel," I say. "Died back in '37."

He gives me a look, one that says I'm a nut case, but I'm much too old—and cold—to care. He takes out a big brown ledger, thicker than the Boston phone book, and he turns the pages slowly, sighing and grunting. At last he shakes his head yes, and tells me where to go.

"Any other time, I'd be happy to drive you in the golf cart," he says in a way that does not convince me, "but I can't use it in the snow."

"Not a problem," I tell him, and go back outside, the wind and cold snatching away my breath.

Just a few minutes later, on the far edge of the cemetery, I find Da. His plot abuts a chain link fence that runs along the backyards of the houses on the street next to the cemetery. On the other side, behind Da's plot, there's an aboveground pool and a deck with a barbecue grill attached, a clothesline with frozen blue jeans hanging on it. Da's stone doesn't quite make it up through the snow. I kneel down to clear it and then I see his name: *Joseph Daniel Sheehan, August 10, 1896–July 4, 1937.* Daddy, dead a month shy of his forty-first birthday. I scrape away more snow, expecting to find Flanna's name and her date of death. But all that's there is Da's; the dates of his birth and death, and some silly line from a Yeats poem. No hint whatsoever of what happened in between those dates, or of what happened to her.

"Why did you let her go, Daddy?" I say the words loud and clear because nobody's around to hear. I don't even have to say Fagan's name. Da knows who I mean. "Why didn't you try to get her back?"

I feel better having asked. Kneeling in the snow, knowing I'll pay big when I try to stand back up. I take hold of the stone. "Will you tell me?" Poor Da. He's dust by now. Old bones, no longer capable of answering. I hold the slab of cold stone anyway, and promise I'll come back in spring, to plant daffodils and violets.

Fourteen

BAUBLES, BANGLES,
AND BEADS

Keeley's birthday, the big six-one, is right around the corner, and as soon as the roads are clear enough for us old girls to get behind the wheel, Cass plans a celebration. We would have celebrated last year, the big six-oh making more sense, but her husband preempted us; took her on a two-week cruise along the Mediterranean, the type I've always dreamed about but have given up on ever experiencing. Big treat, we're going to the new Marriott in Quincy even though we don't have any coupons. We'll have to pay full price. But we figure, what the hey, we'll blow a couple of extra bucks to make things really nice. In one of her morning phone calls, Cassie insists that we go shopping.

"You can't wear those old-lady clothes of yours if we're going to the new Marriott."

"My old-lady clothes?"

"You know, those pull-on pants you get in the mail. And the baggy over-blouses with the big flowers and the sailboats."

"Thanks a lot." What every mother needs in her golden years, a brat like Cassandra working on her personal style.

"You used to be so stylish, Mimi." She sighs. "Never leave the house without looking your best. You drilled that into us. And now you're letting yourself go. I just can't believe you're letting yourself go like this."

"Letting myself go like this?" Something Jack would say. "I'm not letting myself go. How many times do I have to tell you? I just don't care anymore."

After being forced into retirement, and with the little that I'd settled for from Jack, I had to pick and choose what mattered, and I decided that beautiful clothes didn't. Not at my age, on my budget.

At least Cassandra puts her money where her mouth is. A couple of days before the brunch, she takes me to the Little Lady, a pricey boutique at the mall, and treats me to two outfits, a dressy and a casual, at prices that give me palpitations. "My dime, my dime," she keeps saying.

First she asks the salesgirl to take a guess at my size. A moment of mortification, with those two staring me up and down.

"Twelve, petite," the salesgirl guesses.

"Short and round, I could have told you."

Cassie shakes her head, then roots through all the racks, enlisting the salesgirl's help, hunting for clothes she thinks might look good. Actually, "presentable" is the word she uses. Presentable. That's a notch or two below good. We're there for ages, with me trying stuff on while Cassie sits in a comfy chair in front of the three-way mirror, and the salesgirl stands behind her. At one point I come out in a navy skirt and sweater with red trim on the sailor collar and a big red bow in front. "Well, I've always been small," I say, turning like a runway model. "Am I sophisticated now?"

"Mimi, you're impossible, just impossible." Cassie yammers to the clerk about how difficult I can be, no matter how generous she is. In the end, we choose gray slacks and a matching blazer, a pinstripe shirt, and a little silk scarf and earrings. And I have to admit that these good clothes feel wonderful; I almost feel like my old self again, although that's the last thing I'd tell Cassandra. We also pick out some black dress shoes with low heels that don't hurt my bunions too much, and some navy-blue knit pants and a matching zip-up jacket for working out. "So you'll look decent while you're getting into shape," Cassie says.

"I'll look just like a stewardess," I say when we're at the counter and the salesgirl is wrapping up the slacks. "Fly me."

"Flight attendant," murmurs Cass. Neither of them smiles.

Fifteen

I GUESS I'LL HAVE TO
DREAM THE REST

*M*ixed feelings, that's what I've got about this birthday brunch. Been there, done that, I'm thinking when Cassandra drops me off, and I scoot with my shopping bags into Paul Revere. Don't bother to hang up the new clothes. Instead, I grab the pendant and take a load off on the couch, my aching feet up on a pillow.

Our get-togethers always turn out the same, and the fact that we're celebrating Keeley's birthday won't change anything. One drink, and my sisters are off and running, down the beaten track to the old days in Weymouth and Quincy, back before the roads were paved, when everybody grew veggies in their Victory gardens and swam in the Fore River Shipyard basin, and the big excitement of the week was when the ragman came.

If only my sisters would leave it at that, the good times. But no, they've got to keep on going, straight back to our grandparents, parents, sisters, aunts, uncles, and cousins, both dead and living, and who did what to whom way back when. But once we get there, to who did what to whom, we have serious disagreements. I cling to certain truths, which I hold to be self-evident, and my surviving sisters insist I'm nuts, that I've got it wrong. Now Patty's genealogy is giving them an additional excuse to pick and poke at all those painful places best left undisturbed.

In the early winter of our lives, as Patty puts it, my sisters love nothing better than picking at our past like it's the carcass of a rotisserie chicken, oohing and aahing when they find a juicy morsel, a bit of crispy skin. It's a love that came upon them, one by one, after the Change. Maybe it's a side effect, like night sweats and hot flashes. But to me, it's just charred bones. It's always the same, and I, with my rotten memory, have memorized the script. First we'll meet for Mass at Our Lady Queen of Peace, what's left of us: Patty and Josephine, the real twins, fraternal; the baby Keeley; and finally me, the oldest of the survivors.

After Mass, we'll head out in Keeley's brand-new Avalon to one of those all-you-can-eat Sunday brunches cardiologists warn against, with crepes, bacon, sausage, cheese Danish, and at least four kinds of potatoes. Using coupons from the Entertainment Book, especially the buy-one-get-ones, we check out all the good Sunday brunches on the South Shore. They always seat us by the kitchen door, or maybe a table with a window that overlooks the parking lot, guessing, incorrectly, that we're so far over the hill we won't know how to tip. We're used to it by now.

On my first trip to the buffet, I'll grab some eggs Benedict, my favorite—love that Hollandaise—but I'll be hoping for a Belgian waffle before we are through. Enough food for a week, but no doggy bags allowed. You've got to eat it all right there.

I always look around the table a couple of times to get my bearings, to see what's left of the glorious Sheehan girls. Four sixtysomethings in knit pantsuits and me with the Rockport Walkers, only Keeley still in pumps, with little diamond earrings and a snazzy silk scarf tied around her neck. Patty and Keeley with puffy hairdos from their weekly wash 'n' sets, and Jo with the same pixie cut she's worn for thirty years or more. Me, I go for the short perm, extra-curly, so it lasts longer. Wash-and-wear hair. The glorious Sheehan girls.

"Alberta was such a card," Josephine will say, speaking of one of our departed sisters, the second oldest, and the second one to go. As Jo sips her drink, her cheeks will begin to glow. "Three husbands: Buddy, Buster, and Bub."

"But four marriages," Patty will say. "She married Buddy twice."

"No," Jo will argue. "It was Buster, not Buddy, she married twice, wasn't it?" She'll look to Keeley for support.

"But isn't Buster the one who knocked out her front teeth?" Keeley will ask. "And he's the one she loved the most."

"Poor Alberta!" That will be Patty, who still has her red hair and freckles—a worn-out version of the doll she used to be, and on the verge of tears. "She really let herself go those last few years."

Letting oneself go, a recurring theme.

"She couldn't help it." Jo will take Patty's hand. "She was broke."

"And broken," I'll throw in. Because she was, Alberta. Shattered, physically and emotionally. No getting around that fact, no matter how hard they try. Alberta, brunette like me and well-built. She loved nothing better than a good laugh, but never seemed to get them with her Buddys, Busters, and Bubs.

"If Eden had seen her, she would've been heartbroken too." Patty's reply. And every time it's true.

Eden and Alberta, the top of the line, both gone before their time; Eden at forty-three of a female cancer, no health insurance, and Alberta of cirrhosis at forty-six. And all that heartbreak before the two of them moved on.

"Eden kept herself up until the very end," one or the other of them will say, all of them so impressed that she didn't let herself go.

"I can still see her," someone else will say, "with her lipstick and her earrings, right up to the day she died."

Now, relaxing on my sofa, lighting up a True Blue, I see Eden too—darling Eden, baptized Aiden, a boy's name for the son my parents longed to have. She's in the spare room of my house, our house, the house Jack built for me. On her deathbed, weighing less than seventy-five pounds, her famous silky skin the color and texture of a turnip. Shriveling from the inside out. Eden, thin and silent, still lovely. Early on, she changed the spelling of her name, just as Patty later did. The new way, she said, would make everybody think of Eden, the garden of. Spent her whole life drifting from man to man, most of them married, and from job to job, most of them beneath her. Wandered from place to place, Baltimore, Miami, Las Vegas, always coming back to the South Shore, lovelier and more hurt than ever before. I always kept that room for her. I always let her in.

"They're happy together, in heaven, I'm sure of it," one or the other of them will say, the cul-de-sac at the end of every meeting of the Yik Yak Club. They repeat it like a litany. The two of them are happy together in heaven, Eden and Alberta, life eternal, happy, happy, blah, blah, blah.

Sixteen

COME RAIN OR
COME SHINE

*C*ass picks me up in her Bimmer, me wearing my new outfit, shoes included. Per usual, and against my better judgment, I'm joining my sisters for brunch. I couldn't hurt Keeley's feelings.

"You look great, Mimi," Cass tells me when I climb in, smiling a grateful smile because she doesn't have to be embarrassed to be seen with me. "Like a new woman," she adds, happier with the new one than the old. But maybe I am new. The clothes are a big upgrade, the type Jack used to buy for me. Don't even recognize my feet in the new pumps. I hope God the Father, not to mention His only son, will recognize and remember me.

We drive the few blocks to the church instead of walking them. Sunday Mass at Our Lady Queen of Peace. Wouldn't miss it for the world, and I haven't once for as far back as I can remember. The cathedral's right in downtown Quincy, surrounded now by so many bars, banks, clam shacks, drugstores, and doughnut shops that the Blessed Trinity must have trouble squeezing in. Our Lady Queen of Peace, with its vaulted ceilings so high your prayers can float straight up, and the smell of myrrh and incense so you know for sure you've been to church. Oh, and the stained-glass windows of the Stations of the

Cross—Jesus dragging the cross, Jesus falling under the weight of the cross, Jesus hanging from the cross, the weeping women all around him. An act by which he redeemed all of humanity and gave us all eternal life.

When it's sunny, like today, light streams through the stained-glass windows and splashes pretty colors, a benediction over all of us. We take a pew close to Veronica Wipes the Face of Jesus, number six, my favorite station. But today I have trouble getting into the prayers. Lots of unwanted company stopping by, like at night when I can't get to sleep. My dead sisters, Eden and Alberta, up in heaven now, and Fagan Sent Away. We go to the altar for Communion, no point to Mass without the sacrament. We take the Eucharist on the tongue, we Sheehan girls—forget that in-the-palm-of-the-hand malarkey—*Body of Christ, amen*, but I don't get my usual lift from swallowing the Host. Today it's just a dry wafer sticking to the roof of my mouth, leaving a sour aftertaste.

At long last we're at the restaurant of the Marriott, on a big hill overlooking Beantown, to celebrate Keeley's big day one year late. The room is beautiful, two or three stories high, and a guy in a tux sits at a grand piano playing soothing music. "Moon River." "I Enjoy Being a Girl." Here, we're taken to a lovely window table, covered in pink cloth, with a vase of bright pink roses in the middle.

"Tea roses," says Cassandra.

And surprise, surprise, the window doesn't overlook a parking lot but instead a landscaped courtyard with a fountain in the middle. But the fountain isn't flowing and no flowers are in bloom. The trees are crusted with ice, the shrubs wrapped in burlap against winter kill. We order Bloody Marys, and I'm betting we'll go through another round or two before we finish with this celebration.

First thing, we raise our glasses to Keeley. Her fiery tresses have darkened over the years, aided and abetted lately by L'Oréal. She's worth it.

"Cheers, many happy returns of the day," all of us say at once.

"You didn't have to," Keeley answers, embarrassed to be the center of attention but also loving it.

"We did, yes, we did," we cry.

"You're more than just my godmother, Keeley," says Cassandra, smiling at my sister in a way she never smiles at me. "Summer vacations at your house were the best times of my life." That would be at Keeley's second home, her Cape house on the beach in Chatham.

"Hear, hear," the others chime.

Now Keeley holds out her hand, her wrist cuffed with a gold bracelet set with amethysts and diamonds, a gift from her husband, Frank, who's done all right, working his way up from letter carrier to postmaster of Weymouth.

"Beautiful," says Cassie breathlessly, fingering the gems. Keeley takes it off and hands it to Cassandra to try on, which she does. She holds out her arm so the bracelet glitters. Worth a fortune, and I figure that sooner or later, if Cass plays her cards right, she'll inherit it— and I've no doubt she will.

"Life is good," announces Patty, the one in charge of life, or maybe only goodness.

"Oh, yes, very, very good," my baby sister answers, smiling her million-dollar smile. She works in the development office of a hospital in Attleboro, throwing parties for rich people, raking in the big bucks. The bracelet matches the sparklers on her ears. She passes it around the table. I pass it on quickly when my turn comes.

"I'd be afraid to wear it. Afraid I'd lose it or get mugged."

I'm not jealous, not a bit. Keeley deserves whatever she gets. She grew up motherless, after all. I must confess, though, that I don't know Keeley as well as I know the others. We never shared a bed, and, therefore, not too many secrets. Instead of kids, she and Frank bred golden retrievers, and built that nice house on the Cape. Once each summer, we're all invited for a cookout. Except for Cass, who's always managed to stay most of the summer. She's done well, our Keeley, if you count having dogs instead of kids.

"Sixty-one years since our mother passed."

The words fly out of my mouth before I know I've spoken.

"How could you, Mimi?" Josephine and Patty chime like bells. They look at me, eyes wide, their mouths perfect O's.

"Mimi!" Cassandra, who's next to me, smacks my hand. The sting wakes me up.

"Oh, my God, I'm so sorry, honey." I try to reach across the table to Keeley, but can't quite touch her. The table is round, big enough for six.

"See?" Cassie wails, so loud that some other diners turn around. "See what I'm talking about? She's losing it. I swear to God, she's losing it."

"I'm losing it?" I'm trying not to blow my stack. "I am not losing it, Cassandra. I haven't lost one damned thing I can't live without. And, by the way, I've kept some things I could. . . ." I reach for my purse, take out the little pouch holding the blue pendant. I slide the pendant out, slam it down onto the table. Cass grabs it, she wants to hide it, but Patty, the pint-sized potentate, holds out her own hand.

"Mam's," she whispers.

"It's her fault." I point to my daughter as the pendant makes its way around the table, on the same path as Keeley's bracelet, the scratch visible to all. Cassandra's face turns the color of the tea roses.

"I only wanted to find out how much it's worth." She starts to cry, tear tracks running through her foundation like cracks in a crust, with my real daughter, the one who hardly ever shows herself, sobbing underneath.

"How much it's worth?" Jo's eyes fill up. "Well, then, Cass, tell us. How much is it worth?"

"Worthless," I interject.

"I didn't know he'd ruin it," Cassandra says. "I know it's ruined, and I'm really sorry, but that wasn't my intention."

"Ruination," whispers Keeley, a word the priest used during Mass.

"Ruination," I repeat, a close relative of deterioration.

The server shows up at our table, worried maybe that we'll cause a scene, a worse one than we already have. Cass suggests we order off the menu.

"I'm not sure I could make it to the buffet table," she says.

All of us agree. We take forever choosing our meals, discussing every last detail of the menu, which offers temptations too numerous to count. I go for the eggs Benedict, one of the few items I recognize, but with a layer of baby spinach in place of the Canadian bacon.

"Get the Hollandaise on the side," Cassie says in a stage whisper, then repeats this order to the waiter. "Do you know how many fat grams are in that?" she asks once he's gone. Nobody answers. "Just dip your fork into the sauce. You save hundreds of calories that way."

But miss out on all the flavor, I think.

The restaurant is full. A lighted candelabra, like Liberace's, decorates the top of the grand piano, though the pianist's tuxedo is plain black. All the well-dressed diners are talking softly, and, like them, we try to behave, yammering on about the weather and our kids and grandkids and dogs until the waiter brings our food.

The Hollandaise is to die for. When Cassie isn't looking, I pour the little cup all over my eggs. Strengthened, after a bite or two, I open my big mouth again. "It's all your fault," I say to Patty, "you and your damned genealogy."

"Stop your cursing. You've just taken Holy Communion."

"And we're drinking Bloody Marys," I answer. "Speaking of which . . ."

Cassandra hails the waiter and orders another round.

"What's Aunt Patty's fault?" asks Cassie once he's on his way. "Don't try to blame her for your bad manners."

"I'm not blaming her for that. I mean this trip I've been taking down Memory Lane. Thinking about the old days. It's an obstacle course, worse than the ones they use to train Marines."

"Well, you're new to it," says Patty. "The rest of us have been training for a while."

"I keep thinking about Flanna." They nod and hmm. "Not that I want to. But all of a sudden, after all these years, she's back."

"Flanna," Jo whispers, nodding, but I can't tell if she's pro or con.

"Once," says Patty, "she sewed matching dresses for me and Jo out of one of her hand-me-downs."

"You mean our mother's," I say. "She took all of our mother's clothes."

"She gave me minty candies shaped like flowers." Keeley.

"You always shared." Jo.

"Da's secret rose." Patty laughs. "He loved her so much."

Da's secret rose. But all I got were thorns.

"Once she told us the faeries took our mother off on a horse." Jo.

"A white horse," adds Patty. "Then the faeries brought Da to her."

"Flanna and her nonsense."

"A white horse?" Cassandra.

"Only explanation we ever got for our mother's death," Jo tells Cass. "The faeries took away our mother, on a white horse, in a white gown, with her hair streaming out behind her. Believe me, Flanna could tell a story. We lapped up every word."

Like kittens at the bowl.

"She could cast a spell." Patty.

"Which is what she did to Da." Again, they ignore me.

"I thought Flanna was my mother," says Keeley. "What did I know? But sometimes she called me Fagan."

"Fagan?" A chorus, like in church, at the high part of the liturgy.

"I was so confused. Sometimes I thought I *was* Fagan. Not that I ever knew her."

In my memories, too, Keeley replaced Fagan. The hole Fagan left closed up, so there was no loss to feel. But as soon as I think about that closed-up hole, I get an awful feeling, one that comes on me whenever the Yik Yak Club is in session. As if I'm alone, locked in a small, dark place, choking on smoke, and the air is running out. Eden and Alberta are gone. No one's left with me to loathe and fear Da's woman of shining loveliness.

"Loose lips sink ships," Patty declares, like she's just that moment thought of it.

"Keep mum, chum," echoes Jo. They nod over these words of wisdom from posters at the shipyard forever ago—the shipyard, a vast city with countless top-secret contracts, more than thirty-two thousand workers during the war.

"Keep mum, chum? What the hell's that supposed to mean?" I have trouble keeping my voice under control. "You're the ones who told Cassandra about Fagan. You two let the cat out of the bag." The twins look at me as though I've just run over the cat. "Well, you did. After we promised one another. Best of luck now putting it back in."

"Fagan was our sister," says Patty. "She belongs on the family tree."

"My aunt," adds Cass.

"How can we put her there if we don't know what happened to her?"

"We know what happened to her." Patty, the great historian. "She got sent away and died before we could get her back."

"You and your all-important genealogy." I take another sip of my Bloody Mary, which is what I feel like at this moment—bloody Mimi, mad as hell. "We agreed to let bygones be bygones." I look around the table, hardly recognizing what's left of my own sisters. Now I wonder if we ever actually did agree.

"Remember Alberta's prayer?" I say, not looking at them but at the blue pendant by my plate. "Accept what you can't change, change what you can, and so forth?" The rest of it escapes me, but Alberta couldn't live by it anyway. Too much she could not accept; so little she could change. "We can't change anything that happened."

Patty's silent, everyone's silent for so long, it's as if we've fallen out of time. Time enough for me to realize I've really done it now, I've ruined Keeley's birthday.

"Oh, Keeley," I say, trying to apologize again, but Patty cuts me off.

"Cassandra is your firstborn," she says at last. "She's got a right to know. Why do we have to keep pretending?"

"Pretending? Who's pretending? I erased her. Ages ago."

"You can't just erase one of your sisters," she says.

"You girls need group therapy," Cass announces, as if over a PA system. "I know somebody who's done a lot of family-of-origin work. Maybe he could fit you in, I mean the bunch of you together. The glorious Sheehan girls."

"'Family-of-origin work'?" A moment of comic relief. Patty, Jo, and Keeley crack up. Their laughter silences Cassandra. Family-of-origin work. It's the only kind of work Cassie's ever done.

"I'm so sorry, baby, I really am," I say again to Keeley, but she stops me.

"No, Mimi, you're right," she says. "It's the anniversary of our mother's death, and we've never said it before. Not once in sixty years. I'm glad to have it out there." Her eyes fill with tears. I could kick myself.

"I never knew Mam, not like the rest of you." Keeley twists her cloth napkin. She doesn't look at us. "I never knew anything about her. But from day one, as far back as I can remember, you girls, plus Eden and Alberta, took care of me. You never wanted me to suffer. You were always trying to make it up to me. But our mother died the day I was born. My birth stole her from the rest of you."

Bam! My ticker starts to whine and sputter like my old Mixmaster just before I tossed it out. I'm looking at, listening to my baby sister, but my heart spins and stalls in my chest, a tire stuck in ice and snow. Keeley, Patty, and Jo fill their coffee cups from the silver pot on our table. I watch like it's *Search for Tomorrow* on an ancient black-and-white TV. They yak and yak but the sound's muffled, the volume stuck just above a whisper, the picture snowy. I'm slipping away, pulled under, as if by a wave at Nantasket Beach. Out toward Eden and Alberta, who slipped beyond my reach so long ago. Who struggled so hard out there in the deep water, my old sweethearts. The other dead are out farther, heads like buoys bobbing, warning of the water's depth, its shallows and submerged obstacles.

The lights flicker and dim. A power outage, I think, but no, it's my lights on the verge of going out. Jesus. I'm having a myocardial infraction, or something else I'm not sure how to spell, right here at the table, my arteries clogged from all that Hollandaise.

I push away my plate. Rush, fast as I'm able, to the bathroom. Almost run into the men's. Bump into a slick young fellow coming out.

"Watch it!"

He gives me a dirty look, like I'm polluting his environment. No respect at all. Knocks me back to my senses.

*   *   *

In the ladies', I pee and splash cold water on my face. I lean against the sink until the trembling stops. Not a myocardial whatever, but one of my old episodes. Claustrophobia, like in that MRI machine. My ex used to pick on me about it, my fear of the dark, of enclosed places; the trouble I had with closets and cellars and sometimes, with sitting in the car at night, when I'd be alone waiting to pick up one of our girls someplace. This awful feeling would seize me, hands reaching out of the dark to grab my neck and squeeze it hard. No air, no light.

When our daughters were very young, I took the doors off all their closets. "What the hell?" my husband asked. "So nobody will ever be shut inside," I answered. "Wacky," he said, twirling his index finger by his ear. But that was back when he still loved me, so I won. Once our girls were teenagers and could take care of their own things, Mr. Malloy Himself put those doors back on, cussing up a storm as he lined up the hinges with the drill holes in the frames.

Way back when, when my ex still cared, he would tease me and call me Scaredy Cat. He'd comfort me, and we'd end up doing it wherever we happened to be. But in later years, he lost patience. "Get over it," he told me. "Don't pass your craziness on to our girls." Good point, I figured, but I couldn't help it. That's the part he didn't get.

Mimi's Episodes, a running gag between my husband and my daughters the whole time we were together. Then all of them were gone, my girls into their own lives, my ex into the arms of the new wife. I moved into an apartment without a cellar and just the one big closet all along the bedroom wall. With a sensor light so you couldn't ever get caught there in the dark.

I take a hard look at my face in the mirror. Oh, Mimi, not again, I tell her. No more episodes. No more claustrophobia. Been there, done that. I slap my cheek, good and hard, so it stings, the way I used to keep my daughters in line when they got snippy. A harmless crack on the cheek. It almost always did the trick. What's real is real, I tell that old gal in the mirror.

When I get back to the table, it's clear that none of them even noticed I was gone. "So, Mimi," says Patty, smiling like the cat that just ate the worm, "we've done a little research and it turns out that we Sheehans—yes, us—we really were somebodies back in the day. Not just poor potato farmers, landless peasants who crossed the ocean in desperation."

"What on earth? . . ." I try to ask.

"Not by a long shot." Jo's so excited, her hands are out like the priest's during the Consecration. "It turns out that, a few centuries ago, we had a castle up there on Northern Ireland's coast."

"Ages before the Troubles." Keeley's eyes sparkle like the gems on her ears and wrist. "Before there was a Republic and this other northern country."

"How on earth did you get here?" I missed two hundred years of family history while I was going to the bathroom. "A minute ago you were talking about Fagan."

"The genealogy," says Cass, glowing, smiling like she's just gotten something she's longed for her entire life. "We had a castle. We were somebodies."

Swell, I think, but bite my tongue while the others clap their hands and sigh. The Sheehans really were somebodies. Just wunnerful.

"The Sheehans through two centuries," Patty declares, her cheeks the color of her Bloody Mary. "Growing like clematis along the South Shore, through Quincy, Weymouth, Braintree, Hingham."

Then a ruckus breaks out. Keeley and Jo and Patty and Cassandra argue about who gets to tell which part of the story. Then they start to blabber about a feature film, a television miniseries.

"We could call it *Those Glorious Sheehan Girls from Quincy*," says Jo.

"You mean the Nobodies from No Place," I say.

The bunch of them fall silent, give me the gimlet eye.

Seventeen

HOW DEEP IS
THE OCEAN?

Story of my life, the ringing telephone. I take my time getting to it, pick up on the fourth or fifth ring, expect to hear about a cruise to nowhere I've just won, or a request for a donation from the PBA. Instead, it's Duffy.

"Mrs. Malloy," he says, "if you're not too busy, I wonder if you'd like to take a ride with me? I've got to check up on my best girl, see how she's holding up in all this cold weather. I'd like to introduce the two of you."

"Your best girl?" See how she's holding up? Duffy can't see me, but I'm red as boiled beets. I'd rather have a stranger trying to sell me thermal windows or lightbulbs they swear will last forever.

"Can you meet me outside in an hour?"

Can't think fast enough to say no. What to do? Never dreamed it would come to this, me meeting Duffy's best girl. After hanging up, I get out some Lancôme Cassie bought for me at Filene's and try to do my face the way she showed me, outlining my lips, putting mascara on my lashes. Afterward, I check it in the natural light, like Cassie told me, to make sure the blush isn't too bright and that my lips are on straight. I spray on the Trésor that Delilah got for me, the two of them in cahoots—sprucing up the old girl—for my last birthday. Then I put on the casual outfit Cass bought me, at least a cut above the other things I own. If I'm going to meet Duffy's best girl, the least I can do is stand my ground. I'd hate to meet her looking frumpy or not smelling my best.

Another bitter day, with a cutting wind, but the sun shines like it's summer. Duffy does a little double-take when he sees me. Not sure if that's good or bad. He holds the door of the Caprice for me, and as we head out, his face turns a little redder. I begin to wonder if there's something wrong with mine after all. Or maybe it's the perfume. I look at the visor, hoping there's a mirror, but no such luck in the old Caprice. I'm imagining my lipstick smudged, or my mascara streaked, and I can't do a damned thing about it. So I hold my head high. I pretend I'm twenty years younger and twenty pounds lighter, with my face on straight.

I've always believed you can tell a lot about a man by the way he drives a car. My ex, hunched over the wheel in his late-model luxury sedan, expected everything else on the road to get out of his way, and, for whatever reason, they almost always did. I can't tell you how many times the streams of traffic parted when I was with him so that Jack F. X. Malloy could glide through.

It's how I knew Cassandra's future husband, Mike Sr., was a stinker back when they were dating—I could tell by the way he drove. Made Jack Malloy look like a turtle by comparison. Weaving in and out in heavy traffic, cutting people off just for the fun of it, speeding down the breakdown lane if he felt like it, running red lights. No consideration for anyone else. Would Cassie listen? No, she knew best. My oldest daughter knew it all. She was pregnant with their second kid, a girl, when Mike used his rotten judgment at a busy intersection in Weymouth. He escaped without a scratch, but Cassandra's pelvis was broken in three places. She lost the baby, and the doctors told her she'd never have another.

"Don't say a word. Don't say anything," she cried when I walked into her hospital room. "I know what you're thinking, but don't say it."

Of course I wouldn't. That day, when just the two of us were in the room, she broke down, and I held her for a long time while she cried and cried. "Let it all out, baby," I kept saying, and she did, rivers of tears, until the nurses came to give her an injection. I'm the only person in the world whom Cassandra would cry with like that, wordlessly, the two of us together mourning her lost child. Not too long afterward, she filed the papers.

We have thick crusts, Cassandra and me. Thick crusts with many layers, like an Armenian pastry that's impossible to make without many years of practice. Often, these layers rub, one against the other, generating an awful friction between the two of us. Then, without warning, a layer of crust will crumble, hers or mine, or both of ours at once. That's when we'll find the soft layer beneath the crumbling crust, the real mother and real daughter. That's how it was when Cassandra lost her baby.

Duffy's a different breed of cat, though, nothing at all like Cassandra's ex or my own. Never in a rush, never driving above the speed limit. He's got all the time in the world. Anybody wants to pass, and he'll do what he can to let them. He yields when he's supposed to, always cuts the other guy a break. He keeps the radio tuned to a smooth-jazz station out of Boston, so whenever I get into the car, I know I'll be hearing my boy Frankie, or maybe Sarah Vaughan, or Tony Bennett. If we get stuck in traffic, he'll light up, crack the window, listen to the music—peaceful, like the old Caprice is a refuge, not an unguided missile. Today, as we head away from downtown Quincy, out along Shore Drive, ancient neighborhoods crowded on one side, the Atlantic shining on the other, I'm thinking Duffy knows exactly who he is and what he's doing. He doesn't have to prove anything to anyone. He's comfy in his own skin, no small achievement in times like these.

Once, not long after I got laid off, I tried Senior Bingo over at Our Lady Queen of Peace. Big mistake. A roomful of blue-haired biddies with greedy eyes behind their bifocals. Many from my complex, Centennial Square. A couple of times his name came up, Duffy's, these antediluvian women gossiping about the only man nearby who was still warm and walking. Whispering about how cute he was, and also about his troubles, his burdens. Whispering. I didn't listen. I hold to that old maxim, *Whispering, whispering is a sin; when you get to heaven, God won't let you in.* I've got better things to do with my time. Like take a ride with Duffy to visit his best girl.

I begin to regret the Trésor. It's too heavy for this enclosed space. Also realize that Duffy's best girl must have a place right on the water, maybe in one of those pricey new condos out at Marina Bay.

"She's got a waterfront place?" He shakes his head yes, staring hard through the windshield, his own cheeks bright red. She must be a rich old broad, I think. Skinny, too, no doubt.

"Must be nice." Again he nods. I'm trying to keep it together, wishing I was anyplace but in Duffy's station wagon heading out to meet his best girl with her place right on the water, and me wearing too much Trésor.

There are some nice new condos out there—high-rises—and, I'll admit, I'd envy anyone who could afford one. Then I see the buildings up ahead, glossy pink granite, their big windows facing out over the water, all shiny in the sunlight. Pink elephants, I say to myself. Totally out of place on the South Shore, way too showy. Not my type of thing at all. Give me Paul Revere any day of the week.

We're driving down Victory Boulevard, almost there, when Duffy makes a sharp right. Next thing, we're at Marina Bay's winter storage facility for boats. On both sides of the road, as far as I can see, pleasure craft are up in dry dock, shrink-wrapped against the elements. Cabin cruisers, luxury sailboats, little yachts. Rich folks' toys, wrapped tight in plastic, like leftover meatloaf or ham. Duffy gets out and punches in a code to open the gates. Once we're inside, he parks, and I let him open the door for me. I wonder what else I can do to put off what's coming next.

"She works here?" I ask him as we walk along the rows of boats, looking for an office or some such thing where a human being might be working. He grins and shakes his head, no this time. "I wouldn't say so, no," he says. He stops to light up, cupping the flame from his Zippo with his hands. We walk farther, down a row of shrink-wrapped boats up on platforms. It's exactly how I feel at this moment, shrink-wrapped, my skin too tight. We stop at the end of a row, right above the water, next to a nice big cabin cruiser. This one isn't shrink-wrapped, but instead is wrapped in a green tarpaulin and protected by a canvas tent instead. The tarp has come loose and is flapping in the wind. When we get closer, I see the name, *Miss Nomer,* printed in big black letters across her backside.

"Here she is," says Duffy, exhaling a puff of smoke into the cold air. "My best girl, *Miss Nomer.* Isn't she a beauty?"

I start to laugh, can't help it. I'm dying of embarrassment. Duffy's smoking, inhaling deeply, staring straight ahead at his best girl, his eyes twinkling, like he can't hear me laugh. Oh, he got me but good, and he knows it, but he'll let me keep whatever little shred of pride I have left.

"She's gorgeous, a knockout." I stifle more laughter. I run my hand along her hull. It's wood, dark and shiny, with white-painted decks and nice chrome fittings here and there.

"She's a Chris-Craft," he says. "A twenty-six-foot Express Cruiser. Semi-enclosed. Built in 1957."

"You do like old things." The minute I say this, I think, Me and my big mouth.

"Not all old things are created equal," he answers. "This is vintage Chris-Craft. Mahogany. They don't make 'em like this anymore. Everything's fiberglass now. Me and my boys rescued her in the '70s. Bought her for almost nothing at an estate sale. Fixing her up was our project. Kept us sane, or me, anyway, during Virginia's illness."

"Nice name. *Miss Nomer.*"

Again Duffy nods. "In junior high, my oldest, Thomas, turned into a real pain in the ass, a know-it-all. Every time I turned around, he was correcting me. Every word out of my mouth was another misnomer. According to Thomas, anyway. So when the boat was finished, that's what I christened her. The *Miss Nomer.*"

"She's elegant, a classic." I take in her gleaming wooden sides, her graceful hull, her windshield and red leather seats. "She must be worth a fortune." Duffy owns a cabin cruiser he docks at Marina Bay. Who'd a thunk it?

Duffy shrugs. "Maybe. I haven't checked, because she's not for sale. But the whole point of Chris-Craft, in its day, was to make quality pleasure boats affordable to working people."

"In its day?"

"Fiberglass killed 'em. Well, it didn't exactly kill 'em. They sold the company for millions. Wood boats were their thing. They didn't want to deal with glass."

Duffy starts to replace the tarp, and I ask him why he doesn't shrink-wrap her, like all the other boats.

"You can't shrink-wrap a wooden boat. It'd rot right out. Wood's got to breathe."

"You learn something new every day."

"Stick with me, kid," he says. "Let's check her out before I cover her again." He climbs up a ladder on her side, his bum leg dragging just a little. He reaches down to help me, his rough hands warm and strong. Take it easy, Mimi, I warn myself as he pulls me up. I try to climb on board with at least a smidgeon of grace.

We stand side by side, looking through the windshield toward the water, which is icy blue with whitecaps here and there. "Here, take a load off," he says, wiping a spot for me on the red leather seats, which are covered in tiny droplets of ice and water. He sits next to me and offers me a smoke, which I accept. The Atlantic stretches out in front of us, the horizon a blue blur. If I weren't so cold, I could almost believe we were out there, sailing, instead of up in dry dock. Then I see the two of us, Duffy and me, on a hot summer day, in the *Miss Nomer*, speeding out across the harbor.

He puts an arm around me. "It's heaven in the summer," he says.

"I'll bet," I say, exhaling. The smell of our cigarettes mixed with the salt air makes my heart race, but in a good way, not like that myocardial thing.

"The first nice day, I'm going to take you out."

"Threat or promise?"

"Oh, a promise, Mrs. Malloy. You can bet your life on it."

I lean in closer to him, imagining myself out there next to him, sunbathing. The image falls apart when I see myself in a bathing suit.

Cellulite. My thighs like candles melting. Got to get serious about getting fit and losing weight.

"Centennial Square's my real life," Duffy's saying, "and the *Miss Nomer* is my dream of life. You know, I don't really fish. I just sit on the deck holding the rod. If something swims onto my hook, so much the better."

"How often does that happen?"

"Often enough to make life interesting," he says, and gives me a little squeeze. I turn to look at him, but he's staring out at the water.

I've lived my entire life surrounded by the water but have never once gone out on it in a pleasure boat. That was something wealthy people did. Far beyond the reach of us Sheehan girls.

"I've never been in a boat like this, Duffy," I say. "Not ever. The closest I got was one of the inner tubes I used to bring to the beach with the girls."

He laughs. "No comparison." I shrug. "Poor Mrs. Malloy, you're deprived," he says. "We'll fix that, the first nice day. We'll take you on your maiden voyage."

"My ex was a marine architect," I tell him, just by way of conversation. "Spent his career designing big ships."

"No kidding?" Duffy's not particularly interested.

"That's how he explained it. He built great ships to ply the waters of the world. But after he came home from the war, the Navy, like you, Jack never again rode the high seas, or the low ones, for that matter. He made his living engineering ships, but he never boarded one again."

"Couldn't live without it, myself," says Duff, nowhere near as interested as I am in this irony. He turns to me. "So, what do you think, Mrs. Malloy? Come spring we'll take a sail?"

"You bet," I say.

Eighteen

LET IT SNOW! LET IT SNOW! LET IT SNOW!

*D*awn. *Cold gloom. A naked child, smoldering, her arms outstretched, her face too close to mine, yet blurred. Stinking of smoke, vomit, pee. She nudges me, shaking me awake. Tries to tell me something without using words. Who is she?* An alarm sounds, but not one for waking up. Where is the alarm coming from? Even in my terror, I know it's coming from the naked child, but how? Why? I sit up, she disappears, and it's my telephone, my own damn phone that's ringing. My bedside clock says 9:18 A.M. Cassandra.

"Don't even think about driving in this," she wails.

"What, in what?" My voice is thick.

"You're still in bed." She sounds as if the eastern seaboard is about to fall into the Atlantic because her mother overslept.

"It's Saturday."

"Don't even think about driving in this," she repeats. "It's a blizzard, a beaut." As if I would. "Stay put. We're supposed to get a foot."

"Don't worry, honey." I use my most soothing Mom voice. "I'm not going anyplace. I've got everything I need right here."

"I'll call you back in a couple of hours to make sure."

Snow. A sudden winter storm. Before the ice and drifts from the last one have even melted. When I hang up from Cassie, I snuggle back under the soft, clean covers of my bed, my Sealy Posturepedic, while the snow whirls around me. I reach out for the blue pendant on my bedside table, squeeze it in my fist, rub my face into my feather pillow. I doze off and another child is there, like a stray cat you made the mistake of feeding once.

I sit up. *Stop haunting me*, I say, or maybe I only think it. The girl's face begins to clarify, like a photo coming into focus. She's a brunette with hazel eyes who looks a lot like me. My sister Alberta, close enough to touch, but I don't touch her. Her face is bruised, her lip swollen, but she's too young for this damage to have been done by Buddy, Buster, or Bub. Her eyes glow like those laser pointers they sell to drive cats crazy. Behind her, a shadow, a black spot. She came out of it—she's going back, and wants me to go along.

My old sweetheart Alberta, standing in front of me, wanting me to go with her, the way I always used to. Something spins inside me, like I'm in a blender on the puree setting. I love Alberta so much, a humming, spinning love, but I don't want to go. I couldn't follow her in life, and I don't want to now. I'd give anything not to go. But I can't stop what's happening. Can't find the right button on the blender. It spins and spins until a younger me emerges, eight or nine years old.

We're in our bed, Alberta and me. Where's Eden? We cling to each other. Where's Eden? She's gone. We have to find her, bring her back. We wait for ages, listening through the wrought-iron heat register in the floor until we're certain Flanna is asleep. We sneak downstairs. Flanna at the kitchen table, her head on its wooden surface, her mouth open, drool like a teardrop falling from her lips, her hair spilling out across her arm. In a shiny blue dress, black high heels. Waiting for Da, waiting and waiting, just like me and my sisters. All of us, forever waiting for Da to get home.

On the table, an ashtray full of butts, each smeared red from her lipstick. The whiskey bottle, almost empty, not far from her hand. "If it was full, I'd brain her with it," I whisper to Alberta. She picks up the bottle, takes a big swallow, coughs as it goes down. I shake my head no when she offers it to me.

Flanna, enchanting beauty. Sleeping, she's as pretty as a saint on a prayer card, all pink cheeks and shiny curls. Still, she has that power. She makes a shuddering sound, her lips vibrating when she exhales. Ever so carefully, I reach into her pocket, take out her keys. She jerks. I jump back. She's waking up, but no, she settles back into her noisy sleep. I grab a couple of slices of bread and a cup of water. Alberta and I head back upstairs.

That old house was full of closets, eaves, nooks, cupboards. Eden's locked in one of them. Sobs when she hears our footsteps. "Amelia Earhart," I whisper so she knows it's us, not Flanna. "Amelia Earhart loves to fly," Alberta chimes. When we open the cupboard door, Eden reaches for us, her face shiny with snot and tears. She grabs the bread and water. She pees into the cup once it's empty. We try to take her with us, back to our own bed.

"Flanna's drunk, she won't remember."

"No, no, no." Eden scrunches up her eyes and waves her hands. No, no, no. She refuses the pillow we brought for her. She goes back into her little prison. "Lock it. Lock it now before she comes."

Snow blows against my windows. The icy bits make a clattering sound. It's 10:15 A.M. I feel a little crazy, seeing my dead sisters sneaking around in the dark like that. I get up and put on coffee. My heart pumps in a wild rhythm. Maybe it's the A-fib, Jesus, the dreaded A-fib. If it throws off a clot, well, I'll be history, another Sheehan sister down the tubes. Every one of us dropping like flies.

I stand by the counter, watch the coffee bubble up into the glass knob of my electric perk. Nothing like a fresh-brewed cup with a spoonful of real cream, one of my guilty pleasures. When we were kids, the milkman used to leave the glass bottles in a metal crate by the front door, before milk was homogenized and bought at stores. My sisters and I used to sneak spoonfuls of the cream on top whenever we could get away with it. Nothing today tastes as good as that cream. I take my coffee to the table. Now, that's my type of memory, a happy one, of days gone by.

Through the curtains, the sidewalk and parking lots glisten with snow. Duffy's already out there, all bundled up with a ski mask over his face, clearing the sidewalks on a tractor with a plow attached to it. I make a mental note to call him, invite him over for coffee, a bite to eat. I could use some company. Then I remember I've got a brisket in the freezer. I'll stick it into the slow cooker, with carrots and potatoes. Pot roast, the perfect meal on a day like this. When his work is done, we'll share a nice hot meal and watch *Family Feud* together, or maybe a rerun of *Magnum, P.I.*

I'm betting that if I don't call them first, every one of my sisters and my kids will call me, everybody worrying about everybody else, but also glad to have this unexpected snow day, a chance to do absolutely nothing and enjoy it. Sure enough, I've just finished my coffee when Patty calls.

I'm fine, I'm fine, I tell her, and she tells me she's fine too. No hard feelings about what was or was not said at Keeley's birthday brunch. But once we get that squared away, I can't help but bring it all up again. That image of Al and Eden haunts me.

"Patty, our past feels like a curse. I like forgetting better."

"That's what some of the old folks said about us, that we were cursed." She chuckles. "But you," she says, "you exaggerate every-thing. You older girls were drama queens." My ears ring with the pain of her words. "Everything was life and death with you, plural."

"That's not fair," I cry. "Eden and Alberta aren't even here to de-fend themselves."

Her remark slices through me, and I slam down the receiver, a blunt instrument silencing her voice. Every time we stroll down Mem-ory Lane, we Sheehan sisters, we end up on opposite sides of the street, shouting back and forth about what happened and what didn't.

I pop an English muffin in the toaster, burn it, and eat it anyway. I'm much too thrifty to throw food away, recalling times when my sisters and I would have killed for a bit of an English muffin, burned or otherwise. In that world, the world of Not Enough, we Sheehan girls held on to one another, gained strength from one another, and that's how we survived. That's why it upsets me so much now that we have this great divide.

My sisters and I shared beds in two little rooms in the back of the house. We three oldest in one big bed, and in the next room the twins and the baby—Fagan or Keeley, whichever one it was—in two small beds pushed together, all of us like honeysuckle, tangled up together; grateful, during the brutal winters, to have each other's bodies to snuggle up to for warmth. After Mam passed, we often climbed into bed with each other at night, all six of us. So close like that, sleeping, breathing softly together, it was like we shared just one body. Lots of arms and legs, but a single heart and soul. Every now and again, this heart would break. The sounds of it breaking—bleats, squeaks, sobs, hiccups—issued from the one body, filling the dark silence of the room.

After all that happened, all things considered, the twins turned out OK. Jo—supposedly the quiet one—was born four minutes after Patty and ended up four inches taller. Grew an inch for every extra minute in the womb, we always joked. Once bossy Patty was born, Jo finally had room to grow. As for her name, I figure they grabbed the closest one at hand, my father's, although Jo insists that being named for him was a special honor, like me with my mother's name.

Both are nurses, Patty a retired pediatric RN and Jo a BSN who supervises a long-term care facility for permanently disabled kids. Not long after the war, they went to nursing school together, paying their own way. Unlike Eden and Alberta, profligate with everything—their money, their bodies, their love—the twins were savers, penny pinchers. Still in their twenties when they bought a house, a sturdy double-decker in Dorchester, worth a fortune now and paid for long ago. "We'll always have a roof over our heads," they said at the time, haunted by our orphan years, when Nana Sheehan would sometimes have to farm us out to other relatives because she didn't always have enough to feed us.

Patty lives on the first floor with her husband, Wesley, and their four kids. Jo, who never married, lives upstairs. No, Jo never married. She could've have had any guy she wanted, but she didn't want. She gave up her glamour-girl ways when she went to nursing school. Keeps her hair cut short and hasn't bought a rouge or lipstick since. "This way," she says, "I'm always driving my own bus." She can take it anywhere she wants, whenever she wants. Not that she's ever been alone. Besides being a second mother to Patty's kids and to a couple of mine, she's always had foster kids, fifteen or twenty over the years, many of them disabled in one way or another, all of them abandoned. "At risk," is the term Jo uses. At risk. She takes them in one or two at a time, lavishing her love upon them, banking their government stipends so they'll have a little nest egg when they move on, and they always keep in touch. She's got more "grandkids" than me. Her refrigerator's covered with their pictures. A saint, that's Jo. When the sun shines just right, you can see her halo.

Pouring another cup of coffee, the snow and wind still howling, I reconsider the silence. Glutton for punishment that I am, I call Jo. She, too, is home safe and sound, doing a jigsaw puzzle with her foster kids. We, too, agree to forget/forgive—take your pick—what happened at Keeley's birthday party, then move on to the subject of our mutual safety. Nobody's going anywhere. Once we get that settled, she launches into what's really on both our minds.

"Patty called and told me you got mad and hung up on her. The truth hurts you too much, she said."

"What's the truth?"

"If we only knew."

"You agree we don't?" No answer, just the sounds of her foster kids squabbling and laughing in the background. "Patty said we older girls were drama queens. That cuts deep."

More silence.

"Jo, we were not drama queens. Not at all. You know that. How could Patty ever think that about Eden and Alberta? Or me? Tell me you don't believe it too."

Jo's too honest and too loyal to answer one way or another. "Sorry, but I can't do this on the phone, Mimi, not now."

I'm about to ask what "this" is, but suddenly I'm exhausted. I drop it. Then Jo tells me one of her kids is doing a fund-raiser for his basketball team, selling gourmet popcorn in a dozen flavors. I promise to buy three packs, six bucks a pop.

"It better be really good."

Jo laughs her sweet laugh. "It will be, I promise."

I hang up, more puzzled now than angry. It's so unlike Patty to cast

aspersions upon her sisters, and especially upon the departed ones—
"drama queens." Again, I think about how we Sheehan sisters held on
to one another, always, all throughout our lives. *Amelia Earhart loves to
fly. Amelia Earhart will never die.* A rhyme we made up, to remind us of
who we were and how we had to stick together, although, in Fagan's
case, we didn't hold on tight enough.

As for Al and Eden, once they passed, I cut them loose. Had to.
Their sad lives, their untimely deaths, weighed on me like cement
shoes, pulling me down, down, down. If I hadn't let them go, I would
have gone under too. Once and for all. So many of those years with
Jack, those middle years at home raising our daughters, I struggled just
to keep my head above the water. I needed a ballast. I couldn't take on
more weight.

Eden never married, but Alberta made up for her, each of her husbands a bigger jerk than the last one, except for whichever one it was
she married twice.

At Alberta's funeral, as the gravediggers lowered that cheap box
into the ground, I collapsed with grief, ready to climb down there with
her. That's when Jack F. X. Malloy whispered, "All Alberta ever did
was cry into her whiskey, feeling sorry for herself. Drank herself to
death, just like your father," a point he never tired of making. Jack had
nothing to say when Eden died from the cancer, not a single word.

"Girls as beautiful as those two had to work really hard to make
such messes of their lives," Jack once said.

"What do you mean by that?" I was furious in a way that only Jack
could make me.

"Life is easier for good-looking people," he said.

"Oh, you should know." I spoke sarcastically, but Jack took it as a
compliment.

"Well, it's a fact." I don't remember where we had this conversation, but I do remember he was breathing on my neck, rubbing my hip
in a way that always weakened me. "Also, common sense if you think
about it," he went on. "Any number of successful men would've been
happy to take care of them. But they always found the losers."

"Speak for yourself," I said, pushing his hand away. I felt shredded like carrots in a coleslaw every time he bad-mouthed Eden and Alberta. "Anyway, you always had a thing for Eden. Maybe you wish you'd married her."

He shrugged, blushed. "She was a knockout, a movie star, but she didn't know how to get out of her own way."

During Eden's last weeks, in a room with lots of sunlight where she could see the water, my daughters kept running in and out to keep her company. She loved it when they climbed into bed with her; she held them like they were her own. Jack, known far and wide as a cheapskate, paid to keep fresh flowers in her room, bouquets of lilies and white roses that covered up her dying smell. He sat with her and held her hand, feeding her orange sherbet with the little spoon we used for baby food. It was the only thing she could keep down.

By then, Eden's worldly goods consisted of a driver's license and two small suitcases stuffed full of cheap clothes with lots of lace and sparkles. After she passed, my daughters found the suitcases and played dress-up in them. They loved pretending to be Eden. They'd take me by surprise, Cassandra, or Celestine, or Ruthie, in Eden's sequins and high heels, like she'd dropped by for a quick chat. My heart stopped every time. More than anything I wanted to throw those clothes away, but the girls hid them so I couldn't.

While the snow blows and the wind howls, I give Duffy a ringy-dingy, leave a message about the pot roast. While I chop the carrots and potatoes, I listen to the TV. The blather about storm tracks and cold fronts and icy moisture in the upper atmosphere calms me down. Pretty soon, my apartment smells of nice rich stew, bay leaf, onions, and thyme. When it's almost done, I'll throw in some dumplings.

After that, I turn off the TV, pick up the pendant, take it to my recliner. Sit there holding it, rubbing my finger on the scratch. I hear the thrum of those deep and dreaded feelings. Fear and longing, flies buzzing around the black spots.

Some things, like sneaking cream from the milk, I remember perfectly, and I hold on to these memories as proof positive that I didn't spring full-grown onto the Earth as a mother in my twenties, hitched to Jack Malloy. Which is what I often felt like as I raised my girls, that I'd just been born that day, without any experience or memory.

No idea at all what I was doing as a mother, but I couldn't tell anyone, not my sisters, and least of all Jack. Boiling glass bottles for the formula—no breastfeeding, Jack's eleventh commandment! My breasts belonged to him alone—mixing big pots of formula on the stove; soaking the soiled diapers in the toilet, wringing them out, flushing; laundering them by the dozens, hanging them outside on the line . . . no dryer, not yet. Not knowing what to do when Cass or Ruthie or Cellie wouldn't stop crying, and Jack was never there. I just muddled through.

Yet I loved that house by the water, where, from the clothesline in the yard, I could see way across the bay to the shipyard, where Jack was working. And I knew that, no matter what, he would come back home to me.

A house not anything at all like Da's in Quincy, with its cupboards, closets, crannies, cellar, hiding places, places to be scared. No wonder we all slept together in one bed. But Flanna put an end to that. She separated us, kept the six of us from sharing a single bed. Turned Da into an enforcer, something he'd never been. She sent him to check on us, and often checked herself, a swooping shadow. "Stay put, you stinkers," she'd hiss after Daddy was asleep. Like if we got back together, we'd plot against her. *Thick as thieves*, she called us.

I had so much trouble sleeping after Flanna came. No more one body. Even with my eyes closed, snug under the covers, I couldn't fall asleep. Couldn't keep my eyes closed for any length of time. The slightest sound—a sigh, a rustle, a whoosh through the registers, a creak on the stairs—would jerk me awake and ages passed before I could close my eyes again. Sometimes a cold gust awakened me, and when it did, I smelled sharp stinging herbs, nothing like those in my pot roast, no; instead herbs that burned my eyes, and I'd believe a ghost, not a holy one, had come into our room, might be there still. Sometimes, after waking up and checking to make sure the coast was clear, I sneaked into my sisters' room just to count the lumps in the bed. Sometimes I counted wrong. An overactive imagination, my father and my sisters said, and then my husband, too.

World War II may have been hell on Earth for everybody except me and my sisters. Those were our glory days, or as close to glory days as we'd ever get, we glorious Sheehan girls. One by one, we finished high school and went to work at the shipyard, where our father, along with various uncles, cousins, and other relatives, had worked back when Joe Kennedy, the father of the future president, ran the place. Girls replaced the boys who'd gone off to war, Jack Malloy among them, although at the time I hadn't met him yet.

As in World War I, the Fore River Shipyard had countless naval contracts, turning out aircraft carriers, destroyers, landing ships, and heavy cruisers at a crazy rate. Triple shifts, the shipyard in full operation 'round the clock. Workers grabbing extra shifts, as many as they could handle, for as long as they could stay upright at their task. As fast as one ship was torpedoed, another would slide off the ways and into the water, chugging off to the European or Pacific theaters.

While under construction, the ships had hull numbers instead of names; from the 1400s up past the 1600s when I was there. Like babies, the ships got their names when they were christened. I remember a group of heavy cruisers with the names of American cities: *Boston*, *Baltimore*, *Pittsburgh*, *St. Paul*, *Providence*, and, of course, the *Quincy*, torpedoed in 1942. That same year, the battleship *Massachusetts* was christened—the heaviest ship ever launched at the yard—nicknamed Big Mamie by her crew. The types of ships, their names, were my poetry, taught to me first by my father and then my husband. When the *Wasp*, a magnificent aircraft carrier—cutting-edge, a wonder—was torpedoed in '42, we mourned her as though that craft were one of us. The men who built those ships were classified as essential and did not have to serve. But thousands of them, men like Jack, volunteered for combat, and off they went.

I suppose we Sheehan girls really were beautiful back then, with

clear eyes, shiny hair, small waists, nice bust lines. Oh, and pretty ankles! Must not forget the ankles, all that I've got left. During school, we
wore saddle shoes and bobby socks, pleated skirts and sweaters. But when
we started at the shipyard, some of us, depending upon our job, wore
sweaters, skirts, and heels like Lana Turner, and others jumpsuits like
Rosie the Riveter. For the first time in our lives, we had a buck or two
to spend, even after we paid Nana Sheehan for our room and board. We
bought lipstick and nail polish and shiny pumps.

We Sheehan girls made quite a splash over there. So many of us,
and everybody raving about how alike we looked despite the various
colors of our hair, brunettes and redheads, and Eden, the drop-dead
gorgeous natural blond. Those days, my sisters and I fought about everything, from the underwear on out. First up, best dressed. We'd claw
one another's eyes out to wear the blouse we wanted. We had so few
belongings, and we longed for everything! Not that our fights were
ever serious. My sisters and I forgave one another everything. *Amelia
Earhart loves to fly. Amelia Earhart will never die.*

What we didn't understand is that it didn't matter what we wore,
what color we painted our lips. The entire bunch of us could've gone
out barefoot in potato sacks and all the doors that opened to us would've
opened anyway. Because the war had given us a future, and we had our
youth, if not our innocence.

My phone rings again and I grab it. Duffy.

"That's a sweet offer, Mrs. Malloy, one I can't refuse."

"Well, all right then, great. How about six?"

"Can I bring anything?"

"Just yourself. I've got everything else we need."

"Looking forward to it." The line goes dead, but I still feel like
we're connected. Duffy, I feel so comfortable with him, in a way I
never felt with Jack. Not worried sick about meeting some mysterious
standard, one so high it was impossible to reach.

Looking back, it's hard to believe how Jack Malloy swept me off my
feet. Our romance was as fast and thrilling as the roller-coaster ride
at Nantasket Beach, where we often went that first summer we were

dating. Jack, a handsome devil—tall, with slicked-back hair, wire-frame eyeglasses, and shiny cufflinks on the wrists of his starched, pressed shirts. The spitting image of Artie Shaw, his idol.

The first time I saw him, he was walking into the drafting room at the shipyard, where I was a clerk. I fell head over heels for him, a regular Kodak moment: Jack, just back from the war, walks in and everything stops. Bright light shines all around him, and I know without the slightest doubt that he's the One. Oh, yes! A sweet memory I keep on hand for troubled times. And I wasn't alone in my conviction. Every girl at the shipyard, and there were dozens of us, felt the same way. All the girls had the biggest crush on him, but I'm the one he chose. Jack, a big shot, the one who finally figured out how to move great ships through the shallow channels of the Fore River into Quincy Bay, and beyond that, the great Atlantic. His words. And he was always happy to tell anyone who'd listen.

Jack might've been my father's boss if my father were still alive. Not laboring beside Da in the dark, hot hull of a ship, but working high above him at a desk in the drafting room, which was bigger than a football field and surrounded by sparkling windows with great views of the water.

Even our wedding was spectacular, with Jack's parents picking up the tab, a reception in the church hall of their parish, St. Jerome's, a three-tiered cake, and Jack's musician buddies—a real swing band—playing halfway through the night. All of my sisters were bridesmaids, each in a pastel satin gown. We sewed them ourselves on Nana's treadle machine. Alberta, the maid of honor, in lavender, and me, a virgin, in pure white satin with a sweetheart neckline, a train, a flowing veil, and dozens of white roses.

Eden and Alberta figured I'd hit the jackpot when I hitched up with Jack. That's what Alberta called him, even to his face, Jackpot. Why, he'd built a brand-new house for us, a little Cape Cod cottage across the street from his parents', above the Fore River. A new house of our own! My sisters couldn't get over how lucky I was. My future was assured, they said, and I wouldn't even have to work. Outside the home, anyway. I was the one who was going to "make it," the two of them kept saying. But those girls didn't have an ounce of good judgment between them. If you asked them what "it" was, neither of them could have said.

No doubt my life looked great compared to theirs. Eden, always searching, never finding. Alberta, finding losers, one after the other. By the time she reached her thirties, her nose had been broken more than once, her eyes blackened, her smile marred by missing teeth, and her bank account, the little she had, emptied out. She had a son and a daughter, half-siblings. Miracle of miracles, the daughter's a high school history teacher, married to another teacher now, and the mother of three. She doesn't keep in touch, much as I'd love to see her. But who could blame her?

Alberta's son, Danny, the cutest kid, the first boy born into the family in ages, died at eighteen. A dead ringer for Da, Alberta always bragged about him, so proud of this fact. *Smart as a whip, and so good with his hands.* Alberta's sun rose and set on him. He died alone, on a sidewalk in Brockton, of a heroin overdose. His druggie friends got scared and took off, leaving him alone, convulsing in an alley. The medical examiner said he was alive for several hours after the convulsions started. If someone had intervened, Narcan, a simple shot of Narcan, would've saved him.

The rest of us chipped in for his funeral, as we would soon after for Alberta's. In spite of everything else Alberta had been through, she kept functioning, but the death of Danny crushed her. *Left to die there like a dog.* She couldn't stop saying it, couldn't get the picture out of her head. After Danny's death I didn't see Alberta much. Couldn't handle her grief—a depth charge, so many bad things exploding to the surface, the sludge and slime of our early lives.

Since the two of them have passed, my sisters, I rarely talk about them, try not to think about them. No point. I get all tangled up in the messes they made out of their lives and while I'm tangled there, I hear Jack Malloy: *A drunk and a slut, that's what you've got for sisters.* I tried so many times to explain to him that it wasn't always like that, but he didn't want to listen. He liked his version better.

* * *

I set the pendant down. Go stir the stew even though the point of the slow cooker is to turn it on and leave it be. The potatoes are still hard. I take the Scrubbing Bubbles from under the kitchen sink and head into the bathroom. I spray a nice foam over the tub, the toilet, and the sink in case Duffy has to go, let it set while I Windex the bathroom mirror. Then I give the toilet bowl a good go-round with a brush, working up a lot of suds, getting up under the rim and as deep into the hole as the curved handle will let me. I lift the lid and wipe it, and when the toilet's spotless, I flush, certain that it will pass muster even if God Himself has gotta pee.

I'm in the kitchen peeling off my rubber gloves when the two of them return to me, Al and Eden at seventeen and eighteen. Bobby-socksers. A blonde and a brunette, at the height of their beauty. My heart skips when I see them, my old sweethearts. Nobody who saw them like that, in their pretty skirts and sweaters, with their shiny Breck Girl hair, would ever have had a clue how they'd already suffered in their lives. I try my best to ignore them.

I get out the vac, a nice little Dirt Devil that Ruthie and her boys gave me last Christmas. Lightweight, so I can lug it around without throwing out my back. My kitchen, bath, and entryway are tiled, so I sweep them, but the living room and bedroom are wall-to-wall, a comfy shag my daughters say is hopelessly out of date. But it's in such good shape, I tell them, it would be a shame to replace it. I start in the bedroom, working up a sweat. Aerobic exercise. I'll have to tell Cassandra.

I hope the noise of the Dirt Devil will drown out my sisters' pleas. No such luck. They hang around, and keep telling me without words to look, look, look. No, I say a million times. Look, they demand again, and in a moment of weakness, I obey. I look. I see through their clothes. Marks on their bellies, backs, and thighs, the work of Flanna Flanagan. Flanna with her garden shears, pliers, wire cutters. Her spatulas, paring knives, soup ladles. Her mortar and pestle. Her matches and cigarettes. You learned fast not to rile her.

Flanna, Da's secret rose, in our mother's clothes, mumbling prayers we didn't understand. Right off the boat, they said about her, and we

girls, right off the bat, we understood that she was nuts. We also understood that Daddy loved her, more than he loved us. He forgot all
about our mammy. Never spoke her name. Put Flanna in our mother's
bed—even in her underwear for all I knew—in all the places where
Mam used to be, and thought the rest of us should do the same. That
way, none of us would have to feel the pain of loss. He'd found a
mother for his daughters, a wife for himself. We tried to stay out of her
way, but it hardly ever worked. She found us, always.

I get down on my knees to run the nozzle of the vac all the way
under my bed. Can't stand dust bunnies, never could. The Terminator
is what my daughters call me. I take it as a compliment. But it's my late
sisters, not my daughters, who wait under the bed. The Dirt Devil
does not suck them up. They stand and watch me with their sad bright
eyes. *Go away,* I tell them. *Let me live in peace.* They bow their heads
like nuns in prayer. *What did I ever do to you?* I ask, but on second thought,
I don't want an answer. Don't want to know how I failed them. *Don't let
our suffering be in vain,* they chorus in high voices, like it's a hymn. I
think of Duffy by the Dumpster, closing my hand around the pendant. Out of sight, out of mind. Pull shut the pouch of memory. That's
what I'll do. But when I try, Alberta cries, *No, Mimi, no. . . . Keep trying
to remember.*

"Cut me a break," I whisper above the howling snow. I could
howl too. Because Patty didn't go through what we went through.
And we did our best to keep it from her, from all of them. Didn't
want the younger ones to know what we knew.

I trip on the vacuum cord and fall, end up on my bottom on the
bedroom floor. But the floor gives way beneath me. I keep tumbling,
down, down, landing in a darker place.

*Flanna pushes me down the stairs, into the coal cellar. I bump and bounce
and flop, a broken doll, wearing only panties. Flanna stripped me, took my
clothes. Left me naked and ashamed. "That'll teach ya!" Flanna hollers. "Ya
stinkin' brat!" I land with a thud, a hard landing that shakes loose something
inside of me, a mystery as dark as my surroundings. I howl so everyone will
hear. Howl loud enough to wake the dead, hoping Mam will come back for
me, but the dead do not awaken. Howl until I cannot howl anymore. Lose my*

voice, lose track of time. It slips away. I'm hungry, and so thirsty, my mouth dry as ashes. "Da, Da," I cry both inside and outside myself. "Da, Da." But Daddy, Da, my father, doesn't answer.

I try to get up from the floor of my bedroom, with its outdated wall-to-wall and the beautiful quilt Ruthie sewed for me. Home. It's a long way up, though, and every joint and muscle's creaking. I don't quite make it, and down I go again, collapsing the way I did in the cellar long ago. Maybe I should start with the glucosamine and chondroitin. Duffy swears by it, though he tells me it's expensive, and Medicare won't cover it. He buys it, two for one, when it's on sale at CVS. Maybe we can share.

The wind's still howling, just like me, and the snow still blows against the windows. I unplug the Dirt Devil. God, I hate to leave my sisters. I hate to leave them again, the way I did before. Hooking up with Jack, going down the path he laid out for us, a path too narrow for Eden and Alberta and their messed-up lives. Not once looking back. I have to get back to my own. Not that it's so great, but at least I know, more or less, what's going to happen next.

Nineteen

ZING! WENT THE STRINGS OF MY HEART

Praise the Lord for Duffy, *Family Feud*, and pot roast. He shows up around six P.M., just in time, because I can't turn off the spigots. I cry and hiccup and cry some more. Me. Mimi with her heart of stone. Bawling her eyes out. Her tear ducts, like the bathroom pipe, have sprung a leak. Before he rings the bell, I try to fix my face, but the telltale signs are there. Red nose. Puffy eyes.

"What's up, Mrs. Malloy?" He puts his warm hand on my shoulder. He's wearing gray slacks, a light-blue shirt with a navy-blue cardigan. His silver hair is slicked back nicely and he smells of aftershave.

"Don't give me any sympathy," I say. "I'll fall apart again."

"It's this awful weather. It'd give anyone the blues."

"Maybe that's it," I say, even though I know it isn't. "Had the whole day to walk down Memory Lane. Big mistake."

He nods but doesn't say a thing. I can talk about it, or not, is the feeling I get from him. I decide not. I'm done for the day. I mix each of us a Manhattan, straight-up, which we sip on my couch while we watch the Weather Channel.

"This'll warm the cockles of your heart," he says, lighting up.

"You betcha." I settle into the cushions, let him light my cigarette. Right away my nerves calm down.

"Good thing we got over to the boat," he says as we listen to reports of all the damage up and down the coast. "I must have had an intuition. If I hadn't fixed that tarp . . ."

"She's beautiful, Duff, the *Miss Nomer*. Classy."

"Almost lost her a couple of times," he says, looking at the TV, not at me. "Put her up for collateral, and almost lost her. That's when I put my foot down. I realized I couldn't live without her."

I blush, and hope to hell he doesn't see. Because I'm wishing, all of a sudden and very strongly, that Duffy was talking about me. But no, he's got his eye on the TV, on the maps of storm tracks swirling eastward toward coastal Massachusetts. They look almost like the maps that radiologist made of the inside of my skull, except without the black spots.

"Age hasn't diminished her a bit," I say.

"No," he says, glancing at me, then back at the TV, "she's only gotten more beautiful."

Embarrassment and longing collide inside me and my trusty sharp tongue fails me. I can't think of anything to say.

"You know, Mrs. Malloy, you can only lose so much, and then you have to put your foot down. You just can't lose any more." His sad tone pulls me back from another meltdown. Loss and sadness I can handle. I'm an expert on those.

"I hear ya loud and clear." I sip my Manhattan. He nods, still watching TV, but his eyes are shadowed with that darkness. The subject's closed for now.

When we've finished our drinks, I whip up the dumplings, one of my ex's favorites—a thought I wish I didn't have—and, minutes later, I serve the pot roast on my best white Corelle. We eat at my table with the TV on. But as soon as I dig in, I'm disappointed.

"You should be able to cut this with a fork." I struggle with a steak knife to cut my meat into little bites.

"It's the gravy, and the dumplings, Mrs. Malloy." He smiles at me with his eyes. "Best I've had in years." He chows down like a trooper.

"You can really put it away." I'm pleased by his appetite. Who wouldn't be?

"Cold weather and hard work. That'll do it every time."

When we finish eating, he helps me with the dishes, washing while I dry and put away. While we clean up, we listen to the news, not talking much. We don't even get in each other's way, which is quite a trick in these small kitchens.

"My ex never helped me with the dishes," I remark when we're almost done, and Duffy turns bright red, then I'm embarrassed too. Me and my big mouth. There's an awkward silence and I put on a pot of coffee.

"You still attached to him, Mrs. Malloy?" he asks. I want to die. Attached. I think of buttons on overcoats. Stamps on envelopes. IV lines in a vein.

"Attached?"

"You still carrying the torch?" Duffy's voice is kind and curious.

"The torch? Uh-uh." I take out the mugs, set them by the percolator, keep my back to him. Don't want him to see the color of my face. "No way. That flame died out long ago. I still love a good torch song, though. 'Am I Blue?' 'Cry Me a River' . . . 'Here's That Rainy Day.'"

"'Can't Help Lovin' That Man of Mine'?" Duff adds to the list, but still kind, still curious.

"Nope. I know for sure I don't love him anymore." Even the thought of it appalls me. "Been divorced for fifteen years. He remarried years ago."

"But you never got over him?" His question probes deep as a plumber's snake. I can't help turning around to look at him.

"I was with him thirty years. Married him at nineteen. He was ten years older. We had six kids. I don't love him anymore. That flame died long before we parted, but it's also true that I'm not over him."

"You wish you were."

I shake my head yes. "And you, Duff, you're not over Virginia, are you? You weren't ready for her to go, and you haven't ever let her."

He nods slowly.

"You can't when you've got kids. Even grown-up kids."

"Much as you might want to. Healthy as it might be if you could."

He nods yes, the two of us on the same page, even though we're holding our own ground, on opposite sides of my kitchen.

"I can't bring her back," he says. "And you can't make Jack any better than he was for you."

The coffee's ready, and I pour each of us a cup.

"Remember when we went out to the *Miss Nomer*, and you said you don't really fish?" I ask, my back to him. "You just drop your line into the water to see if anything comes along?"

He's chuckling, the nicest sound. He sees my point before I make it.

"Am I a fish who just happened to swim onto your hook?"

"Oh, I don't know about that, Mrs. Malloy." He picks up our cups and carries them into the living room. "Before we could say for sure, we'd have to know which one of us put the line in the water first."

"Oh, but I've never fished in my life," I tell him, refusing to laugh. "Never even been out on the water. Told you that before. I wouldn't know a hook from a lure if my life depended on it."

"Well, in that case, it couldn't have been you," he says, teasing, as we settle onto the couch for our after-dinner cigarettes and coffee. We're just in time for a rerun of *Magnum, P.I.* We sit close to each other, Duffy's thigh touching mine. I feel peaceful, such a relief! Next thing I know, I'm waking up during the eleven o'clock news, my head on Duffy's shoulder.

"You missed Tom getting the bad guy," he says, shaking me ever so gently. "You've been sleeping like a baby. But now I've got to go. Work tomorrow."

I sit up, laughing, embarrassed all over again. "Jeepers, aren't I great company? I was out like a light."

Duffy laughs too. "I'm the one who's great company. Bored you to sleep."

"No way," I protest, walking him to the door. We pause there for a moment.

"Mrs. Malloy," he says with his sweetest smile, "could you give an old man a little squeeze to send him on his way?"

"My pleasure," I say, and so I do. Standing in my doorway, I give Duffy a great big hug, and he hugs me back, warm and strong. We stay there for a moment, before we break apart, and I close the door behind him.

Twenty

A MILLION
DREAMS AGO

Cassie shows up on Ash Wednesday and she's got Delilah in tow. Delilah, the head bobber. Pretty as a picture, my Delilah, all smooth and soft and blond, unlike Cassie, who has starved herself into sharp angles, bones sticking out everywhere. Of course, Cassie's ten years older, in her forties, and who knows what Delilah will look like in ten more years. Delilah's been married twice, her first marriage short, anything but sweet, and childless as well. Now she's with a hunky Boston cop named Steve O'Neil. Her second time around seems to be going better. So far, their marriage has resulted in two daughters who look exactly like her—blond beauties, as if Steve, black Irish, got left on the deck of the gene pool.

Cassie, without enough to do, her own son Mikey grown if not exactly gone—he lives off the fat of the land in that big house in Hingham—has taken Delilah under her wing. As if Delilah can't fend for herself. Every time I turn around, Cassie's up there, at Delilah's lovely home in Reading, telling her how to run her house and raise her kids and probably what to do in bed with Steve. Delilah just smiles and nods like it's fine by her. I've already told Jo and Patty, this one's gonna blow up in a year or so. The cop will have had it up to here with

Cassie's meddling and Delilah's head-nodding, and I hope I'm living on another planet when it does.

The three of us get ashes at Our Lady Queen of Peace, where the priests make a big deal out of burning last year's palms. We carry in our palms from last year, my daughters' covered with a furry layer of dust, but mine is clean as a whistle. It spent the past year wrapped around the crucifix hanging over my bed, and was dusted on a regular basis. We stand around praying while the priest sets them on fire in this special marble bowl in the front of the church. My daughters watch, but I turn away. I hate the sight, the smell of anything burning. Never been one for candles, or even cookouts. Never wanted a fireplace. *Ashes, ashes, we all fall down.* The fire in the marble bowl burns out, small wisps of smoke rising in the chilly air, wafting away. We stay for Mass, take communion, then go to lunch at my favorite seafood place over at Marina Bay, McCrann's, my daughters treating.

Driving from the church to McCrann's in Delilah's SUV, an Excretion or Exterminator or some such thing—a vehicle I need help climbing into—I keep thinking about the words the priest whispered as he rubbed ashes onto our foreheads: "Remember man that thou art dust and unto dust thou shalt return." *Remember man that thou art dust.*

The hostess leads us to a leather booth where we can see Quincy Bay out the window, the three of us with smudges of ash on our foreheads. It's a cold gray day with occasional flurries, and I tell my girls we should've done lunch the day before, Mardi Gras, when we could eat, drink, and be merry before the fasting began.

"We're eating fish, aren't we?" Cassie asks and looks at Delilah, who nods her answer, yes. My girls order broiled scrod and salads with the dressing on the side. They also order a bottle of white wine and the waiter, like the priest with the palms, makes the biggest deal out of opening it, giving Cass a taste.

"What the hell," I say, smiling at the waiter. "I'm dust and unto dust I shall return. Bring me the fried clam platter." My daughters' faces turn bright red.

Turns out, however, that the lovely lunch with my daughters isn't a random act of kindness. I realize this when they're halfway through their scrod, which they supplement by snitching my fried clams, their forks darting out to stab one every few minutes. Not that I blame them. A deep-fried Ipswich clam, belly and all, dipped in tartar sauce, has to be one of the world's great delicacies, especially at McCrann's. I could never finish all of them.

"There's a new apartment complex for senior citizens going up just a few miles from Delilah's," Cassie announces.

"Squantum River Two? Another storage facility for unwanted antiques?" I say, trying to warn them off.

"Oh, no, it's even nicer." Cassandra's oblivious, or she pretends to be in a convincing way. "Federally subsidized, and you pay based on your income." She takes a pen and notebook out of her purse, and, sure enough, she's figured out my monthly income, and what I'd have to pay.

Last summer, just to appease my daughters, we went to a so-called open house. Everywhere we looked, down the long hallways, with numbered metal doors, grown-up children were visiting their parents, but nobody smiled. Irritation radiated off of them like heat off the pavement in July. In one empty hallway with no view, a man old enough to be my own father if he'd lived a normal life span sat and rocked in a wooden chair. His eyes were open but empty. No reaction whatsoever to all the people walking by. That's what the offspring do to you when your useful days have ended. Not mine. No way, no how.

"Remember that last place we visited?" I ask. "I couldn't get out fast enough. I decided then and there that I wasn't going to move. Ever."

"You should see the plans," she says, as if I haven't spoken. "It's gorgeous. Like a Club Med, right in the Boston burbs. Valhalla, I think it's called. It'll have a health club and a screening room right on the premises. They also have an assisted-living wing that you can move into when you're ready."

"Oh, and let me guess, another wing for those lost to Old Timer's disease. Another three-winged creature."

I sip my wine and speak softly, but my blood pressure, Old Faithful, is shooting upward. My daughters never stop.

"You'd be right around the corner from me," Delilah chimes in, proving, after all, that she can speak. "I could bring the girls over anytime you want. And they'll have full-time medical support, to make sure residents take their pills, stuff like that."

"I'm not decrepit. I know when and how to take my medications."

"We know people," Cassie adds. "We could get you moved to the top of the list."

"The developer owes Steve a big one," says Delilah.

"I thought we'd been through this." I feel angrier than I sound. "I thought I'd made myself clear on this point."

They shrug in unison, as if they'd practiced.

"We're worried about you, Mimi," Cassie declares. To my chagrin, several other diners turn around to look at us.

"We want to keep you around for as long as possible," adds Delilah.

"I'm happy where I am."

"You're in denial about your health situation." Cassandra.

"Am not."

"Are too."

"You're not safe where you are." Delilah.

"Not safe? Why not?"

"Even Steve says so. He says those windows are so flimsy, and with those shrubs around them, you're asking for a break-in."

Great, now we've got the cop in on the act.

"Plus it costs too much." Cassie.

"What if something happened?" Delilah.

"What if you slipped in the tub?"

"I put down those sticky butterflies."

"Or fell down in the bedroom?"

"I've got a phone in there."

"What if you couldn't reach it? You could be there for days."

"Without anybody knowing."

My chance to tell them about Duffy, but I won't.

Then Del launches into a story about her ex-husband's sister-in-law. Her elderly mother fell down in her bedroom the day after Christmas, her arm wedged between the headboard and the wall, and she was unable to reach a phone. For three days nobody called her because they'd all just seen her on Christmas. By the time one of her kids figured out the mother was MIA and got the super to let her into the apartment, the mother's more than half dead; semiconscious and dehydrated with the broken arm, which a week later had to be amputated because of all the damage done during the days she lay there helpless on the floor slipping in and out of it.

"I'm not elderly," I say, as if they'll listen. "I'm pretty good on my feet. I'll study tai chi. They've got senior classes at the Y. And how on earth did her arm get stuck behind the headboard?"

"She was chasing dust bunnies." Cassie. "Behind a couple of Martinis."

"That's what they said." Delilah.

"I'll give up my Manhattans on cleaning day."

"Now she lives with one of her kids. They built a bedroom and a bathroom onto the back of the house, with a separate entrance. Nice place, but a major, major guilt trip."

"She's bitter. Angry and depressed all the time because of the lost arm."

"She lived for golf."

"Can you imagine? No more chipping or putting."

In my mind's eye, I see this gray-haired granny, in a visor and a golf skort, trying a one-armed swing. It just about kills me not to laugh.

"A tragedy that could have been avoided if she'd had appropriate living arrangements." Cassie.

"For a woman her age." Delilah. "In her situation."

"A built-in support system." Cass.

"You mean those alarm thingies you can pull in the bedroom and the bathroom? Or that thing you wear around your neck?" They nod together.

"And people to check up on you." Cassie. "On a daily basis."

"Nosing into my business."

They shrug again, a syncopated move.

"It's only because we love you, Mimi." Cassie. "That's the part you don't get."

"And we worry about you all the time." Delilah.

"We've got a great superintendent, a fellow named Dick Duffy," I hear myself say against my own better judgment. "He's there 24/7.

Keeps an eye on everything, just to make sure everything's OK. If I forget to pick up my mail, even for a day, he'll come check on me." That's all I'm going to say, and I hope I don't regret it.

By now Cassie's eyes look moist, and a tear is dripping down Delilah's lovely cheek. They're good. They're really, really good, my girls. First-class connivers, just like their old man.

"Put me in a pine box," I tell them now, but in a calmer voice. "That's how you'll move me out of my place. I've told you that before, and I mean it. The only way I'm leaving is in a pine box."

Last summer, on the way back home from that open house, so much fury raged in Cassandra's car, I'm surprised the windows didn't blow out. Me alone in back, the two of them in front, talking about me as if I wasn't there. As if I was just a memory, a bad one. Stubborn. Secretive. Sneaky. Self-centered. Cold.

So today, in the restaurant, looking out at the water, I make a promise.

"Cross my heart that I will never, ever be a burden to you." The two of them look at me with their beautiful blue eyes. "You, my lovely daughters, owe me nothing. I do not expect, nor would I ask for, end-of-life care from you. I want you to move forward, expect you to. Live your own lives. But please, let me make my own choices while I can."

Lunch goes smoother after that. We finish the wine and clean our plates, Cassie and Delilah ruining my plans to take home a doggy bag. Stuffed to the gills, we can't even think about coffee or dessert. We're heading back in Delilah's gas guzzler and again I hear the priest, *Remember man that thou art dust*. We'll be driving practically right by Gate of Heaven, and I think, Hey, why not introduce my daughters to their grandfather?

"Would you like to see where your grandfather is buried?" I ask. They try to catch each other's eyes, but it's tough with me riding shotgun and Cassie in the back. "Gate of Heaven. It's on the way."

Delilah says she knows how to get there, and next thing you know, we're at the gate. Most of the snow has melted, though icy mounds still shine against the stones. I look out across the acres of gray, glinting with old snow and ice.

We park and make our way along the concrete pathways, but this time I know where I'm going. Cassie stops before we've gone very far.

"What a dump," she announces. She's standing, one hand on her hip, a manicured finger on her chin. Turning this way and that, shaking her head, like a movie star from the '40s. Bette Davis or Joan Crawford. "This must be where they buried the poor people."

Delilah is looking all around too, but at least she doesn't bob her head. "It isn't taken care of very well."

"Well, it's an older cemetery. Lots of the people buried here don't have anyone left to tend their plots. That's what happens, sooner or later."

"Still." Cassie's snotty tone tweaks a nerve. Then I realize that's how we raised her, to believe she was privileged, a princess. To expect the best, to demand it. I helped make her who she is.

"I guess I never showed you." My voice sounds thin and cold. Suddenly I'm flooded with sadness, like a cellar after weeks of rain.

Up ahead, beyond a chain link fence, is the backyard with the barbecue grill and the aboveground pool. In the background, not fifteen feet from where Da lies buried, is the clothesline, one of the round ones that spins on a metal pole. Underwear, frozen stiff, is hanging on it, men's cotton boxers in crazy prints—tigers on one, hearts on another—and women's bras and undies.

"Victoria's Secret knockoffs," says Cassie from behind me.

I kneel down to wipe dirt and snow off Da's stone. Instead I see his face, his shame and sorrow, a face he doesn't want me to see. He covers his face with his hands.

The ground's covered with icy slush. My knit pants soak it up. My girls reach down to help me up, one on each side, pulling me away, as if from something not one of us can bear to see. They stand close, not letting go. The three of us stand for the longest time, looking down at Da's grave and holding hands.

Joseph Daniel Sheehan
August 10, 1896–July 4, 1937

. . . the world's more full of weeping than you can understand . . .

Four decades between the dates, me in his life for only eleven years.

Del's voice breaks the cold silence. "He died at forty," she says. "He didn't even make it to the prime of his own life."

People aged faster then, I'm thinking, but what I say is, "I want to be buried here. Put me here when I pass."

"Would you stop?" Cassie screeches. "You're so fucking morbid."

"Don't use that language around me!" Can't tolerate the F word, never could, and Cassie knows it.

Cassie's looking to Delilah, her ally, for the nod, but Delilah's blubbering. What's gotten into her? I wonder.

"We never knew him," she gasps, "we never knew anything about him."

Then I see Da in the parlor, the cornet to his lips, his music slipping and sliding all around us. No, they never heard Da's music nor saw his laughing eyes.

"Time to go." Cassie tugs on my arm. Delilah's still snuffling. I want to comfort her but don't know how. By the time we reach the Guzzler, she's going strong again, weeping and repeating, "We never ever knew him. You never told us anything," over and over.

"I'll drive," says Cass.

Delilah hoists me into the backseat, and the whole way to my place she weeps and snuffles. Reaching from the backseat, I pat her shoulder.

"We never had him in our lives, Mimi," she says again when we arrive. "I'll never know who he was. Neither will my girls. None of us ever will."

"I wish I could tell you more about him," I say, and in that instant, as Cass turns off the ignition, I'm overwhelmed with remorse. What would my girls' lives have been like if my father had been in them? "I don't even have his picture."

Twenty-one

PENNIES FROM
HEAVEN

A couple of days later, Patty calls to tell me her grandson's project, the genealogy, is due, wailing like the earth might stop
spinning if he doesn't get it in on time.

"We still have unanswered questions!" Including me in that first-
person plural, though I do not include myself. "We've gotta call your
dreaded Yik Yak Club into session."

"So what if we leave a few things blank?"

"Where can we meet? Not in public. No repeats of Keeley's birthday party."

A bust, the three of us plus Cassie, bawling at the pink table with
the tea roses in the middle.

"How about your place?" she asks, like she's just that moment
thought of it. But I know better: payback for wrecking Keeley's birthday.

"Sure, why not? I could make lunch." When I make this offer to
Patty, I'm thinking only of us, the surviving Sheehan sisters—the Fab
Four, Ruthie calls us. But Patty tells Cassandra, who immediately in-
vites herself and then she calls a couple of her sisters to invite them,
too. And they all call Patty—not me—to say they'll be there.

In a few hours, after countless phone calls and endless datebook checking, it's settled. Me and my sisters and a few—not all—of my daughters will get together for an official meeting of the Yik Yak Club. At my place, with the stipulation that I don't light up while the meeting's going on. The plan is, we'll bring our rag bags, we Sheehan girls. We'll piece the scraps together, try to stitch up the holes—not just in Aidan's genealogy, but in our lives as well. Not that I care all that much. I'm happy to go on as-is, holes and all.

As the big day approaches, I'm a bundle of nerves, like a pageant contestant facing the final judges. My daughters and my sisters. Well, not my sisters, really. I usually don't have to prove myself to them, except when they call me a drama queen, which makes me see red, and, when that happens, I cannot think, let alone prove, anything at all. But my daughters are another story. A harsh group. Exacting. Not anything like yours truly, who's always willing to cut a guy a break.

As grown-ups, my daughters have become divided into two camps, and each, for different reasons, finds me full of faults. Celestine and Ruth Ann on the one side; Cassandra, Siobhan, and Delilah on the other. I don't count Malvina, who's all by her lonesome in the Bronx.

Two peas in a pod are Celestine and Ruth Ann—a brainy but critical pod, self-certain, and one I prayed they'd break out of at Boston College, Jack Malloy's alma mater, where they graduated from, one year after the other. But no such luck. The pod got thicker. Trust the Jesuits to shape a really fine mind, and they've shaped four out of my six—five if you count Malvina, a Fordham dropout. Cellie, who tends to be a nitpicker, runs a copy desk at a newspaper in Philadelphia. Once she tried explaining what she did to me, and how important it was. Crossing t's and dotting i's and putting in periods and commas where they belong, plus checking facts, like is Nome or Fairbanks the capital of Alaska. All day long. So they can put it in the newspaper. What I got out of it is that my daughter bosses around a bunch of other nitpickers, and that she's paid well for it.

Ruth Ann is, or was, a folklorist, an expert in American quilts, though I usually think of it as guilts. Now, she's mostly just a mother who sews all the time, stitching together bits of bright fabric in patterns so complex I get a headache just from looking at them. But who knows, maybe it's a skill that will come in handy for the Yik Yak Club.

Then there's Cass, who married well if income is your measure of success, a CPA with a big corporate practice named Michael Broome. You go girl, I said when she finally dumped him. Sweep him out of your life, Mrs. Broome. Once, at Christmas, all of us—me and Cassie and Mike Sr. and Mikey—went out to a Christmas tree farm to chop down their tree, which we would then drag home and decorate, celebrating the spirit of the season. This splendid tree would fill the big front window of their Georgian colonial, showing all their neighbors and the passersby how joyful they were. During the fall, they'd gone and tagged one, and now the day had come to chop it down. We rode around in a golf cart with a chain saw, and finally found the tree with the tag that said Broome Family. Right next to it was a bigger, nicer tree. Mike checked the tag. It was somebody he knew, a big-shot lawyer he couldn't stand. So he switched the tags and cut down the lawyer's tree and that's what we took home. The three of them thought it was hilarious, but I was mad enough to spit. When I told them so, Mike Sr. called me a killjoy. "What's your problem?" Cassie asked me. "Have you forgotten how to laugh?" Little Mikey, grinning, topped them both. "Get a life, Mimi," he said.

As for my two youngest, Del and Siobhan, the blond betrayers, they're still floundering around in their lives, with Jack Malloy always rushing to the rescue. Del's an efficiency expert at BankBoston who is always short of cash. And Steve buys the groceries and pays the household bills because, despite her MBA, she can't ever quite get her act together. So fragile, Delilah—bursts into tears at the slightest provocation, her lovely face and perfect body a container for unending sorrow, but you'd never guess by looking at her. And finally, the second youngest, Siobhan. A feminist scholar in Irish studies, her education dragging on, year after year, no end in sight. She's ABD, our Siobhan. That means, she explained to me, All But Dissertation, which is like a book she's got to write, but not one that I would like to read. Heading back to the old country every chance she gets, Siobhan is, with me reminding her, "Honey, you're going in the wrong direction. The ancestors couldn't wait to leave. They were lined up at the docks."

I'm a wreck over this all-important powwow, and I don't think very well when I get nervous, but Duffy, that prince, he helps. He suggests a deli platter, so I order up a nice big one with turkey, roast beef, baked Virginia ham, and several types of cheese; sides of pickles, potato salad, and coleslaw. We go together to pick it up, along with bags of chips and sodas and wine coolers and all the paper products I'll need to serve them. Everything fits nicely in the back of the Caprice.

We're heading back to Paul Revere, slowed, as usual, by the congestion in downtown Quincy, when I notice a white envelope half wedged in the crack between the seat and the seatback. Without thinking, I tug it out and see it's unsealed, with cash inside and the name Christopher J. Duffy handwritten across the front. Quicker than a wink, Duffy snatches it from my hand and sticks it into his own pocket. I want to melt into my seat.

"Thanks for finding that, Mrs. Malloy." He smiles, but he keeps his eyes on the road in front of him as we pull into the parking lot at Centennial Square. His cheeks are pinker than usual, his eyes a brighter hue.

"No problem," I answer, afraid I've just trespassed against him, finding an envelope full of cash with his son's name on it. I wish he'd meet my eye. He doesn't. *Forgive us our trespasses*, I pray to myself as we unload the Caprice, as if the incident didn't happen. We carry the bags inside and put everything where it goes, me clearing a big space in the fridge for the deli platter. After that, we walk to Hanrahan's Bakery in the Square for rolls, the very same bakery where Da used to buy those pastries. It's run now by the great-grandchildren, and still a first-class place. They've really kept up with the times, selling things I personally wouldn't dream of eating, breads filled with olives and sundried tomatoes and cheeses whose names I can't pronounce. I stick with my old favorites, the snowflake rolls and Parker House rolls, hot out of the oven. The smell of warm bread from that bakery drives me crazy. On the way back home, Duffy smiles with his eyes and says, "I won't tell if you don't," and we dip into the bag and share a warm roll. I've been forgiven, or my trespass has been forgotten. When the roll is gone, I take his hand and squeeze, and we walk home that way.

The morning of our meeting, Duffy brings over folding chairs and a card table that he keeps in storage for just such occasions. He puts orange cones on the parking spaces nearest to my place so the girls won't have to walk too far, or drive around looking for a place to park. He attaches little signs to them with duct tape that say "Malloy Party." Just before the girls arrive, he shows up with a bouquet of cut flowers: mums, dahlias, and yellow roses. I open the door and he's standing there, holding this big bouquet from the florist down the street, his face bright red. Suddenly, my heart warms up, like it's wrapped in clover.

"For your table," he says, shoving the flowers at me, then taking off like a shy little schoolboy.

As I arrange the flowers in a vase, Lenox crystal—another gift from you-know-who—I forget about my dread of spending time with these women whom I love but do not always trust. It tickles me, the way Duffy shoved the flowers at me and took off, and it keeps tickling me every time I see them on my table. Before the others arrive, I sniff the flowers, convincing myself that I can get through what's coming next. Of course I won't say one word about him. Duffy and I agree on this point. We're just good friends. No big deal. Why drag the kids into it?

Twenty-two

I'VE GOT YOU
UNDER MY SKIN

Keeley is the first to arrive, in one of those shiny jogging suits Cassandra favors. I give her a big hug. "I didn't mean to ruin your birthday," I say.

"You didn't, not at all," she insists with her sweet smile. "That happened a long time ago."

"I love you, Keel. I wouldn't hurt you for the world."

"I love you too, Mimi. You were the wind beneath my wings when I was growing up."

"The wind beneath your wings?" I'm about to make a crack when I realize Keeley's sincere, one hundred percent. I bite my tongue and hug her again. Realize, maybe for the first time, that Keeley is more precious than any of that fancy jewelry Frank buys for her. She helped me raise my girls, though I don't believe I've ever told her. Keeley gave them things I couldn't, like fun and her rapt attention: *Keeley's the best aunt EVER*, a continual refrain I heard throughout their childhood, although it hurt sometimes when my daughters didn't want to come back home to me.

Cassandra shows up with the twins, Jo and Patty, dressed in

turtlenecks and sweatshirts and fur-lined boots. Patty's carrying a big box of pastries from Hanrahan's.

"Cream puffs and éclairs. A taste from childhood," Patty says, putting the box on my counter next to the deli platter.

Cassandra, in her pricey Talbots weekend wear, eyeballs me up and down, her lips curling. I'm back in my Rockport Walkers, my black pull-on pants, and a polyester top with purple flowers.

"Just want to be comfy," I say, not meeting her eye. "And besides, I'm not taking it public."

I carry their coats into the bedroom, and when I come back out, Ruth Ann's arrived but without her sidekick Cellie, who lives too far away to come.

"I like the orange cones, Mimi," Ruthie says. She's in jeans and a crewneck sweater, like she's still in college. "You must have good connections here."

"Oh, I do. Friends in high places."

"That Dick Duffy character, right?" says Cass, and my insides realign themselves. When did she meet him? What does she know?

"Dick Duffy? Who's he?" asks Ruthie.

"The super," Cassandra answers.

Just then Delilah and Siobhan arrive, short-circuiting that line of conversation (yay!) and yapping about the traffic through the city and how the Big Dig is only making matters worse so far—all of the usual Boston laments, plus their gripes about the smell of tobacco in my place.

"I'm allergic, you know," says Del.

"I've opened the windows. You can sit right next to one."

"Daddy sends his best wishes," says Siobhan while I'm taking her coat.

"Yes, he told us to give you his regards," adds Del. Both are wearing full-length leather, butter soft, one caramel, the other forest green.

"Tell him he can stuff it."

"The least you could do is be polite, Mimi," says Delilah, outraged. "He's polite to you. It would make our lives so much easier."

"Less stressful," chimes Siobhan. "I don't know what you've got against him anyway."

"Against him? Shall I write a list? Send you a memo?" They shoot daggers at me. "Oh, I'm sorry, I'm sorry." I don't want to rekindle the old rage, but I can't help it sometimes. Its embers still glow hot beneath the ashes, ready to burst into flame at the slightest provocation. I lay their coats across my bed, take a few slow breaths, get myself together.

"I'll try to control myself."

"Please do," they say together.

Everybody comments on the pretty flowers, Cass happy because I've used her vase. "The crystal does those lovely flowers justice. Where'd you get them?" she asks. Everyone's waiting for the answer.

"A secret admirer," I say, but I know they don't believe me. It doesn't occur to them that anyone might buy me flowers, not even the lowly super.

Pretty soon, everybody's helping themselves and finding a spot to sit down, my daughters at the card table and my sisters at my window table, more people than I've ever fed in my place. They tell me how great the food is, and I tell them, "The only thing I did was drive over to the deli to pick it up. That's me, slaving over a hot takeout window."

When the time comes, when everyone's eaten and dropped their paper plates into the trash, we move the chairs into a circle in front of my couch as best we can, with the coffee table in the middle. Everyone except Delilah, that is, who keeps her folding chair by the open window in order to breathe clean air. I look around at the two generations, my sisters and my daughters, blondes and redheads plus Ruthie, the brunette. The younger generation is well groomed and lovely, done up right, the way I taught them. We older gals, Keeley excepted, are somewhat dowdy—Cassandra's word—having let ourselves go. Approaching our "use-by" date, or maybe past it. I look around my crowded living room, and those old bad feelings start to seep into me again.

If they could, they'd have me put away.

"Let's get back to Aidan's project," says Patty, who's wearing her WORLD'S GREATEST GRANDMA sweatshirt. She pulls a notebook and some files out of her tote, clicks her Bic, and looks at us.

"Yes, let's figure out what happened to Fagan and when it happened," says Cassandra, even louder, like she's the one in charge. She, too, has a notebook—a fancy little moleskin, along with her gold pen.

"Don't think it's any wonder we don't know," Patty says to Cass. "Our lives were in chaos when she was sent back."

"To Cullyhanna, County Armagh." Jo

"Leaving a big hole in our lives." Me. "Filled by Keeley."

All of us turn to Keeley, who looks at least a decade younger than her years, maybe because she raised golden retrievers instead of kids. She flushes, shaking her head no, when Siobhan cries, "Cullyhanna, County Armagh?" The words roll like music off her tongue.

"It's so beautiful there," she raves, her eyes lit up as if the words have flipped a switch. "You should see it."

"You've been there?" I can hardly contain my surprise. That's how much I know about my kid.

Siobhan nods.

"We don't know exactly when she left," says Patty, getting all excited too. "And we don't know when she died, only that it happened before Nana could send for her."

"We were grown-ups when we finally learned the cause of death. Marasmus." Jo looks around the room.

"Who told us?"

"Nana." Patty frowns at me, her pen and notebook at the ready. "On her deathbed."

"You were there, for heaven's sake," says Jo, her halo not on view today. Another black spot.

"Marasmus means starvation," Cassandra interjects. "I looked it up. Failure to grow. Emaciation as the result of protein energy malnutrition. It's fairly common in developing countries among young children."

"Fagan was five when she got sent away," I throw in.

"Fagan starved to death in Ireland?" asks Siobhan, and the pain of it almost knocks me over. Poor Fagan. And me, I let her go without a peep. Now, I swear, her warm breath is on my neck. She's on my lap after one of her tantrums, and I'm rocking her to sleep. Baby Fay.

"When she lived with us, she was anything but wasting," says Jo. "She was a spitfire, full of energy."

"Chubby," adds Patty, scribbling down a few words. "Something happened after she got sent over."

"Fagan, the holy terror," says Jo. "It came down to Fagan or Flanna. The war of the worlds."

"A death match?" asks Delilah, still by the open window, trying to breathe unpolluted air.

"Da had to choose, one or the other," Patty says. "He chose Flanna."

He chose Flanna. These three little words pitch me backward, pull the floor out from under me, make me lose my footing. Fagan: here today, gone tomorrow.

"Da gathered the rest of us together to explain," Patty says. "In the parlor, all of us sitting on the shiny sofa. 'We had to send your sister, Little Fay, away to Ireland to grow up,' he said. His face was wet with tears, and Flanna was crying too—the picture of desolation."

I take over, hearing Da's voice and imitating it: " 'She'll live with family, she'll learn how to behave, and then she'll come back home.' "

" 'Learn how to behave'?" asks Siobhan. "In Cullyhanna, County Armagh?"

"Someone's family was taking her in, Nana's or Flanna's. Nobody remembers."

"Then Da took out a map," Patty interrupts. "He pointed to a spot on it, the point in Europe closest to America, 'Not so bad, huh, my little beauties?' he told us"—Patty imitates his accent perfectly—"and he ran his finger on the map from Boston to Belfast, just a few inches after all. 'She's really not so far away. We'll send her letters and packages, OK?' "

Hearing Patty, my skin feels burned, the way it would after one of Flanna's punishments. She'd draw scalding water in the bathtub, force us to bathe in it, we three oldest girls together. She'd dare us to make the slightest sound: *You do, and I'll warm your little bottoms for you.* A joke, maybe, since our bottoms were already burning, and would for hours afterward.

"There must be someone left who'd know," says Cass. My sisters shake their heads.

"Flanna took all of our birth and baptismal certificates, whatever was left in Da's house, after Da died." Patty. "The house and all inside it, that's what Nana used to say. Da's uniform, his cornet, our mother's things, whatever few belongings we girls had."

"Then the house got torn down, for an exit ramp on Route 3A," I add.

"Our mother's things?" says Jo. "Flanna took them over the minute she arrived."

"Back then, you didn't throw good things away," says Patty.

"She didn't get the blue pendant," I say, "though who knows how it ended up with me, on my closet floor of all places."

"She smelled funny," says Jo.

"Like the herbs she was forever boiling." Patty. "She grew them in the yard, in a garden where we weren't allowed to go."

"Not anything like Mam's." Jo. "Her smell."

"What did Mam smell like?" asks Keeley.

"Like a Hanrahan's pastry," says Patty. "Sweet."

"You never knew when that hand of hers would fly out, smack you on the cheek," says Jo. "Or whatever body part was reachable."

"Flanna, not our mother," Patty clarifies.

"She'd hit you with whatever she was holding." Jo. "A hairbrush, a spatula."

"A soup ladle, a spade." Patty.

"Her cigarette." Me.

My daughters hum and chirp, their lovely feathers ruffled. Mine are ruffling too, a peculiar sensation deep under my skin. "Patty, how can you call us drama queens when you know all of us were hurt?"

Hurt. This hard little word ricochets around the room, repeated by the older and then the younger generation.

"Hurt," my daughters echo.

"Beaten or burned." The twins shake their heads no, but I hold my ground. "Or both."

Now my girls are whispering to one another, like I'm making it all up. I look at them, beautiful birds perched on the shaky limb of our family tree. Suddenly I'm furious at them, with the safe lives Jack and I worked so hard to give them, keeping everything from them so they'd never have to know. Made sure they'd never have bad dreams, never be afraid. Not once did I ever ask them for sympathy—and certainly not for pity—but a little bit of respect would go a long way. I roll up the sleeve of my big shirt with its pretty purple flowers. I hold my arm out so they can see a spray of scars.

"That was fat splatter from the stove!" wails Patty.

"Fat splatter," repeats Jo, looking like a bobble-head doll, nodding so hard just to agree.

"Daddy was cooking bacon," the twins recite together. "You were standing too close to the stove when he dropped the spatula and the fat splattered and burned your arm. That's what Daddy said."

Nope. I find the correct black spot inside my head: Flanna grabbed me and held me close to the stove. Slammed the spatula into the bubbling oil on purpose. She screeched when it hit my arm, not my face. I tried to run, but she grabbed my arm again. Looked at the blisters bubbling. Did this without anger, without any feeling I recognized. Her brown eyes were so beautiful—a place for getting lost in, the way Da did. But when I looked into her brown eyes, I refused to get lost. Refused to cry. Put on my plaster of Paris mask, the one I used so often growing up. A plaster mask that pushed Flanna closer to the edge. She reached for the pan of hot oil, ready to throw it at me. I broke away just in the nick of time. Whatever that means, the nick of time.

"It wasn't Da. It was Flanna. She burned me on purpose."

"When?" asks Patty. "When did she do that?"

"I don't know when. Can't remember."

"Traumatic amnesia," babbles Cassandra, scribbling into her notebook.

"Stop it, Mimi, just stop it," Patty begs.

"Things were bad enough." Jo. "Don't make them worse by making things up."

The twins glare at me, their faces white and hard.

My daughters steal glances at one another. Mad Mimi, telling another whopper, like the one about the secret admirer who gave her flowers.

"I'm not making things up. Eden and Alberta had scars too. Worse ones, and you know it. Flanna was jealous of their youth, their beauty. She didn't want to share Da with us, with anyone. She refused to let him love us." At least that's my theory, all I could come up with.

I roll down my sleeve, hiding the scars, closing off that memory, at least for now. To hell with my sisters' version of our lives. Other memories roll toward me now like waves on the shores of the Fore River, after a big ship had been launched. I'm stepping right into that swirling cold water. I'm going to tell it like it was.

Twenty-three

LAST CALL
FOR LOVE

Ruthie gets up and grabs a wine cooler, one of those fruity kinds that looks and tastes like soda. "Alcohol content, three point two percent," she reads. "I don't think that's strong enough to get me through this."

"I've got a box of something stronger in the fridge," I say. Next thing you know, my Franzia Chardonnay is out there on the counter, and they're all lined up, holding paper cups up to the spigot, even Cassie. I'm way too hurt to join them.

I watch while they fill up, my sisters and my daughters. I wish they'd all leave. I'd like nothing better than to light up, mix myself a Manhattan, call up Duffy, and turn on Sinatra's "If You Go Away." The last place in the world I want to go is back to Flanna hurting us, or to Fagan Sent Away.

But while I'm thinking this, Eden and Alberta show up and press against me, one on either side. They've got my arms, the three of us together, the way we were so often growing up. I remember Flanna chasing after Eden and Alberta with her Lucky Strikes. *Reach for a Lucky instead of a sweet*. Flanna's words to live by. I try to break free of these memories, to push them away again like I did before, but Eden and Alberta won't let me go.

"Flanna wasn't always vicious," Patty says, her face no longer icy white but flushed. The room is heating up now, even with the open window.

"That was the crazy part." Jo. "She could be sweet and caring, curling our hair, ironing our dresses, parading us in front of Da, showing off how well she took care of us."

"You never knew which Flanna you'd get." Patty.

The memory of the other Flanna cuts through me. I might've keeled over from the pain, but Al and Eden hold me up. *They take me into a terrible dark place, but it's familiar, with fearful sounds and smells. I gag. Switch off my ears and nose. Alberta holds my wrist, her little hand a clamp. Eden, on the other side, holds me too, but gently. She leans her head on my shoulder. Her silky hair feathers my cheek. "Amelia Earhart loves to fly," they whisper, and I join them. "Amelia Earhart will never die."*

I stumble between them, leg bones melting, until I recognize the place where they are taking me, the coal cellar of our house. The stink is worse. My throat closes up. I cannot breathe, no air. I struggle to break free, but Eden and Alberta hold me until Flanna steps out of the shadows. She holds aloft some type of pole, the poker, its tip glowing in the dark, red hot. "I'm your mother now," she says.

"We loved the good Flanna," says Patty, jolting me back in to my living room. "We wanted her to be that way all the time."

"That's why we never told on her." Jo.

"Fagan got the worst from her," I say.

"Worse than being burned with hot oil?" Ruthie asks.

"Fagan couldn't go with the flow," says Patty. "She was always fighting."

"Defiant." Jo. "It was her nature."

"Oppositional defiant disorder?" asks Cassie, the expert, using the new lingo.

"A brat," I answer. "Don't you remember when Fagan burned the shoes? The blue Mary Janes? Back before Flanna came?"

My living sisters chuckle, then I have to tell the story so my daughters get it. Fagan throwing the hand-me-downs into the fire, Da trying to pull them out, then buying her new red ones. My daughters love it, so I haul out another.

"Remember how Fagan was always taking off her diaper because she said she was a big girl, not a baby? Then she'd pee the bed again."

"Hey, that's my story, not yours," Patty cries.

"You didn't have to share a bed with her," Jo adds, like the two of them hold a copyright.

"No, but you two tried to climb in with us whenever she wet yours."

"We learned our lesson after Flanna came, though," says Jo. "The first night we told on her, she poured the chamber pot over Fagan's head."

"Showered her with pee," adds Patty. "Wouldn't let Fagan wash. Fagan had to sit in the corner all night, covered with pee."

"Chamber pot?" says Delilah, turning to look at us, risking an intake of foul air.

"That's right," I say. "That's how ancient we are. When we were growing up, people still kept chamber pots in the bedrooms at night. Houses didn't have fifteen bathrooms, not like now." Delilah's house had four at last count. She and Steve are planning major renovations.

"She poured it over Fagan's head?" Siobhan asks.

"Yes, she poured pee over Fagan's head when she wet the bed at night."

Fagan, wet and smelly, whimpers in the corner of the bedroom. I sneak over to her so she won't be alone. Fagan, wet and whimpering, and me, a few feet away, whispering nonsense. "Wee Willie Winkie runs through the town." I can't hug her or even touch her because if I do I'll get her pee stink on me, and Flanna will find out.

"Flanna couldn't control her. Sometimes I could, and so could Da, if he was home. But not Flanna."

"Fagan never missed a chance to get Flanna's goat," says Jo. " 'You're not my Mammy, not Mammy.' She said it half a dozen times a day."

"Not Mammy."

The words ignite a fuse. It sparks and hisses in my skull.

"Flanna couldn't have children of her own." Patty. "Nothing made her madder than to be reminded of it."

"If only Da had known enough to stay single." Jo.

"That wasn't an option," says Patty. "And besides, he really did love Flanna."

"He was always spouting Irish poetry." Jo looks at my daughters, who watch us like we're actors in a foreign film and they're having trouble with the subtitles.

"Yeats," adds Keeley.

"Yeats shmates," I say, snapped out of my trance by their nonsense.

"He thought Flanna was an angel, or a creature from a poem." Patty. "His secret rose. That's what he called her. He worshiped the ground she walked on."

"Da and his poetry," cries Jo. *"A man that had six mortal wounds, a man violent and famous, strode among the dead . . . "*

"And that other one he used to read us, something about *No better than a beast, upon all fours?*" says Patty. "It was Da's favorite."

"That's when he was worshiping the ground Flanna walked on." Unbidden, Da appears to me like that; on his hands and knees, clutching at the ground. But where? Maybe in some sort of garden? But not Flanna's. Flanna isn't anywhere around.

"What was Da thinking, reading us that stuff?" Jo asks.

"Other kids got Mother Goose and we got 'Cuchulain Comforted.'" Patty.

My daughters watch, flushed and alert. Then Siobhan, almost always silent, speaks again. "Yeats? Your father read you Yeats?"

"Your grandfather," I say. "Even if you never knew him."

"The Rose, The Wind Among the Reeds, The Tower, his favorite books," says Jo. "He always had one with him."

Da's poetry. I put it in the same category as Flanna's mumbo-jumbo.

"Awhile back, just for the heck of it, I picked up Yeats's collected poems," Jo says. "Flipping through the pages, I saw all these poems Da used to read to us, so I bought the book." She shrugs. "It isn't airplane reading, but it sure did bring back memories."

I shake my head. "Sinatra's all the poetry I need."

"Sinatra has never written a word," argues Ruthie. "Not one word."

"He only sings them," says Cassandra.

"Not even 'Nancy with the Smiling Face.'" Ruthie.

"Who cares? He sings my own feelings," I say. *"How far would I travel to be where you are? How far is the distance between here and a star?* I don't get that other stuff. Makes my brain hurt."

And again, I see Da, right there in front of me, just like my sisters, but unshaven, his blue eyes rimmed red and a crusted cut across one cheek. He's on his hands and knees, on the ground, a place that seems familiar even though I can't place it.

"The Ahearns never stopped blaming him for our mother's death," says Keeley. She gets up with the box of Chardonnay, and walks around the room, slim and shapely, holding it up so the others can help themselves to refills. "Knocking her up so many times, I guess. Seven kids in eleven years. And then not having enough money to bury her. They paid for her funeral, the Ahearns did, and never forgave Da for it."

"When Da remarried, forget about it." Jo. "They were outraged. He didn't even wait a year."

"A year?" Patty laughs. "How long did he wait? No more than two or three months."

"After that," says Jo, "they didn't give a rat's ass about us." It's the strongest language I've ever heard her use.

"Flanna expected us to fall all over her with love from day one." Patty. "Alberta and Eden did. At least at first."

"Look where it got them."

Again, Siobhan speaks. "You said Flanna was right off the boat."

My sisters and I nod.

"We don't know where she came from." Patty.

"She was supposed to be some type of healer," I say, thinking about her garden, her awful concoctions. "The old folks were always coming by the house for remedies. Healing potions."

"And also for help with their bad luck." Jo. "Can you imagine?" She and Patty laugh. "Flanna, making their lives better."

"She gave them herbs, elixirs, prayers to say." Patty.

"Flanna might have been a *cailleach*," says Siobhan, who, after all, is ABD in Irish Studies.

"A what?" we chorus.

"Kyle-yuck?" I try to copy Siobhan's pronunciation, but the word won't go deep enough into my throat.

"*Cailleach*," Siobhan repeats, the strange word tumbling all through my childhood, like when Flanna pushed me down the cellar stairs. "A faerie healer."

"Faeries? Jesus," chime her sisters.

"What was that word?" I want to hear it again, this word I can neither pronounce nor spell.

"*Cailleach*," Siobhan repeats, yet again, and looks at her sisters. "Laugh if you want, but faeries weren't always funny leprechauns, wee folks on cereal boxes. Back in the last century, in rural Ireland, an entire preliterate cosmology—"

"'Preliterate cosmology'?" Cassandra and Ruthie echo, a sharp edge to their voices, a warning. If Siobhan gets too big for her breeches, they'll cut her down with her own words, a life skill the Sheehans and the Malloys have both perfected.

"An entire world view was built around this belief in faeries, the so-called good people, who weren't always good but could also be sneaky, spiteful, and treacherous. Kind of like the Irish themselves."

Speak for yourself, I want to say, but stop.

"I thought it might relate, you know, faerie belief," Siobhan adds. "You said Flanna poured the chamber pot over Fagan's head."

"What's that got to do with it?" I ask.

"Maybe nothing. But it is something a *cailleach* might do if she thought the faeries had taken over a human child."

"The revenge of the faeries," says Ruth Ann.

Del and Cassandra giggle. "Taken over a human child?" Delilah asks.

"Laugh if you want," says Siobhan in a snippy voice, like she's arguing that Tom Cruise is better-looking than George Clooney and nobody agrees. "But I'm telling you, it was powerful stuff. It kept the peasants in line long after the Catholics converted them."

"Flanna used to tell us the faeries took our mother off on a white horse." Patty looks at Jo, then Keeley. "She died from toxemia, but Flanna said the faeries took her."

"She said the faeries wore shining white robes and had beautiful long hair." Jo. "I thought faeries were like angels. I thought it was a good thing."

"Some faeries are like angels," says Siobhan. "According to the myths, they were angels before they got kicked out of heaven. They kept their wings."

"Kicked out of heaven? Kept their wings?" Cass, Del, and Ruthie think that's hilarious. Their cackles cut right through me.

"Thanks for the lesson, Professor Smarty-Pants," says Cass. "Very edifying!"

Again, Del and Ruthie chuckle.

"She said we had a *piseog* on us," says Jo. "Flanna did."

"A *piseog*?" Siobhan perks up again. A *piseog*. That's news to me. More language I don't understand.

"Faerie nonsense," Patty says. "That's what Nana called it."

"No, no," says Siobhan, her eyes bright, her fingers fidgeting. "It's a spell, a curse. Like voodoo. Somebody puts an object in or near your house. Rotten meat, say, wrapped up in something belonging to your family. Maybe a towel or a diaper stolen from the clothesline. A lock of hair from a dead child. They'd put it in the cellar, or under the front steps, make an evil wish. Its spell would keep working unless someone found it and burned it to ash."

"A faerie healer," several of them murmur, turning the words over like precious objects they desire, even though they can't quite appreciate their worth.

"Yes," I say, "a faerie healer who brought every last one of us to heel."

"Healer, my tush," says Jo. "She was a drunk, like Da."

Now you could hear a pin drop. Dead silence. Poor Da. I never told my girls. Not a word about Flanna or my scars; not a word about Da's drinking. Not to mention Fagan. No point. I couldn't stain their lives with so much shame and sorrow.

"Well, it's true, isn't it?" Jo says. The Chardonnay has gone straight to her head. "Much as we all hate to admit it. We're all ashamed."

"Shame is toxic," says Cassandra, our own resident healer. "Always toxic."

"I was wondering when we were going to get to him," Ruth Ann interrupts in that tone she used on me at Dunk's. "Where was he in all of this? Didn't he take any responsibility?" Her cheeks too are flushed, and her eyes shine the color of the sky outside.

"He was the kindest, the most loving man I've ever known," I say, and I glimpse him on the steps of our old house, passing out our cookies, teasing us with magic, his spiky hair, his dimpled smile.

"But weak, obviously, and irresponsible," answers Ruthie. She looks to Cass. They nod in agreement. I'd like to smack them both.

"I wouldn't say that at all," interrupts Patty, the potentate. My daughters wouldn't dream of talking back to her. "He did the best he could under terrible circumstances, most of which he couldn't control. Don't forget the Depression. Everyone was out of work."

"When our mother was alive, he was always working," says Jo. "He was a riveter, a hellish job, hot and dangerous, all through the Depression. That's how he bought the house, and kept it, even in the worst of times. He had a second job, part-time, as a chauffeur for a wealthy family, the Mortons. Not to mention playing his horn whenever he had the chance. He provided. He treated us like queens, or maybe princesses. At least until Mam died, and *she* came along."

No need to specify who "she" is.

"Called us his bouquet of beauties. Remember, Mimi?" says Patty. And I nod, because I do. Words I'll never forget, nor the sound of Da's voice when he said them. *My little bouquet of beauties.*

"Then everything fell apart."

"The shipyard just about shut down in the '30s," Patty says. "The workforce reduced to a few hundred. The Mortons lost everything in the Crash; our mother died. He married Flanna, who couldn't handle Fagan. Fagan got sent away. The rest is history."

"He turned into a drunk?" asks Ruth Ann.

"That's what some people said about him," I say. "But the way I think of it, Da just couldn't chew and swallow all the bitter pills life dished out to him. He got a handful, all at once."

"Bitter pills," Jo repeats.

"What about everybody else? Your aunts and uncles? Your neighbors?" asks Ruth Ann.

"The other grown-ups?" Patty shrugs. "All of them had troubles of their own. Hard times. We grew up during hard times, honey, not like now."

She looks at my daughters who are all, I see, quite beautiful, the way my sisters and I used to be. The difference is, they've never once gone hungry, or worried about how to make ends meet. They've never had the rug pulled out from under them just when they thought they'd finally found their footing.

"No, we didn't talk about it." Jo. "And nobody, not our aunts or uncles or grandparents or neighbors, asked us anything. Nobody wanted to know. Da had married a beautiful young woman to give his girls a mother. We had a mother. It was official. That's all that seemed to matter."

By now the sun is setting. My apartment, sterile with its beige walls, the sheer white curtains at the windows, is full of shadows, plus the spirits of Eden and Alberta. Then there's Da, on his knees, in that strange place of earth and stones. Behind them, in a darker place, is Flanna—enchanting Flanna, our stepmother.

But where could Fagan be?

"How about some coffee?"

I get up to put on a pot, hi-test, just what everybody needs. I end up making a second pot to have enough to go around. I swear my black spots throb.

When everybody's got coffee and are settled back in their seats— me in my throne, the La-Z-Boy—Cass grabs the box from Hanrahan's and picks out an éclair.

"Hog," says Ruthie before she takes the box and grabs one too.

The box makes its way around our circle, nobody worried about plates or napkins, or about carbs or fat grams or calories. We've got bigger fish to fry. Soon all of us are drinking coffee and pigging out on those scrumptious treats.

"The world's more full of weeping," says Delilah, out of nowhere. She turns toward us, forcing herself to breathe the air in my apartment. She chews thoughtfully on a cream puff. *"The world's more full of weeping . . ."*

"Than you can understand," adds Cass.

"That's a Yeats poem, 'The Stolen Child,'" says Siobhan.

"The stolen child," Jo and Patty chime.

"That's written on his gravestone," says Delilah. "Your father's."

"Your grandfather's," corrects Patty.

"Mimi brought us to the cemetery on Ash Wednesday," Del explains to Ruthie and Siobhan, like they missed out on something big.

"Mimi brought you to the cemetery?" Ruthie points to me as though I'd committed a sin.

"Da always used to read that poem," says Keeley. "I remember the weeping part."

"It's so depressing. Why would he pick that for his headstone?" says Cassandra.

"He didn't pick it." Patty is outraged. "How could he pick it? He keeled over at forty. Right in front of us. He wasn't planning to die."

"Come away, O human child!" Siobhan recites. *"To the waters and the wild, with a faery hand in hand, for the world's more full of weeping than you can understand."*

Come away, O human child! I've heard those words before, but the sight of Da keeling over, right in front of us, collides with them. My late sisters, Eden and Alberta, give me a good hard shake. Flanna. She's the one who said them.

Twenty-four

LOOKING FOR
YESTERDAY

*N*ext thing I know, Ruthie's gathering her purse and parka. "Gotta go be a soccer mom," she says, blowing air kisses to her aunts and heading toward the door. "I'm not all that into Yeats."

She pauses and looks back, gesturing to Delilah and Siobhan, expecting them to join her. I do too. Thanks for the memories, Mimi. We're outta here. Then they'll stand outside in the parking lot gabbing about all my shortcomings. But the blond betrayers stay. The truth about Da's death has got them riveted to Duffy's folding chairs. They don't even wave good-bye to Ruthie.

The minute she's gone, Cassandra pulls a folding chair next to my recliner. She drops her pen and notebook; holds one of my hands in two of hers. "Your father keeled over right in front of you?"

The twins and Keeley nod.

"He died on the Fourth of July," says Del. "In 1937. It's on his gravestone."

"Two days after Amelia Earhart disappeared." Patty.

"Amelia Earhart?" Del.

"It was all over the news." Jo gestures to show the big headlines.

"Amelia Earhart and her copilot, Fred Something, disappear over the Pacific."

"Without a trace. Until a year or so ago, right?"

Jo nods. "An explorer found a rubber heel and an empty whiskey bottle on that island in the South Pacific where they supposedly went down."

"The copilot having been, supposedly, a drunk." Patty. "More booze on board than fuel."

"That whole first week of July, it was all anybody talked about." Jo. "Biggest news ever."

"Amelia Earhart, the beautiful, high-flying aviatrix, disappears without a trace." Keeley. "Not that I remember. Too young, but I've read a lot about it."

"Remember Nana in the kitchen?" Jo asks. "With the RCA Victor radio turned up loud so she could hear it while she worked? She wanted every detail."

"We lived with Nana then." Patty. "We girls got up and got dressed to go to the Independence Day parade. Nana had ironed our best dresses, and we got to wear our shoes."

"We couldn't wait to go, but Nana wasn't in the mood to celebrate anything." Jo.

"She'd seen enough parades."

"She made us toast and eggs, and sent us off." Patty.

"While we ate, the radio was on, Amelia Earhart gone." Jo. "We kept looking at each other."

"We three oldest were thinking about our silly rhyme. *Amelia Earhart loves to fly. Amelia Earhart will never die.*"

"But she did," my daughters chorus as I slip back to that hot bright Fourth, humid with a pounding sun.

"We heard the drums before we even got there." Keeley.

A pulse that ran through my body as we squeezed our way out to the front, the six of us together, holding hands. Eden, Alberta, Maire, Josephine, Patty, and Keeley, the glorious Sheehan girls, in our pretty summer dresses, our faces shiny bright, our hair curled and tied with ribbons, our patent leather shoes buffed to a high shine.

"There were floats, marching bands, baton twirlers, and old soldiers with pins and ribbons on their chests. They marched right by us," says Patty, the great historian. "The parade went on and on. Sousa marches. And finally, a military band, like the one our father used to play in."

"That's when we saw Da." I see him again, emerging slowly, as if from one of those Polaroid cameras, the picture blurred at first, then turning crystal clear. "He ran out behind the military band, trying to catch up." Wire-thin Da, running, running, running, trying to catch up to the parade. The jacket of his uniform! I know it from the cedar chest upstairs, but its shiny buttons are unbuttoned. The sides flap out like broken wings.

"He ran and ran, holding on to his cornet." Keeley.

"I couldn't wait to hear him play." Patty. "I felt so proud, Da joining the parade."

"But the minute people noticed him, they started to laugh." Jo.

"I wanted to run out to march with him," Keeley says. "But you, Mimi, you pulled me back."

"I called out to him, right?" I ask my sisters. "Didn't I call out, 'Daddy, stop, it doesn't matter,' but he didn't hear me." The people around us just laughed harder.

"'We don't care about a stinky old parade!' Jo and I yelled," says Patty, all excited, this shared memory keeping us together, Da keeling over right in front of us, his life over and ours hardly yet begun. "We kept yelling, but he didn't hear us, never saw us."

My late sisters nudge me, longing to be included.

"Eden and Alberta were paralyzed, weren't they?" They press against me once again, just like they did that day. "Even Alberta, who loved a good laugh better than anything." They clung to me and to each other, watching Da run.

"All around us, everyone laughed. 'Joe Sheehan, drunk again.'" Patty. "'Look at Joe, that fool.'"

"'A shame, with that beautiful girl he married,'" adds Keeley. "'If I'd been lucky enough to get her, I'd behave myself.'"

"'Oh, yes, the second Mrs. Sheehan is a beauty.'" Jo imitates those awful accents, those brogues we Sheehan sisters refused to speak. "'And him with all those lovely girls to raise.'"

Slow down, slow down, it doesn't matter, I screamed, or wanted to; the way he was running made me afraid.

"He ran right past us," says Patty. "A short way down the street, he fell." He fell flat, like a tree that's lost its roots, all at once. Slam, onto the ground, facedown. "Like in a cartoon. Splat!"

"Laughter, a great roar of laughter," says Jo. "'Joe Sheehan, that drunk.'"

Nobody moved to help him, not even us. The others talked and pointed and snickered as if we weren't there.

"Their words cut deep," says Jo, hugging herself, protecting herself from those still-sharp blades.

Cassandra squeezes my hands. Across the room, Delilah and Siobhan huddle against the window, clinging to each other. They stare at us as if they are looking at a wreck on the highway. Rubbernecking. Curiosity factor, clogging traffic everywhere.

"Everything stopped when Da fell." I realize this as I say it. "My life ground to a halt and I had trouble starting it up again."

"The parade kept going." Jo. "Another damned Sousa march."

"Down a street lined with red maples." Keeley.

"Nothing I hate more than a Sousa march," says Patty. "Makes my blood boil."

Not a single Sheehan sister disagrees.

"Da-didda-da-da-da," Jo stutters, a Sousa tune, "Da-didda-da-da-da!"

"Shut up!" commands Patty .

"You'd think we'd be wailing like banshees," says Keeley, looking at my daughters, "but not one of us made a sound."

"It took forever for the parade to pass," says Patty. "Then we ran across the street to him."

I remember somebody rolling him over, but I looked away. Da lying on the ground, peaceful, like he was sleeping, but I knew it was something worse.

"I couldn't look at him. I looked at the grass around him, soft and green, like the grass he raved about in Ireland. The grass where Fagan lived."

All of us are stuck there, in the sunlight, on the roadside long ago.

"Faerie struck!" Siobhan's voice rings out like a bell, calling all of us to attention. "Your Da was faerie struck."

"Faerie struck?" Delilah elbows Siobhan, a good hard jab.

"Zapped by faeries. Having a stroke."

We stare at Siobhan. Her silky pale skin turns pink, her eyes a deep, deep blue.

"That's the etymology of the word 'stroke.'"

"Etymology?" Cassandra grimaces.

"Sounds like a disease." Delilah. "Contagious."

"Its source," Siobhan explains. "Isn't that what he died of? A stroke?"

"Of drink," I say. "Drank himself to death. Pure and simple."

"You don't keel over like that from drink."

"Since when did you get a cause of death?" Cassandra reaches for her sparkly pen and notebook.

"I could hardly think about it, ever," I tell Siobhan. "Thinking of my father dead drunk on the roadside. No. It made me so ashamed."

"We were only kids." Jo. "What did we know?"

"Then Aunty Alberta followed in his footsteps," says Cassandra, like she understands everything. "She carried on the family tradition, substance abuse, and after her, her son, my cousin Danny."

"I'll bet it was a stroke, not alcohol," says Siobhan. "It goes back to the faeries."

All eyes turn to her. I'm relieved, can't help it. We've got another lunatic in our midst.

"Is it any wonder I needed therapy?" says Cass, scribbling into her notebook. "Or that I keep recommending it?"

"Before anybody understood a thing about brain hemorrhages," Siobhan continues, ignoring her, "or any other type of cardiovascular issue, if someone suddenly became paralyzed, experienced aphasia, or maybe even dropped dead in their tracks, they were called faerie struck."

"You were orphans, you and your sisters." Delilah, on the brink of a breakdown.

"We never thought of ourselves like that," says Jo. "We had Nana. She took us in without a second thought. Lace curtain, not shanty, that's what we Sheehan sisters were. Plus we had each other. That made us as good as anybody else. At least, we thought so."

"Nana refused to give us any pity, and we didn't pity ourselves." Keeley.

"Wasn't your father born in Ireland?"

"Your grandfather," somebody corrects.

"In the north, County Antrim. The family worked in shipbuilding. For a while, his family went back and forth. But his mother, Nana, once she settled here, she wouldn't allow any talk about the old country or the old ways. 'We're here, now. Look ahead.' Nana meant it, believe me."

"Half our roots are missing." Siobhan looks pained. Maybe that's what she's searching for every time she goes back to Ireland. "When we were growing up, you never said a word about our grandparents. Never once mentioned your own father."

It's true, I didn't, but I didn't plan the silence. I didn't do it on purpose; it just happened.

"He was a lovely man, but life just didn't go his way," I say. "That's all you need to know."

"But we're just now finding out about him." Delilah.

"We've got holes in our family history." Cassandra.

I shrug, afraid she'll start to cry again. All of them on the verge of a meltdown, the room a bubbling pot of anger and sorrow.

"What did you do?" Delilah, face scrunched, holding back the tears. "I mean, with your father, on the roadside, dead. What happened next?"

"We just stood there," says Patty. "We didn't know what else to do."

"We didn't do anything, only looked," says Jo.

"Everyone forgot us. We were standing in plain sight, but it was as if we'd been erased." Keeley.

"Finally a couple of our uncles, Leo and Teddy, got to him." Patty.

"I saw his cornet in the grass. I picked it up." Keeley.

"Our uncles hoisted him up and rushed with him back to Nana's." They lifted him from the ground carefully, lovingly, and without a sound, cradling Da the way he'd carried me that time he took me to the doctor's.

"We followed them back to Nana's house, running down Commercial Street, away from the parade."

When we walk through Nana's front door, it's like entering an ice cloud, a place where I can't see or feel. The only sense I have is sound, and what I hear, through hushed voices of frantic grown-ups, is Nana's aching cry. "No, God, no. Please don't take my Joe. No, God, not my Joey, no."

"Our uncles sent Jo and me upstairs to find a clean white sheet in the hallway closet," says Patty. "We stood there for the longest time, maybe hoping that if we froze, right there, we could stop what was coming next."

"We looked through stacks and stacks of crisp and neatly folded linens, ironed by Nana on the mangle in her kitchen." Jo. "One of our uncles hollered from downstairs. 'Whatcha waitin' for? Hell to freeze over?'"

"We chose a sheet with yellow flowers along the edge, flowers Nana embroidered for her dowry," says Patty.

"Years before Da was born." Me, because Nana told me, showed me all her beautiful linens in that closet. Tried to teach me to embroider, with silky threads and a flashing needle, but I was all thumbs; couldn't ever learn. "That's what they used to cover Da before the undertakers came and carried him away." Everyone's so quiet we hear the hum of my Frigidaire, the slamming of car doors in the parking lot. I toss in two more cents' worth. "The whole world wept for Amelia Earhart, but we were the only ones who cried for Da."

"The rest is history," says Keeley.

"History? What history?" Cassandra holds her pen, her fancy little notebook, ready to take it all down.

Slowly, Jo and Patty start to unwind the rest of it, a film with hazy pictures, but I'm stuck in Nana's house, my da covered in the sheet, even his face, especially his face; his handsome, handsome face, the one I'd built my world around. Sun and moon. Stars and planets. The entire solar system. No matter what he'd ever done or failed to do, Da remained the center of everything. He was the known world.

Within hours, Flanna Flanagan claimed him. She barred all of us, even Nana, from the wake and funeral. There was no way for us to say good-bye. Flanna buried him according to her own wishes, and ages passed before Nana found his plot in the Gate of Heaven Cemetery.

"When Da died, we weren't allowed to cry, so I used to think about how he put his beloved horn away."

"His ritual," Jo says, smiling.

"Everything had to be done just so." Patty.

"At night, to keep myself from crying, I'd imagine the hands of angels getting him ready to be put away, with the same care he used to put away his horn. They would bathe him and shave him and comb his hair and change his clothes. They would turn him back into handsome Da, the man who always made me laugh and always made me proud."

"The riveter, the chauffeur." Jo.

"The musician, the poet." Keeley.

"The good father who ran with me to the doctor's when I broke my arm."

"Who walked us home, up the hill." Patty.

"Who brought us treats on payday." Jo.

We're all silent until Delilah demands, "That's it? The end? The angels cleaned him up?"

"Oh, these angels were so beautiful," I say. "Like on the cards Cassie sells. They took their time, working with great care. They laid Da out in a beautiful box lined with red velvet." I give my girls a chance to pick on me for being such a nut. They don't. "The angels stretched him out in this box, and I could see him snug and safe. Nothing could hurt him anymore. Like his cornet in its case. Then the angels closed the lid and snapped shut the brass clasps, just the way Da did with his horn."

"Before last week, you never even took us to the cemetery." Cass.

"You never said a word about him." Del.

"And all this time, Mimi," says Siobhan, her face lit by the late sun and her own strong feelings. "I could have been looking for Fagan. I was right there, in the place she got sent to. I might have been able to find the place where she's buried."

Twenty-five

BEGIN THE
BEGUINE

It's after dark by the time my sisters and my daughters have sobered up and gone. The box of Franzia is empty. So's the box from Hanrahan's. I throw them into a giant trash bag, along with all the paper cups and plates. The bag of trash is full, but I get that old empty feeling. The Yik Yak Club accomplished nothing except stirring up more sorrow. Eden, Alberta and Fagan, Mam and Da, Nana—all gone. Which is exactly why I prefer to look ahead instead of back. And the Yik Yak Club never even figured out the date of Fagan's departure, the main purpose of our meeting. I head out to the Dumpster with the bag and toss it in. I'd like to do the same with my childhood. Back inside, I go to close the windows and the blinds and see Duffy outside, picking up the cones. He's had his share of losses, but he always seems to know exactly what he's doing, and what he has to do next. That bum leg doesn't stop him or even slow him down. It must be badly scarred, with all that shrapnel in his thigh. Scars everywhere. . . . Nobody escapes.

I go back to cleaning up. A few minutes later, he's knocking on my door. I know the sound by now.

"Mrs. Malloy," he says as I open it. "I hope I'm not disturbing you."

"That happened awhile back," I say, flushing while he grins. "You'll be picking up those chairs and the table?"

In a sec, we've got them folded, ready to go. I carry the table behind him as he takes the chairs to a storage closet at the end of the hallway.

"How about a cup of coffee?" I ask him when we're done. "I just brewed a fresh pot."

"Can't turn down a cup of your coffee, Mrs. Malloy," he says, but I know what he really wants is company, my company. As I want his. Next thing you know, we're back at my place, and I turn on Sinatra. Nothing like good, soothing music. No torch songs tonight.

"You've got some hungry women in your family," Duffy says when he sees the little bit of cold cuts left. Two pickles. A tablespoon of potato salad. Not a chip or a crumb of pastry in sight.

"You know it. Just enough left to make you a sandwich."

"Twist my arm."

When we're settled on the couch, and he's digging into the nice, thick triple-decker I've built for him, he asks how the get-together went. I shrug.

"They yak and yak, but we never get to the heart of what happened. At least, I don't think we do."

"You could just let it alone, Mrs. Malloy," he says, taking a long swallow of hot coffee. "Happened so long ago. Let sleeping dogs lie."

"My philosophy precisely," I tell him. "That's what I've done all my life, but the dogs aren't sleeping anymore. They're awake and howling."

"The silver pendant with the blue stone," he says. It's almost, but not quite, a question. I nod again.

"Not to mention Patty's damned genealogy."

I curl up next to Duffy on my couch, smoking and drinking coffee, while he finishes his sandwich. With my remotes, he switches off Sinatra, and switches on the television news to catch the weather report. I tell him how Fagan was sent away and died before we could get her back; sent to Cullyhanna, County Armagh, but nobody knows when she passed, or even where she's buried.

"You've got to keep track of where your dead are buried," Duff says, and I think about his chore during the war. How he kept track of the bodies of those boys, no matter what condition they were in, every bit and piece, to make sure they got back home. Their families got to keep whatever was left of them, and to know where they'd been laid to rest. I'm lost in thought when Duffy grabs the remote and turns up the volume on the TV.

I watch him watch TV for several moments before I tune in, something about the high-tech prison complex, on thirty acres of rural land in Bridgewater. A state-of-the-art place, the Bridgewater Correctional Complex, aka the Old Colony Correctional Center.

The reporter, a young Asian woman, stands in front of a high fence and a sprawling brick building. "Even the name 'Old Colony,'" she says, "signals what's going on here, a new type of corrections. In deference to our early settlers, its name fosters a sense of hope and renewal."

"Good lord," I say, but Duffy's mute.

"In keeping with the theme of hope and renewal," the reporter continues, "each of the housing units within the institution is named after a Revolutionary War hero." Among them, Paul Revere, naturally, plus Patrick Henry, William Dawes, and Crispus Attucks.

"Can you believe it? Just like Centennial Square," I say, but Duffy just stares at the screen. The most innovative part of the complex, the reporter informs us, is the Treatment Center, capital letters, the place for sexually dangerous persons. Rapists, pedophiles, predators, sex traffickers.

"Here, men committed both civilly and criminally are mixed together, treated together, in the most humane but rigorous way possible."

"'Sexually dangerous persons,'" I murmur, just to try it out.

"The only problem so far," the reporter says, "is overcrowding. There are now more inmates than the most generous projections allowed for, and almost more than the facility can handle. Most of the men are double-bunked in single rooms."

Microphone in hand, the reporter strolls up to the fourteen-foot-high chain link fence, which is topped with razor wire. She pats it with her pretty hand. "Behind this fence is another identical fence," she says, and the camera zooms in close so we can see the second row of fencing.

"In between the fences are motion sensors, connected to a microwave system that alerts the towers the moment an intruder is perceived." She smiles and steps closer to the camera, which zooms in on her face.

"It's impossible to get out of here until they decide to let you go," she says. Then the program segues to an ad for tartar-control toothpaste. Duffy clicks off the TV and clicks back on Sinatra.

"Maybe your daughter wasn't so far off," he says, as if the past few minutes hadn't happened. He puts his arm around me, pulls me closer. "I mean, when she said you have some kind of post traumatic stress disorder."

"Maybe I do," I answer, not exactly willing to concede the point, yet feeling myself softening in the sadness of all these recollections.

"Not a flaw, just a fact," he murmurs, hugging me tighter. I lean against him, a thrill to press my cheek to. Sinatra croons and we smoke and drink our coffee, not talking for a while.

Twenty-six

I'LL NEVER
SMILE AGAIN

The next morning, the phone starts ringing before I even get a chance to pour my first cup. I've got no desire to chat with Cass or my sisters. Not interested. But I give in on the seventh or eighth ring.

"I'm so glad I caught you, Mimi," cries Ruthie, panting, her voice edged with a siren's squall.

"Is everything OK?" I ask. "The boys? They're OK?"

"Do you know who your super is?"

"My super?" I feel the air whoosh out of me, her question like a puncture wound. I grab hold of the kitchen counter.

"Dick Duffy. I met him outside yesterday. We introduced ourselves. Well, I introduced myself to him and we talked for a while. I wanted to make sure he keeps an eye on you."

Oh, Duffy, don't, I'm thinking. Don't betray us. Don't break our promise to each other.

"The name, his name, rang a bell, a distant bell, but still I had to check it out."

"There's millions of Duffys. It's like Smith or Jones. Common as common could be."

Not a black spot, but a black hole, opening up this time. *Last night when you came over, you didn't even tell me you'd met my Ruth Ann.*

Ruthie has always been our doyenne of disaster, our catastrophe collector, forever calling with some horror story or another. She's addicted to true crime books and reads at least three newspapers every day, and always the most gruesome stories. She'll retell them to anyone who'll listen: The mother who left her kids in the car on a hot day while she shopped and came back to find them roasted like capons; the boys in her town who sledded down a steep hill right into an oncoming SUV; a kid who committed suicide by hanging himself from the mouth of the soccer goal at the school where his mother was the principal. Her latest, pedophile priests, one of them from Fall River who admitted to molesting more than a hundred boys and girls, an equal-opportunity offender. She goes on and on about them, half the time quivering with fear and the other half marching into battle. This time, it's battle.

"No, Mimi, I did my research before I called. I saw the news story about the new prison. I put two and two together. Your Dick Duffy there is the father of a pedophile."

My Dick Duffy.

Ruthie pauses to let her words sink in, and I sink down the side of my counter. I crumple into myself, like those accordion cups they used to sell so you could take your pills even if you weren't at home. They had a little cover and collapsed to fit right into your purse or pocket. I'm small enough to do that now.

"His name's Christopher. Convicted on multiple counts of sexual assault on minor children. You remember. Don't you? He was a martial-arts instructor, and you know how pedophiles always find ways to be with kids. That's a fact. Now he's doing, like, twelve years at Bridgewater. Not half enough in my opinion. Do you know how freaking hard it is to get a sex-abuse conviction?"

I don't. "Not a clue," I whisper.

"So damned hard," she goes on, suddenly an expert on the criminal justice system. "From what I've read, the evidence against him is overwhelming. So many victims. He—"

"No. No, I don't want to hear."

"Most child abusers have themselves been abused as kids—"

"Stop, baby, please stop."

"Mimi, are you OK? You're not in some kind of relationship with this guy, are you?"

"No. No I'm not," I'm able to declare with a bit more strength.

"Be careful, Mimi. Just be careful. You're so vulnerable."

"I'm ancient, honey, not a child. Who'd want me? Anyway, the sins of a son, should they be visited upon the father?"

"It goes the other way," my daughter contends, as if I didn't know. "The apple doesn't fall far from the tree. We've always agreed about that. I thought you'd want to know."

No, I didn't. I didn't want to know. But she hangs up before I get to tell her. I sit there, on my kitchen floor, my little hopes and dreams in pieces all around me. Nobody to help me put them back together, or to even get back up.

I have no idea at all of what to do with Ruthie's news—which I'm sure she's already shared with all her sisters—when the phone rings again. It's Duffy. "Feel like taking a ride?" he asks.

I hesitate, not sure I do. "Mmm, no thanks," I say.

"I'd really appreciate it," he urges in a voice that sounds as sincere to me as a man's voice can sound. "I just . . . well, there's something I want to show you."

"You've got another best girl?" I hate the brittle sound of my own voice.

"No, I don't."

"How far?" I ask. I'm swallowing, can't help myself, even though I'm leery, and longing for some downtime.

"We'll be gone a couple of hours. No more. I promise. I need to do this."

"Need?"

He doesn't speak, but in my mind's eye I see him nodding yes, and I feel his hope that I won't let him down echo through my receiver.

We set a time, and I clean myself up, but forgo the Trésor, the makeup, the fashionable upgraded clothes. All the while, doubt and fear, hope and longing brawl inside me, fighting for control. Should I go or should I stay? OK. OK. I'll go. I decide to go because Duffy's earned that much from me, but it will have to be a "come as you are" party. Plain old Mimi is the one he's going to get.

I meet him outside. He opens the passenger-side door of the Caprice for me, then slides behind the wheel. We don't speak. I can't think of anything to say. Once we're under way, he stays focused on the road as we navigate through the complicated arithmetic of local and state roads until we reach I-495.

"We're heading south," he says, a redundancy, because I've read the big green highway sign we've just followed. I expect him to tell me more, but he doesn't. Mum's the word. Then he turns on a soft jazz station out of Boston, Nat King Cole, the smoothest of smooth crooners, but I don't feel the least bit relaxed.

"Smoked three packs a day," Duffy says out of the blue, like I'm supposed to understand what he's talking about. I frown at him, a first. "He believed it made his voice sound better."

Got it: Nat King Cole. *I found a dream that I could speak to . . . A thrill to press my cheek to . . .*

"Before every recording session, he smoked one after the other— Kool menthols."

"It killed him," I say, recalling my sadness over Nat's untimely death. I realize both of us are smoking, our windows cracked. "Lung cancer in his forties."

Duffy turns off the radio.

In the quiet, our journey feels more urgent, Duffy driving faster than usual. Thinking of Nat's demise, the silencing of his inimitable voice, I smush out my cigarette in the little ashtray but leave the window cracked. Shopping strips, industrial parks, and housing developments blur past. In this rare silence, it only takes a few minutes for me to figure out where we're headed: Bridgewater.

At last we get off the highway, follow a bunch of twisting roads. Duffy drives more slowly, squinting straight ahead. I get the feeling that he could drive this route blindfolded, that he's done it so many times, and over and over again in his dreams. But I don't say a thing.

Loose lips sink ships. Then, in the distance, huge and shadowy, is a place I've never seen in person but recognize right away. Concrete buildings surrounded by miles of chain link and razor wire, its guard towers glowing in the light of the setting sun. The infamous prison and loony bin, the Old Colony Correctional Center—historical, like so much else around here. It's where his son must be incarcerated—a word I've never used before or even thought about. "Incarcerated." Your body, your soul confined in a place it does not choose to be. The unlighted place in Duffy's eyes.

I wait for him to tell me about his son. He doesn't know I know. He stops in the parking lot but leaves the motor running. His hands grip the wheel. We're as close as we can get, but still quite far away. The prison's gloomy; no interior lights are visible. Armed guards pace its towers, their weapons silhouetted against the sky.

"Medium security." Duffy's voice is weak and scratchy, like it might, at any moment, break. Medium security, like it's some kind of triumph.

"Before this thing goes any further," he starts to say, then stops. "Before this thing goes any further . . ."

Now his face is red, not pink. His nose and ears look scalded, like Flanna got to him with one of her potions. For the first time since I've known him, he's having trouble spitting out what he's got to say.

"What thing?"

"This thing." He nods to me, taps himself on the chest. "Our thing."

"OK, our thing. What are you trying to say?"

He hands me a folded piece of paper, an official notice of some type, stamped with the seal of the Suffolk County Superior Court. What on earth, I wonder until I open it and read the words: "Level three sex offender," and below them, a mug shot of a younger Duffy. Christopher Joseph Duffy. Now forty-two years old. Convicted of indecent assault and battery on a child under fourteen years of age. Three kids. Nine counts. Like Ruthie told me on the phone, he's the father of a convicted pedophile.

Then, in a voice from far away, a voice shaky with sorrow, Duffy tells me how his son had been arrested, tried, and convicted on trumped-up charges of child molestation. How the past decade of Duff's life has been bound up by the tribulations of his son, a Vietnam veteran, a hapless but good-hearted guy, a black belt who'd owned a karate studio in a shopping center in Rockland. He names it and I have the vaguest memory of having passed the place.

"If he has a weakness," Duff insists, "it's women, not little boys." I look at the handsome fellow in the photo wondering, can't help it, if what Duffy says is true, or if he's in denial. His son was convicted, after all.

"He messed with some of the young mothers of the kids at his karate school, true, one of them the wife of a cop. No big deal, in his opinion. They're all consenting grown-ups. That's how he looked at it. The cop caught them, right in the act, in an office at the school. Next thing you know, he's arrested, charged with umpteen counts of sex abuse. For touching his students inappropriately during classes. When he'd actually been touching the cop's wife. But they've got the kids, including two of hers, lined up to tell their horror stories."

"Teaching karate, you'd have to touch the kids," I say. "How could you teach them without touching them?" He nods, exhales a long stream of cigarette smoke.

"Three trials, three sets of charges," Duffy says. "Over three years. He could've taken a plea. Could've done a sexual-predator rehabilitation program, eighteen months in and out, instead of hard time in prison. But he tells me, 'Dad, I can't plead guilty to something I didn't do. I can't admit I'm a child molester if I'm not.' He took his chances at the trial, and he lost. Had a public defender, all we could afford."

Anyone who lives in Massachusetts, especially in Suffolk County, is familiar with our attorney general. He got his start as an ambitious DA a few years back, the same one who prosecuted Duffy's son. Sexual predators were his thing, and he found them everywhere. Routed them from all their hiding places, determined to make the Commonwealth of Massachusetts safe for children. That was his slogan, and by everyone's account, he succeeded. On TV they brag about how the Commonwealth of Massachusetts has more sexual-predator convictions than any other state, and that Suffolk County has the most in Massachusetts. Now it's only grown-ups who need to worry.

"Here's the thing," says Duff, flicking his butt out the window, then opening the door to stomp on it, make sure it's out. "Christopher's new lawyer knows for a fact that during the first set of interviews the three boys who testified insisted that nothing inappropriate had happened, ever. But the recordings disappeared. Don't forget, the husband of the woman he had an affair with was a cop. In later interviews, the boys changed their stories, and their stories were identical, down to the last detail."

"Why three trials? Why didn't they do them all together?"

"The DA figured he'd get more mileage from three trials than from one. Which he did. He was right. More media coverage, more outrage. Dragged it out as long as possible. Now the new lawyer says the DA did it that way because the kids' stories were identical in all three trials. He's got the transcripts. And that's a sure sign of false memory. Even the wording was the same. If the same jury had heard them all, they'd have realized something was up."

"False memory? How can a memory be false?"

"Kids remembering things that didn't happen. The precise details of things that didn't happen because they were fed to them by adults. It's a common phenomenon, even in families. It doesn't just apply to crimes.

"I read the transcripts from the pretrial interviews, which lasted hours, with a parent always present. They asked questions they could not ask in the courtroom. Like, for instance, 'Is that when Christopher Duffy, the karate instructor, put his hand on your right buttock and squeezed?' That sort of thing."

Chris had been appealing on the grounds of prosecutorial misconduct, arguing that the prosecutors themselves, aided and abetted by the boys' parents, had planted the false memories. Recently, a young defense attorney with some connection to an advocacy group for the wrongfully convicted—a lawyer as ambitious as Mr. District Attorney but fighting for the other side—was only too happy to take his case pro bono.

"And, already, through these advanced therapies they do, showing, if you can believe it, different types of pornography to the offenders, to figure out what . . . what rings their bell and they've demonstrated conclusively . . ."

Duffy looks away, at a loss for words. I doubt his face could get any redder. I understand his shame.

"Don't explain," I say, pained by his pain. A sad old Billie Holiday song. "Don't Explain."

"I need to tell someone," he says, turning to me, looking at me eye to eye, in a way that somehow thrills me, in spite of everything he's just said, and even in the dimming light. He trusts me. And I decide to trust him back. Despite my panicked moments earlier today, my fear of betrayal.

"They cover these guys with electrodes, like in an EKG, and then show them pornography." Duffy pauses, gathering strength. "They do brain imagery, measure a million bodily reactions . . . Costs a fortune. The state wouldn't pay, but the lawyer got a grant from some foundation for the wrongfully convicted. And the tests demonstrate that Chris has no sexual interest whatsoever in children. He had the opposite reactions—anger, disgust, nausea. No matter how many times they tested him, the results were always the same. His lawyer will use this as new exculpatory evidence."

"Exculpatory," another new word. I roll it around in my mind. Exculpatory. Duff sits silent for a minute, exhausted, I think, but the silence is OK. I put my arm around him and rub his shoulder, for whatever that might be worth.

"By the time they hear the case, Chris will be released," he says. "He'll have served his time. Good behavior."

"Then what's the point?"

"His name. No 'level three sex offender' next to it for the rest of his life. He had a new girlfriend, and they'd been going steady for a while. He was ready to settle down when all this started. She tried hard to stand by him, but she had to move on. If his name is cleared, Chris, too, might be able to move on." That notion hangs there, Duffy's son being able to move on, a small bright spot in the darkening parking lot, the prison a forbidding edifice, way too close for comfort.

"That envelope, in the Caprice that day," I start to ask.

"Chump change." Duffy laughs a bitter laugh. "Money for Chris to use at the prison commissary."

Chris, his son Chris, a grown-up; incarcerated, but with a chance, however slim, to clear his name. Redemption. What all of us are hoping for. I look at Duffy, and he's still looking straight ahead at the place where his son is doing time, hard time, the only kind a man can do at Bridgewater.

Duffy holds up the flyer. "Every police station and post office in the state has one of these. And, when he gets out, unless he's cleared, they'll inform everyone in the neighborhood, wherever he decides to live, that a pedophile is living close by. I wanted you to know." He's looking at the flyer, not at me. "Before we go any farther with this thing."

"This thing?"

He shakes his head, repeats himself.

"This thing. I didn't want you to hear it from anybody else."

"Like my daughters?"

"One of them buttonholed me yesterday."

"I know. She called." Duffy doesn't answer. He looks at me, and I see an old guy, the lines on his face a map of all he's been through. But he still has a child's eyes, full of wonder and longing, and I can tell, even in the shadows here, that he's gotten to a place where he really wants to be. With me. And in a quiet place inside myself, I make a decision: I believe him. I'm on his side, no matter what his son has done or not done. Duffy. I trust him.

"Well, now you'll have somebody to keep you company on court dates and visits. If you want her to. Only if you want her to."

"Too late to visit today. They're very strict. And when I do, they've got this Plexiglas wall between us."

I take his hand. "We'll come back another day. Just say the word."

Twenty-seven

AIN'T SHE
SWEET

Another morning, another ringing telephone. I've no sooner put my coffee on and plugged the phone back in when it starts. Last night when I got home, I'd unplugged the damned thing in case my daughters or my sisters were in the mood to gab. I wasn't. I was all gabbed out. I had some new vocabulary—"incarcerated," "false memory," "exculpatory"—and these words hung in my mind, blotting out anything else I might want to say. We went our separate ways when we got back, Duffy and I. Didn't even talk on the way home, just listened to the music. A warm and necessary silence, as if we were still communicating, not like that colder silence on our trip south. At last I pick it up.

"Hi, Mimi, it's me," says the voice. "I've been trying and trying to reach you."

"Oh, Cassandra, I'm fine. I just needed a little time off. I mean, from the phone."

"Cassandra?" the voice wails. Whoops. Which one is it?

"It's Siobhan, your fifth child," she says, all huffy.

"Who gave you my number?"

"Very funny."

"Well, when's the last time you used it?" Silence. She can't remember, but I can, me with all the black spots. Not once in all the years I've lived here has Siobhan called to say hello or for any other reason.

"When do you call me?" she asks.

"Once in a while."

"A great, great while, Mimi. To remind me to send a birthday card to Aunt Keeley or some such thing. You never ever call to ask me how I am. Never."

"Well, how are you?"

"Very funny."

We could waste the whole morning, pointing out what I've done to her and she's done to me, or what we've failed to do.

"OK, what's up?" I pour my coffee, the phone cradled by my ear. "What's so important you had to call?" Her breathing still sounds funny, but, hey, the truth's the truth.

"Can I come over?"

"Sure, why not?"

"I've been thinking . . ."

"About what?" I stifle the mean retorts my lips unload so easily.

"I'll be there ASAP."

Siobhan lives on the other side of Beantown, in Andover, not far from Delilah in Reading. It'll take her an hour or so to get here. While I wait, I drink coffee at my table by the window and think about her, something I've hardly ever done over the past fifteen years or so. Siobhan, a feminist scholar in Irish studies. Of course, I also wonder what she's been thinking about, why she has this sudden urgent need to visit me. Maybe it's about what a rotten mother I have been.

Siobhan and I, we never spend time together. I mean, time alone together. When I left Jack, I left the way you leave a burning house—in a mad rush, knowing some things will be lost to you forever. Siobhan was one of those things, but I couldn't let myself feel anything about it. I had too many other things to feel.

Siobhan, the only one of my girls without a nickname. When she was little, she pronounced her name Shibbon. We tried out Shibby on her, but she wouldn't have it, wouldn't answer to it. Siobhan or nothing.

Siobhan is what she insisted upon and it's what she got. This name, I think, is what got her into Irish Studies in the first place, though the truth is, I haven't paid close enough attention to know for sure.

She's soon to be Dr. Siobhan Sheehan Malloy, because, being a feminist, she's keeping my name too. Which makes me proud, though I've never told her. She swears that if she ever marries, she'll keep this name. Though she's already told her sisters, she doesn't plan on having children, a tidbit they've passed on to me. She's doesn't want to do what was done to her to an innocent and helpless child. Whatever that might be.

Siobhan's the biggest of my girls, taller and wider than the rest of them. Not that she has a weight problem, not by any means. She's just bigger boned, like the women in Jack's family, instead of mine. Plus, she's perfectly proportioned, and carries her size well, but she's always been jealous of the others, especially Del and Cass, because they're so fit and thin. Size 4, where she's probably a 10. No biggie, in my book, but it practically kills her. That's what her sisters tell me, anyway. She does spinning and peelatays and a million other things to stay in shape. And she's always on one weird diet or another. She's also into fang shway, and everything in her apartment is placed perfectly so she gets the best vibrations. Siobhan does it by the book. Or so her sisters say. I wouldn't know because I've never been there. Never been invited.

Siobhan's a control freak, I'm pretty sure, though she tries to keep this part of her personality under wraps. Or maybe she doesn't even recognize it. No doubt about it, she's a brain, our Siobhan, quiet and studious all her life—hiding in her room, reading, trying to stay out of the line of fire. Smart, but without a clue about herself. It's funny because she's older, bigger, and better educated, but Del leads her around by the nose, telling her what to think and how to feel. Then, when Cassie gets in on the act, forget about it. The three of them together. Whoa. Or maybe woe.

Siobhan shows up in jeans and a beautiful Irish sweater she picked up on her last trip. She's already thirtysomething, although she looks much younger. It's that gorgeous skin. Where did the time go? I wonder when I look at her. She was in high school when I left Jack, and now she's all grown up, a woman I hardly know.

We don't hug. Never do. I invite her in, and right away she starts coughing and waving her hands around because of the cigarette smoke.

"How can you stand it?" she asks.

"I don't notice." I open a window, trying to keep my cool.

I pour her a cup of coffee, and we sit at my table. Neither of us speaks. The old hurts and betrayals push us apart.

"You've never forgiven me for leaving you." This sentence is out before I even think it. It thrashes in the air between us, a snake about to strike.

Siobhan bursts out crying. She stands and spins around, her hands over her face, howling like one of those car alarms that go right through you and seem to never stop. I stand up too. I want to go to her but can't. She might push me away. I watch her have this fit, spinning like Rumpelstiltskin after the princess guessed his name. Not the shy, chubby teenager I left behind, but a grown woman, sad and smart and so confused. Wailing like a broken car alarm. Did she really come out of me?

"Come on, sit down," I say, enfolding her as best I can given the difference in our sizes. I lead her to my couch and sit beside her. I keep my arm around her, and make soothing sounds. *Now, now, sweetheart, now, now.* She's still crying, but it turns into a more normal type of sobbing, tears running down her cheeks, hiccupping—the type of sad that I can handle.

"After you left, you never cared a thing about me," she says between the hiccups. "You never paid attention. You wouldn't even go to my high school graduation party because it was at Daddy's house, and I was the valedictorian. I had a scholarship to Georgetown. And my own mother was MIA."

"That was fifteen years ago, for heaven's sake," I say, staggered by her first blow. "It's ancient history. Water under the dam. Or the bridge. Wherever water goes."

But it's also true. I went to the graduation ceremony, but hung out in back, refusing to sit up front with Jack and Miss Piggy, though Siobhan had reserved a seat for me there. And I refused to go to the party at Jack's house because, of course, Miss Piggy would be there, playing hostess in my former home, with my former husband, and my good china and silverware.

"You were too busy hating Daddy to think about me. You still are, Mimi. You're eaten up with bitterness."

"Am not!" Leave it to your offspring to tally up your failings and remind you of your every weakness. "And leave your father out of this."

"We can't leave him out," she says. "He's here whether we want him or not. And you don't have any idea who I am." We're sitting close together, and I've got my arm around her, but we're not looking at each other.

"Do you know me?" I ask.

"You don't want me to."

"I don't want you to?" I take her chin and force her, gently, to turn toward me. We look at each other, Siobhan and I, her eyes that same lovely blue as her father's, her head crammed full of learning.

"You're full of secrets." She shrugs. "Always hiding."

I drop my hand. I can't even answer that. I've said it all before, so many times, to one or another of her sisters. All of my daughters. I've got no secrets, not a one. For a time, we're quiet, except for the occasional sob or hiccup.

"Siobhan, I know I got off track with you, and I don't know how to get back on. I don't know if it's possible. All these years, I thought you didn't care. I thought you hated me so much you didn't want to get to know me."

"I never hated you, Mimi. Never, ever. You ripped my heart out a few times but I was smart enough to know that's not what you meant to do. I just happened to be there. Wrong place, wrong time."

"Would it help for me to say I'm sorry? Truly sorry for leaving you behind?"

She nods yes, but corrects me.

"You didn't leave me behind. You abandoned me."

"I'm sorry for that, too. But maybe we can, I don't know, try to get to know each other now," I say. "Take it slow."

She nods but doesn't speak, her nose red, her cheeks tearstained, like when she was a little girl and came to me with her upsets and her hurts. I pull her toward me and hold her the way I used to, way back when, patting her soft hair. She sobs some more. We sit that way for a while.

"But this isn't what you came here for, is it?" I say at last, unable to deal with Siobhan's hurt any longer.

"No." For once, she agrees with me. "It's not."

We get up and take turns in the bathroom, washing our faces and putting on fresh makeup. When she's finished, Siobhan shoves a big plastic bag at me.

"Got it for you on my last trip," she says. "I forgot to bring it last time I was here."

Inside's an Irish sweater, a light-green cardigan with a pretty design around the neckline and the hem.

"You're trying to upgrade my image too," I say, then want to kick myself.

"No," she says. "I just thought it would look good on you. The color matches your eyes."

I go into my bedroom, slip it on over my turtleneck. Siobhan watches in the doorway.

"It does, Mimi," she says. "I was right. It looks really good on you."

"Wow, it does," I say, smiling at her, seeing how pleased she is. I'm afraid the sweater might be itchy or too hot, but I'll keep my big mouth shut. I'll wear it no matter what.

"Let's get out of here," she says, suddenly taking deep breaths. "I'm having trouble breathing."

Twenty-eight

WITCHCRAFT

We drive over to Marina Bay, where we can walk on the promenade by the water and window shop. After I park and we climb out of my Shadow and into the fresh salty air, I take Siobhan by the arm. " 'Come away, O human child,' " I say, and she smiles. As we walk around the shops and piers, the two of us in our Irish sweaters, the weight of what she's said presses down on me. Even still, I can't help but notice the way my daughter draws attention, clueless though she may be. Men like to look at her, the way they used to like to look at me.

We pass a Vietnam War memorial, a miniature version of the one in Washington—black marble, shiny as a mirror, engraved with the names of the local dead. Siobhan points to a name, tells me it was the younger brother of Del's ex-husband.

"Would've been my brother-in-law if he'd lived. Or if Del had stayed married to him."

"The dead are all around us."

"Just like the faeries," says Siobhan, and she squeezes my arm tighter.

"Is that what you wanted to talk about? Faeries?"

"It might relate," she says, her cheeks going pink.

"To what?"

"To what happened in your family."

Then, scholar that she is, she launches into a lecture, about how, back in the day, in the old country—the one that she's obsessed with, just like the grandfather she never knew—the ancient beliefs of the peasantry got mixed up with stories from the Bible.

"The preliterate . . ." I can't remember the next word.

"Cosmology, world view."

"Right."

"Like when God expelled Lucifer from heaven with all the other rebel angels. The rebel angels were already falling through the sky when Jesus told his Father that heaven might end up empty, with so much rebellion going on."

"Everybody getting into the act."

She nods.

"When God the Father stopped to think," she says, stopping in her tracks so we can stare into the window of a sweet shop where they're dipping big red strawberries into a vat of melted chocolate, "the falling angels stopped wherever they happened to be." She touches the window with her fingertip. The strawberry dippers smile at us. "Yummy," she says, then goes on with the lesson. "That's why you've got faeries in the air, in the water, under the earth, and on top of it."

I look at those luscious berries being dipped into the even more luscious chocolate. I try to imagine God the Father thinking, and the falling angels stopping wherever they happened to be. I can't quite see it. I look at Siobhan.

"So this is that preliterate cosmo-something?"

"Cosmology," she repeats, nodding patiently, like I'm slow but catching on. "Most of the time, they're invisible, the faeries, at least to most people, but if you could see them, they'd look human."

"I'll treat you to a strawberry," I interrupt. My daughter doesn't even pretend to protest. We buy four, two each, picking out the biggest ones on the tray.

It's warm enough to sit on one of the benches by the water, especially in these heavy sweaters. We find an empty one and take a seat. "Most were male," she says, and it takes me a second to catch up. "The faeries. That's why, when they kidnapped, they chose girls and women. Most of the time."

"When they kidnapped?"

"Stole a human child. Replaced a human child with a changeling."

"Folks in Ireland believed this stuff?" I ask my daughter, but I already know the answer. I've always known, somewhere deep inside, though I've kept it there—a dark secret I did not want to figure out. The old folks in Ireland believed some crazy things and built their lives around this craziness, their preliterate cosmology. Some, like Nana, dumped those beliefs into the Atlantic as they crossed over to North America, but others, like Da, held on to them—held on for dear life—into their new lives in the new country, a place where those beliefs would mark them as ignorant and backward, something Nana understood.

"Any disturbance in the predictable order of things could be blamed on faeries. Madness, illness, a deformity. A death in childbirth, like your mother's. Misfortune was interpreted as a form of revenge, a failure to appease the little people."

Siobhan has forgotten her strawberries, though I'm nibbling one of mine. It's a disappointment beneath the chocolate coating, dry and mealy. A lesson in deceiving looks.

"They understood the world through the stories they told each other, sitting around peat fires at night. There was no electricity well into the twentieth century. And remember, the Irish Free State wasn't formed until 1922, and even afterward, most people didn't know how to read or write."

Siobhan glows as if she's sitting by one of those fires instead of on a bench with me, Quincy Bay heaving just beyond us, the sky overhead a clear and gorgeous blue. 1922, just a few years before I was born. Suddenly, I feel ancient; a crone, with this cold breeze stirring up the ashes at the bottom of my soul.

Flanna wasn't an ordinary madwoman. She was a *cailleach*, a woman with special power. *Cailleach*, a word that makes you gag if you pronounce it right. She understood the wee folk, could talk to them, could hear them. Which is why Da chose her. Da himself believed in spirits, faeries, wee people. He believed in Flanna.

"When I was a kid, I imagined Flanna getting off a big sailboat right out there," I point, "right in Quincy Harbor, walking on the water, making her way toward us, with her big black satchel."

"What was in the satchel?"

"Herbs. Whiskey."

"Nice combo."

"She boiled up plants she grew in the yard, and made us drink them. If we didn't, there'd be hell to pay."

"Hell to pay," Siobhan repeats. "Probably purple foxglove, and St. John's wort, both used in faerie medicine. *Come away, O human child*. It all goes back to the line you just mentioned, from the Yeats poem. The same one that's on Da's headstone." Da. She's calling her grandfather Da, and in that way, she's claiming him.

I nod. Without wanting to, I see Flanna rushing through the house, muttering mumbo-jumbo. Hiding things. Finding things. Boiling things. Burning things. Whispering. Listening.

As I think about Flanna parceling out her concoctions to the old folks at the back door, Siobhan tells me about how, back in the day, poor rural families—and almost all families were rural poor—couldn't afford kids who didn't obey. Kids had to do their part for families to survive. Life was just too hard. If a defiant child couldn't be gotten under control, parents and priests and healers might gather to exorcise the evil thing from the child who was causing all the trouble. They'd break the kids' spirits, along with a few bones, if that's what was necessary to get them to behave, to stop wreaking havoc in the family.

"'The Stolen Child,'" I say, and the words work like a wire whisk whipping up my dread. "But I don't see the connection."

What I see is Flanna in the coal cellar, next to the furnace, holding the shovel she used to dump in the coal. The furnace door is open, filled with flames. That's when Fagan shows up beside me, her bright, furious self. Clutches me, as Flanna shovels in the coal. I can't see her, only feel her. Fagan. Hot as embers, even out here in the cold.

"Mimi." Siobhan hugs me. She smells scrumptious, like cinnamon and lilies. A scent that overwhelms the stench of Fagan, filthy Fagan, furious Fagan, hanging on for dear life. I lean closer to Siobhan, inhale deeply.

"Flanna believed Fagan was a changeling," Siobhan says. "That's the connection. I'll bet anything."

"For heaven's sake, Siobhan, a changeling?"

"That the faeries stole the real Fagan and left behind the disobedient monster who looked just like her." I look at my daughter, so smart, and so grown-up and serious, telling me one of the nuttiest things I've ever heard. Fagan, a changeling. She blushes again, her cheeks the color of the bits of yarn in the design around her neckline.

"And if she did?"

She doesn't answer, stares out at the water.

"Siobhan!" I shout, as if she were still an adolescent and I was struggling to control her. "Siobhan," I say again, my voice softer, gentler; I'm calling her back to me.

"Well," she starts to say, "if that's what she believed, she'd do what she had to do to get the real Fagan back."

"'What she had to do'?"

"You said Flanna poured the pee pot over Fagan. That was one way to make the faeries let a changeling go. One of the first things they'd do, drench the changeling with piss. If that didn't work, they'd try emetics. By inducing vomiting, they believed they could force the faeries to release the child."

Flanna in the kitchen, forcing Fagan to drink one of her disgusting concoctions. Fagan pukes into the sink, and Flanna smacks her back to make her throw up more. I see, if only dimly and in flashes, induced nausea, enemas, terrible hot baths—the purifying of our systems, Flanna trying to force the evil out.

"Fire was the last resort."

"The last resort?" No place to vacation, this last resort.

"After the dousing and the emetics. If everything else failed, Flanna could have threatened Fagan with fire as a warning to the faeries."

"A warning?"

"To the faeries. To let her go."

In my mind's eye, where everything now seems to be 20/20, I see the burn can in the backyard, the black stove in the kitchen, the coal-burning furnace in the cellar. Beside it, the shovel for scooping up the coal, the bucket with the slanted lip for pouring coal into the furnace, the poker for stoking up the coals. Like a house, the furnace had a front door. *When Flanna opens it, the flames inside shoot up, red and ravenous, warning us how close we are to hell. Flanna commands all of us to stand behind her, to see how, in just a few minutes, she turns that poker red-hot from the flames.*

"Fire was the last resort," Siobhan repeats. I look into her earnest eyes, her lovely face, the sunlight on it. "Sometimes the warnings worked. Little kids could be and often were terrified into docility."

Eden, unbidden, comes back to mind. Early on, she lost her spirit if not her soul. Turned passive in all things, wouldn't or couldn't stick up for herself. A doormat, we'd often wisecrack. Eden, the beautiful doormat. Alberta and I kept her going, then finally just Alberta.

"Children could have the spirit beaten out of them," says Siobhan. "It was common practice, handed down through the generations. If they were ill, they could get well. Believers interpreted these things as successful faerie interventions."

"Faerie interventions?" The last time I heard that word, "intervention," was from Alberta's daughter, a year or two before my sister's death. She wanted us to help with one, but we said no. We loved Alberta, understood her and accepted her as she was. We could not turn on her. And that was the last we heard from her, our niece.

"Faerie literature is full of stories about so-called wise women bringing mortal children back. About changelings flying up out of their beds and disappearing into the night, leaving the normal child behind." Siobhan squeezes my hand. But instead I feel Fagan's fingers dig deep, deep into me. "Stories about how, when a *cailleach* builds up the fire and threatens to put the child on top, what looks like an ordinary child flies up and out the window."

"I'm so glad she got sent away," I tell Siobhan. "That was the right thing for Da to do. Imagine what might have happened if she stayed."

"Cullyhanna," murmurs Siobhan.

"Why don't we go back?" I ask, stunning myself because the trip never seemed possible to me before. "You could help me look for Fagan. I mean, her grave." Me, Mimi, thinking of going back when I've never ever desired to set a foot there. Ireland, land of mystery and sorrow.

"We could do that," says Siobhan, but when I look at her, she's staring out at the water.

"It's funny. After Fagan was sent away, Flanna would call Keeley Fagan all the time."

"Fagan?" She turns to look at me, and this time the knowledge in her gaze frightens me. "Back then, when a child died, families often blamed the death on faeries. Then, when the next child came along, they'd name it after the dead one."

"The dead one? Fagan didn't die til later, after she got sent away."

Shrieking, hollering, though not one of us actually saw Fagan go. *Not Mammy*, my sister's everlasting lamentation. Flanna chases Fagan through the house. They holler loud enough to wake up the neighborhood, but the only ones who wake up are Eden, Alberta, and me. *Not Mammy*. Over and over again, Flanna grabbed Fagan, but Fagan escaped. The two of them ran and ran, cartoon characters racing around the kitchen table, so fast they were a blur. Comical if you didn't know what was going on.

"The new baby was seen as a gift from the faeries who'd stolen the first one," Siobhan says. "That's what they believed."

Now my own mind might be on fire, the same fuse that got lit the other day. Because I see Flanna caressing Keeley, only she calls her Fagan. *Fagan, my wee love.* Which drove Keeley nuts, because she never once thought Flanna was confused. No, not for a minute. *She's thinks I'm Fagan, but I'm not. I'm me, Keeley.* All that conflict always, over who was who and what was what.

"That's why," says Siobhan, "when you walk through the cemeteries in the countryside, you'll see families with two Bridgets or Annies or Padraics born within a couple of years of each other. The second child replaced the first."

No loss to feel.

But I've never walked through cemeteries in the Irish countryside, and I've never planned to do so. Unless, that is, Siobhan and I go to search for Fagan.

I look around, see how normal we look sitting here, a mother and daughter, enjoying the fresh air in our lovely Irish sweaters. Perfectly normal, that's us. The water's churning, with little whitecaps here and there. Siobhan's squinting out at it. I look at her face with Da's clear blue eyes. My heart swells, a feeling as good as that myocardial thing is bad. I love her, this Siobhan, and for the first time, I realize how much I'd hurt her. Me, Mimi Malloy, who swore deep down in her own soul, and with all her might, that she would never, ever hurt her children.

Now both of us are shivering. We lean closer to each other. An icy gust blows up off the water, and trash flies around our feet. It's so cold, it feels like winter's coming back.

Twenty-nine

SOMETHING'S
GOTTA GIVE

W hen I walk into my apartment, my brain is so full of
sparks I'm afraid it might explode. I get the blue pendant
from my bedroom, sit with it in my recliner. I don't turn on any lights.
The dark feels good right now, and maybe necessary. I've got this dull
ache deep inside, like just before my miscarriage, the one I had between
Malvina and Siobhan. Those ashes at the bottom of my soul send up
clouds, making my eyes water. Everything I see blurs and shines through
a veil of tears.

Instead of thinking about my second-youngest daughter, or my first
baby sister, I think about the baby I lost, though it wasn't, either in my
mind or in my body, yet a baby, not really. I was just far enough along
to feel the baby move, the quickening, a word I've never understood.

I wasn't thrilled about the pregnancy, my fifth in seven years. I was
twenty-seven and hadn't been out of maternity clothes since my teens.
No, I wasn't thrilled, to say the least. I didn't want another baby, I was
already in way over my head with the four I already had, and I knew it,
but I told Jack the opposite. I insisted I was happy: God was giving us
another one. He agreed that we were blessed. We were propagating
the faith, and our faith was everything.

Then, one morning I woke up, sat up, but did not throw up. Yippee, I thought, I'm past the worst part. But over the next couple of days, I realized something wasn't right. No throwing up, but also no more of those feathery tickles down inside. Then, in the middle of the night, I woke up, drenched with sweat and with a dull ache down where the baby was supposed to be growing. "Something's wrong," I told Jack, shaking him awake. "Go back to sleep," he said. In the morning I called my doctor. "You're fine, it's all in your head," he told me. He'd see me the next month. After that, I called my sisters. "Keep us posted," Jo and Patty said. "Whatever you need, whenever you need it. We'll be there." It was the twins who came to help, that afternoon, when I started bleeding. I went into labor, sharp, intense contractions, but no baby would be born.

By the time the twins arrived, I was hemorrhaging, gushing blood. No more pain, just this river of blood, with Cassandra and Celestine and Ruthie hollering and sobbing at the sight of me. Jo called the hospital. She told them to get ready for an emergency D&C. She was bringing me in. Patty packed Malvie's diapers between my legs, cloth ones, from the stack folded neatly in the bathroom. She grabbed an armload for us to take along in the car. One after the other, they got drenched. Blood was flowing out of me, and I couldn't do anything to stop it. Patty stayed with the girls and tried to comfort them while Jo drove me to the hospital. That's all I remember. Nothing about the surgery, waking up, the rest of it, though it's one of the twins' favorite stories when the Yik Yak Club's in session. How they saved my life. Talk about drama queens.

My sisters were furious with Jack and they've always held it against him. Because he never showed, never thanked them, never expressed regret about the baby, or concern about me. But me, I didn't expect any of those things. I wasn't angry, not surprised, either. Jack F. X. Malloy abhors the sight of blood. He doesn't do hospitals, that's just how it is. Yes, I lost the baby; no telling, back then, if it was a boy or girl. The next few months were hard. I went into the deepest mourning, a grief out of all proportion. Strange, because part of me had wished that baby dead, though I never told a soul. I wept for days on end, the last time I'd cry for many years. "Get over it, we'll make another one," Jack kept saying, especially in bed at night when he wanted some. Soon enough, a couple of years later, we did, we made another one, Siobhan, and I forgot about the lost one, the one I didn't want. I tucked it away, neatly, into a black spot, like a sandwich into a Ziploc bag.

Siobhan, the one who came next. Still sitting in my recliner, I put down the blue pendant to check my hands, wondering if they're stained with the blood of her broken heart. Eaten up with bitterness, that's me. That's what my daughter thinks. Oh, and that I abandoned her. My own child. Of course, poor thing, she was my fifth in a decade, with the miscarriage in between. I was worn out by the time Siobhan showed up, that much I'll admit. She didn't get the best of me. But abandoned?

My mind churns around the idea that I've known her all her life without knowing her at all. How does that happen? How can you give birth to a kid and raise her, and end up not knowing her? She's got her father's brains but nothing of me—nothing visible, anyway, unless you count what she considers her weight problem, the one nobody else can see.

When we said goodbye today, we promised to call each other once a week or so, just to say hello. We agreed we wouldn't let Cassandra be our go-between, running our relationship for us. We agreed to let bygones be bygones. To try to trust each other.

Which reminds me.

I grab my personal directory, pick up the phone, and punch in Malvina's number in the Bronx. Cassandra wrote it in my book the last time she was here and now, after all this time, I want to talk to her, make it up to her. I can't help imagining her surprise when she hears my voice, "Hello, darling." We'll make a plan to get together. I'll take the train to New York to meet my grandsons, spend a few days there with them—Mimi in the City. But Malvina's phone rings and rings. Nobody picks up, not even the answering machine. I promise myself to try again later. I hope I remember.

I decide to call Cassandra—press that speed-dial number and ta-da, she picks up after the first ring. "What's up, Mimi? Everything OK?" Worried, always worried, like I'm so flimsy that I'll collapse at any moment.

"I'm fine, baby, just fine. Siobhan visited today."

"Siobhan? That's a first."

"A first, but not a last." Then I'm quiet, unable to figure out how to say what I want to say next.

"Great, but what's—"

"That got to do with you? I want to go on a field trip. I want to go back to Da's house, or where our house used to be."

"Oooookaayy. . . ." She's says it like I'm the real nut she's always suspected me to be. The house, after all, was demolished ages ago. I imagine her rolling her gorgeous eyes, shadowed and mascaraed, wondering what craziness is coming next.

"We ran away and never went back. I want to retrace our steps. I want to see what we can see."

"You ran away? To your grandmother's house?"

"Yes, that's all I remember, showing up at Nana's house." Nana's lovely house in Weymouth, just over the bridge from Quincy. Nana in the kitchen, working, forever making soups and jams and breads, Nana playing the radio, tuning in to the Boston stations, and practicing her American accent by mimicking the announcers: *Coca-Cola, ice-cold sunshine! Wonder Bread! It's Slo-baked.*

"I don't remember anything that happened right before."

"Like traumatic amnesia?"

"Something like that."

"Tomorrow morning?"

"Great."

Thirty

MAKIN'
WHOOPEE

I'm no sooner settled back in my chair than Duffy's knocking on the door, calling in that funny way he has, "Mrs. Malloy, oh, Mrs. Malloy."

When I open the door, Duff's smiling like a little boy, embarrassed, maybe because he's showed up unexpected, and he's brought me a treat. He holds a big brown bag, and a rich steamy smell escapes from it.

"Moo Goo Gai Pan," he says. "Chow Mei Fun."

"My favorites." I smile, too, though I haven't got a clue what either dish tastes like. I'd hug him if he wasn't so loaded down. I drag him inside.

"Lovely sweater," he says, putting the bag down on my counter, taking out the little white cartons. "Looks great on you, Mrs. Malloy." He makes a throaty sound, like I'm so delicious he could eat me up. My face burns.

"My daughter Siobhan brought it to me from Ireland." I hold out my arm for him to feel. He rubs his hand along the sleeve and then puts his arms around me, pulls me close. He kisses the top of my head. I almost start to cry, but stop. Stay in the moment, I tell myself, some of Cassie's psychobabble. But this time I get it. I'll stay in the moment.

"You must've read my mind, coming by with Chinese. I'm starving. Went out with my kid, but all we ate was strawberries. They're always on my case about my weight."

"You're looking fine to me, Mrs. Malloy."

I smile up into his twinkling eyes. The feeling's mutual, but I can't bring myself to say so. He's wearing a pale blue sweater and jeans with a thin white stripe down the front from being pressed so many times. Probably brings them to the Chinese laundry on the corner, next to the takeout place. Kills two birds with one stone.

But now Duff pulls away and hands me a package he must have brought in with the Chinese food. A thin rectangle, too big for my mailbox in the foyer.

"Figured I'd make a personal delivery," Duff says, but in a way that makes my heart go pitter-pat. Of course, he keeps packages for all the tenants, saving us a trip to the PO, but usually he'll just leave a note, and we'll pick it up in his office.

"Thanks so much, Duff." I see the return address: Keeley. I shake my head. Can't escape the Yik Yak Club, no matter what. I set it aside, but then curiosity gets the best of me. While Duff divvies up the food and puts on a pot of coffee, I open the package. Inside is a posed portrait of a family. A black-and-white photograph, unframed, and crudely colorized. A mother, father, and six daughters. Just like us, I'm thinking, when I realize it *is* us, the Sheehans, way back when. I'd know Da and Eden and Alberta anywhere, Mam not so much.

"Oh, Duff, it's us." I look again. A note in the package has fallen to the floor. Duffy stoops to pick it up before reaching for me. He walks me into the living room, helps me onto the couch.

"Let me get the coffee," he says, and while he does, I read.

Dear Mimi,

Katie Bain, that cousin I went to high school with, called last week to say she'd found some things we might want when she was cleaning out her mother's place. This was one of them. Our family minus me.

Katie's the one who came to see me when her mother (our aunt!!!) was a patient. The old lady, our mother's sister Maeve, died before I got to meet her. Not that she wanted to meet me. She was in her nineties, still holding a grudge.

Love,
Keeley

On the back of the photo is a note, handwritten in pencil:

Joseph Sheehan and family
Sea Street, Quincy
August 1932

Joe and Mary, so young, so good-looking. Got the world on a string, that's what you'd think, looking at the picture. Da's got his arm around my mother and we three oldest are standing next to him, crammed together, peas in a pod. The twins, Patty and Josephine, stand, one each in front of each of them, and Fagan is in my mother's arms. Her head's resting on my mother's shoulder and her index finger is knuckle-deep up her nose. Darling Fagan, picking her nose for posterity.

The black-and-white picture has been colorized the old-fashioned way, the colors painted over the print, but bleeding just outside the lines. Each of us girls, brunettes, redheads, and Eden, the only blonde, appear to be wearing a pastel-colored dress, yellow, pink, baby blue, mint green, lavender. Alberta and Eden, at ten and eleven, are just as beautiful as I remember. My mother's lips are red, her cheeks bright pink, and Da's eyes are too, too blue. I wish I could peel back this layer of color to see what they really looked like. Still, I'm grateful for this shot of all of us together.

I don't realize Duffy's next to me until I smell the coffee.

"My family," I say. "My first one."

"Sweet."

"Right before disaster struck."

"You mean the Depression?"

Again I check the date on the back, shake my head no. "My mother was pregnant with Keeley. Her birth was the beginning of the end."

"What a burden for her to bear, your sister."

"I like to think we've helped lighten her load. We tried. She's done well. She's got the love of a good man. They've made a nice life together."

The love of a good man. This part of the sentence echoes louder than the rest. Duff puts his arm around me. His fingers press the soft part of my upper arm. My body burns—embarrassment, not lust, but the one, I'm finding, doesn't necessarily rule out the other.

"Hey, I'm starved," I say. "How 'bout that Moo Goo Gai Pan?" I jump up and turn to look at him. Duffy smiles. I've blown him off, but he can take it. He'll try again.

While we eat, I prop the photo on the window ledge over the table.

"Six daughters," he says once we've dug in, using chopsticks and laughing every time the Chow Mei Fun falls back onto the plate. We've agreed, without using words, that tonight we won't talk about his son; about incarceration, false memory, exculpation. "How'd you manage to duplicate that?" His question hangs there while the two of us turn redder than the peppers in the sweet and sour.

"The propagation of the faith," I say, innocent as could be.

"'The propagation of the faith'?" He takes a sip of coffee and shakes his head.

"Isn't that the duty of every Catholic couple? Increasing the ranks of the faithful? My ex was really big on that."

"We stopped at two, Virginia and me," he says. "It's all we could handle, to hell with the propagation of the faith. Turns out, they pushed us to the edge. Over it a couple of times."

He shrugs, looks at me. I nod, I get it. No more needs to be said.

"Hey, it's good to know your limits," I say. "Neither Jack nor I ever did."

Again, Duff looks at the picture. He can't get over how beautiful Eden and Alberta were. "You look just like them," he adds.

"Time to get your eyes checked."

"My eyes are great, except for the fine print. That's when I need glasses." He takes out his glasses. He puts them on and gives me a hard stare. I swear Duff's look goes right through me, like a shot of whiskey, burning all the way.

"You're lookin' good either way, Mrs. Malloy. Mighty good."

I don't know where to look or what to say. Me, who lost my looks years ago. I pretend I haven't heard him, try but fail to pincer a bit of chicken in the Moo Goo Gai Pan. "I keep wondering about my parents. Who, in the end, had seven daughters in eleven years."

"Only doing their Catholic duty?" Duffy's eyes twinkle.

"Even the propagation of the faith can't account for that level of reproduction, I don't think. And Da wasn't devout. He just went through the motions. What I keep wondering is, did my father and mother have a true passion for each other? Did they risk it all and lose it all because they wanted a son? Or because they couldn't get enough of one another?"

He reaches across the table for my hand.

"Does it make a difference now?" His eyes blaze a trail deep inside me.

"All the difference," I say, although I'm not clear why.

"A true passion," he repeats.

It's a statement, not a question, and next thing I know, we're standing and holding each other. We head toward my bedroom, moving slowly, like children going to someplace we've never been, instead of old folks traveling backward down a familiar but neglected path.

Thirty-one

THE LADY IS
A TRAMP

*D*uffy's up and gone at the crack of dawn. I can tell the time by the way the light comes in around my curtains. I pretend to be asleep, roll over onto his side of the bed, enjoying the last warmth from his body, and the nice smell he left behind. When I roll, the hinges of my body creak, a door that hasn't opened for ages, but I'm oh so glad it did. Aren't I just the lucky duck? I think, finding this at last. Whatever "this" is, "this" will do.

But when I sit up, figuring I'll let the coffee brew while I hop into the shower, my sciatica howls. Sharp, hot pain starts deep inside my butt cheek and shoots all down my leg. Great, I think, I finally get laid and now I can't even hobble out of bed.

If only Alberta were around to tell. The sight of me in agony after rolling in the hay with Duffy would send her into orbit. *Mimi screws an old guy and ends up needing traction.* God, Alberta. She kept her sense of humor through it all, right up til Danny died. We shared more laughs than you could count. If she were alive, I'd call her, just to crack her up. *You made my day, honey,* she'd say.

Once, when we were kids, we were at the kitchen table, all of us together, eating elbow macaroni—one of our favorites—and were laughing our heads off about something, when a piece of macaroni shot out of Alberta's nose and landed in the middle of the table. A complete accident, because she'd been laughing with her mouth full. We—the twins, Eden, me, and Alberta—doubled over at the sight of that piece of macaroni in the middle of the table. Then all of us had to try it, snorting and sucking up the macaroni, but not one of us succeeded. We were in hysterics when another elbow macaroni flew out of Alberta's nose, and she wasn't even trying. By then, we were crying we were laughing so hard, and Alberta laughed the loudest of all. After that, she used it as a party trick, blowing macaroni out her nose. It always got a giggle. God, if she could see me now, with love in the air, and my sciatica screaming in a way it hasn't since I carried all those babies on my hip all day. She'd be tickled pink.

A nice hot bath and some Advil ought to do the trick, if only I can get myself to the bathroom. I haul myself up, make my painful way into the kitchen to put on the coffee, swallow a couple of pills. The coffee hasn't even started to bubble up into the glass knob when the buzzer sounds. Cassandra, I think, remembering our date this morning. But, no, it can't be Cass because she's got a key and always lets herself in. And besides, she's not due for at least half an hour. Slowly, ever so slowly, I go to the intercom in the front hallway.

"It's me, Patty, with Jo." My sister's voice sounds muffled. "You gonna let us in? Or make us stand out here in the cold?"

"I ought to let you freeze, the two of you," I joke, but I'm still miffed at the pair of them for calling me a liar in front of my daughters. No memory lapse in that regard.

"Open the damned door," Patty orders.

I buzz them in, crack my apartment door, then go, fast as I'm able, into my room and throw on some sweats. Getting my legs into the pants is a new form of torture. But I'm glad they're here, those two. I'm going to give them a piece of my mind—a small one, at least, considering what's left of it.

But when I walk out of the bedroom, they're shivering in my foyer like the pair of hungry orphans they used to be, all bundled up in down jackets and fur-trimmed hats. Patty shoves an envelope into my hand.

"Greeks bearing gifts," I say.

"Shut up," she answers. "Sit before you open it."

We plunk down onto my couch. Ouch. Inside the envelope are an embroidered hankie and a lock of bright red hair. Fagan's hair. I'd know it anywhere.

"Nana gave it to us," says Patty. "On her deathbed."

"She didn't give it to us," Jo corrects. "She told us where to look for it. In her bureau, under the lining of a drawer."

"A *piseog*," I say, one step ahead of them. "The *piseog*." I fold the hankie back around Fagan's silky hair, just as soft and vibrant as it used to be.

"I forgot we had it," says Jo.

"Until Siobhan started talking about the faeries." Patty.

"The wee people." Jo tries to laugh, but it sounds like something's stuck in her throat.

"Well now, Patty," I tell her, still holding the *piseog*, "your prince of a grandson can include this with his genealogy. Maybe he can laminate it or something." Can't help it. I'm still miffed.

"Too late," says Patty. "He already turned it in. Got a C+ because of all the missing info." She looks crushed because he didn't get an A, but I feel a small surge of vindication: the Sheehan genealogy, an ill-fated project from the start.

"Flanna brought it over to Nana, after Da was buried," Patty says, grabbing back the *piseog*. "She showed up at Nana's, banging on the front door, calling in her sweetie-sweet voice."

"In our mother's black silk dress, and wearing a black hat with a pink feather." I see it plain as day: Flanna on the porch, pink feather on her hat, *piseog* in her black-gloved hand. She held it out to Nana. We hid in the parlor, all six of us crammed behind the curtains and the couch. Scared. But still, still we wanted to look at her, wanted to see her again, Da's woman of shining loveliness. *You put it there, you,* Flanna wailed while Nana stood there, her white hair in its neat bun, her old face gathered like a fist, her squinted eyes sharp as blades. The *piseog*. Our real mother's hankie, and a lock of Fagan's hair.

"Nana wouldn't let Flanna in, remember, Mimi?" Patty asks, and I do. Made Flanna stand outside, on the porch. "'You'll burn in hell for what you did to Fagan and my Joey,' she said."

The twins slip off their parkas, stand in front of me.

"*Its evil spell is broken,*" snarls Patty, taking on the role of Flanna as the twins act out the ancient drama. Her accent isn't perfect, not like when she does Da, but it's good enough to scare me. She jabs her finger right in front of Josephine's face.

"*I've broken it myself, without even burning it to ash, and now I want my Fagan back.*"

"That's right," I interrupt. "She didn't say Keeley. She called her Fagan. '*Fagan belongs to me.*' That's what she said." A chill wind gusts around me, even colder than out at Marina Bay.

"*Fagan's my daughter. They brought her back to me. You've no right to keep her. I don't care about the rest of them. Brats and troublemakers. But Fagan, she's mine.*"

"*Fagan's gone,*" spits Jo, playing Nana's part. "*You know that better than anyone, Miss Flanna Flanagan. And she won't be coming back. It's Keeley we've got here. And she's staying put.*"

Not for a split second would I confuse my sisters for my stepmother and grandmother. Patty hasn't got a speck of Flanna's glamour and Jo lacks Nana's ferocity. But in spite of their bad acting, they've got their lines down to a T.

Patty: "*She's Fagan and she's mine.*"

"*Ha-ha-ha-ha,*" hacks Jo, imitating Nana laughing in Flanna's face. "*Get out and take your faerie business with you. Take yourself and your faeries and your silly curses back to Ireland. On the next boat, and good riddance to ya.*"

"Then Flanna started mumbling, using words we didn't understand." I see her and hear her, on the front steps of Nana's house.

"*She'll be haunting you all your days, will Fagan,*" hollers Jo as Nana. She raises her arms, shakes them, as if to ward off Flanna.

"That's when Flanna took off," says Patty, back to herself, her eyes bright, her face aglow.

"The last time any of us saw her," I say. They nod. "Let's have coffee, huh? The smell of the fresh brew is driving me nuts." I get up and make my slow way to the kitchen.

"Why are you limping?" they ask at the same time.

"Me? Limping?"

"You're walking funny," says Patty. "What happened?"

"I was throwing the trash from the party into the Dumpster," I lie, fast and slick. "I must've thrown my back out."

"Gosh, nothing works the way it used to, does it?" says Jo.

If only she knew, I think, but my lips are sealed.

Once we're settled back in my living room with coffee, I try to give them that small piece of my mind.

"Last week, you two acted like I'm a liar or a lunatic when you know how Flanna hurt us. 'Fat splatter.' Right in front of my girls."

The twins cling to each other. Sixtysomething years evaporate.

"We came to apologize." Little Patty, with her faded red hair, her mind still sharp and shiny, like those multipurpose tools they sell on TV late at night.

"When we were driving home last week, the car was full of angry ghosts." Jo.

"We felt them flying around inside the car." Patty.

"Eden and Alberta and Da," I say. The twins eyeball me. "They were with us at lunch. Maybe they followed you out." Jo looks around.

"The soul has everlasting life." We learned that in our Baltimore Catechism way, way, way back when, the immortality of the soul. It's one of the few points of Catholic teaching that we all agree about. Couldn't keep going if I did not have that faith.

"Flanna hurt all of us." Jo.

"We pretended to the outside world it wasn't happening." Patty.

"Nobody would've believed us."

"You're shaking," my sisters say together. They move onto the couch beside me, wrap their arms around me, the way Eden and Alberta used to do.

"We knew you were scarred." Patty's hug keeps me from falling apart.

"We knew it couldn't have been an accident." Jo.

"Which means Da lied."

"Or he was lied to." Patty.

"May he rest in peace." Jo.

"He's not in peace," I say, as convinced of this as I am of my own existence. "You two know he isn't either."

Patty nods. "Da knew about your scars. But he went along with Flanna's story, about the accident."

The pain of Da's betrayal still sends convulsions through me, even after all this time.

"Da wanted to believe it, all of us did. We preferred the made-up story." This time, the twins recite their lines together. We were all so good at pretending. Blah-blah-blah.

"But you accused me of making things up, right in front of my own daughters. And you know how hard it's been for my daughters and me . . . Jack always undermining. Giving them permission, right from the start, to put me down. 'Don't make things worse than they were,' that's what you said. You two, who chew over the past like it's an Omaha steak."

"We look for the sweet and tender parts," says Patty.

"You try to make it better than it was," I say.

"Well, Mrs. Mimi Malloy, all these years you've acted as if none of it ever happened." Patty, in her snippy voice.

"You're in denial." Jo.

"Denial? No way," I wail. "Never pretended. I didn't remember. I didn't want to. And now my brain is full of black spots."

"It's those little strokes you've been having." Patty. "With the name I can't pronounce."

"You're waiting for the Big One." Jo.

Their words smack me as hard as Flanna's hand. I can't stand having my health status a topic of chitchat. I'm furious.

"Cassie and her big mouth."

"She's only looking out for you."

"Nothing's sacred in this family."

"She looking out for your best interests." Jo and Patty.

Just then there's a light knock at my door, and then the sound of it opening.

"Mimi?" Cassandra calls.

"Speak of the devil."

Cassandra rushes in, stops short at the sight of her aunts. Huffing and puffing, like she's just run the Boston Marathon, except she's carrying a box of Dunkin' Donuts and looks like she won the lottery.

"I've found a guy, a great guy in Scituate." She drops the box of doughnuts on the coffee table, still panting, then hugs Jo and Patty. "He does repressed-memory therapy."

Repressed-memory therapy, the twins echo. My sisters and I look at one another and crack up.

"He cures psychogenic amnesia. We might solve this mystery once and for all, the mystery of Fagan Sent Away."

"With doughnuts?"

"Not doughnuts, Mimi, hypnosis. He's great, that's the buzz. Hypnosis, but no hard-core drugs."

Cass opens the doughnut box, puts it in the center of the coffee table. My favorite, vanilla crème with powdered sugar, sits right there on top, calling out to me. It'd be rude not to eat it after Cass went to all that trouble.

"Are they coming too?" Cass asks, pointing to her aunts.

"Where we going?" Patty, up for anything, assuming she's included.

"We're following the route you took when you ran away." Cass.

"I can't remember any of it, just showing up on Nana Sheehan's doorstep. The summer of '37."

"Wasn't that a movie?" asks Cassandra.

"No, that was *Summer of '42*." Patty. "An entirely different thing."

"Just after school got out," says Jo. "A hot summer day. All six of us setting out. Sad and scared, but excited, too."

Another of those memories that binds us together, we Sheehan girls, forever. That's when Eden and Alberta press against me, like they've got to certify the memory. In my living room, the twins sit facing Cass and me, all of us with traces of sugar sprinkles, flecks of jelly, on our chins and chests.

"You remember Flanna and her tea?" asks Patty.

"No." When I try, and I try hard as I can, my mind goes dark. Lights out, nobody home.

"It had to be just so, just sweet enough and hot enough, or there'd be hell to pay." Jo and Patty nod together, like it's a story they've told a million times. Al and Eden embrace me now, like they want to hold me up.

"Hot afternoon, nothing to do," I say, the black spot slowly dissolving. All of us in the kitchen, with its big black coal-burning stove. Flanna, the queen of her domain, holding Keeley on her lap—two pink-cheeked beauties, mother and daughter.

"Flanna demands to be served her tea." Patty. "She doesn't care how hot it is outside. She wants her hot tea and she wants it now."

"Alberta makes her tea," I say. "Right?" Slowly, encouraged by my dearly departeds, it's all coming back to me. "She puts the loose leaves in Flanna's tea steeper and we knew, all of us, that if she could have, Alberta would have poisoned it."

"Instead she makes it scalding hot," continues Patty, the historian. "We're watching because we know Alberta's up to something. Alberta sets the teacup in its saucer next to Flanna, as nice as could be, but before she's cooled it down."

"Flanna took one sip and threw it, cup and all." I feel triumphant as the scene unfolds before me, like a drama on *Hallmark Hall of Fame*. "Alberta screamed."

"Flanna dropped Keeley and charged after Al." Patty pauses. "Poor Alberta. She always bore that scar on her chest."

"Like a stain." It never went away, a shadow always over her breast. "'Just as well,' she used to say. She used to joke that, without it, she could've made her living as a stripper, but who'd pay to look at that?"

"She said that?" Cass. "Auntie Alberta?"

"She was only kidding," says Jo.

"Alberta was a card, a hot ticket. That's what the fellas used to call her over at the shipyard."

"She howled like a trapped beast when Flanna threw the tea at her, though." Jo. "Then Flanna chased her down and smacked her."

"Da came home." I remember now. "Al tried to show him, but he wouldn't look. He shook his head, like a little boy, and took off again." A recovered memory. Da refusing to help. Running away.

"He left you with her?" asks Cassandra. We nod yes, me feeling again the pain of Da's betrayal, as fresh as the crocuses pushing up through the snow outside and sharper than a spade.

"He left us with her."

"After that, Flanna gave Alberta a royal beating." Patty.

I couldn't see the beating, only hear it. Those sounds convinced me of what I had to do.

"But the story didn't end there." Jo smiles, her halo glowing.

"That's where you came in, Mimi," says Patty. "After Flanna beat Alberta, she went upstairs for a nap, still wailing about her burned tongue. She took Keeley with her, but the minute Flanna was asleep, Keeley ran downstairs to us. Then you got us organized."

"'Gather a few things,' you told each of us." Jo. "'Shoes, a change of underpants. We put everything in pillowcases.'"

"We waited to be sure she was sound asleep," I say. "Then the six of us took off." Sitting in my living room, stuffed with vanilla crème and honey-glazed doughnuts, I see us, in pairs, creeping out the back door. And for the first time, I also see or understand that I was making a choice that day, a choice to stay with Da and Flanna or to go. It was a choice that rippled through our lives, all of them. If Da was going to run away, then we could too.

As Alberta sat there trembling from her burn and beating, I grew certain she'd be next. The next Sheehan sister to be sent away to Cullyhanna, to learn how to be good. I could not let that happen. We had to run away. We'd be leaving Da, I knew that, knew that we'd be leaving him, the center of our universe—my universe—but he'd just turned his back on Alberta when she was in pain, hurt yet again by Flanna Flanagan. So we left, Eden holding on to Alberta, carrying her things.

"You two were bawling your eyes out." I see the twins as frightened children, jabbering and weeping. "I told you to cut it out so you wouldn't wake her up."

"You said we weren't allowed to cry til we got to Nana Sheehan's." Jo. "Then we could cry all we wanted to."

"You carried Keeley, piggyback."

"We were leaving Da that day," I say. "We were leaving him for good."

"The father you loved was already gone," Cass cuts in.

"No, he wasn't," corrects Patty. "The father we loved was the same one who left us with Flanna. Let her hurt us."

Everything is quiet for a while, all of us thinking about that hot afternoon in Quincy when our family fell apart once and for all.

"How blessed we were to have Nana in our lives," I say. To know that she would take us in, no questions asked. That we'd be welcome in her home.

Now Patty tosses Cassandra the *piseog*.

"Check it out," she says. "The *piseog*."

"That hair, that wonderful hair," Cass whispers, fingering Fagan's locks, the color of flame.

While Cass is examining Fagan's hair, I finally see my chance to escape and grab it. "Let me hop into the shower."

I use the word "hop" very loosely.

Thirty-two

THE BEST IS YET
TO COME

*a*fter my shower, I put on the nice workout clothes Cass bought for me, though I've got no plans to exercise—not on the treadmill, anyway. When I'm done, the three of them are still sitting around my coffee table, eating doughnuts, drinking coffee, and jabbering about memories—repressed and otherwise—hypnosis, and *piseogs*. Everything is moving just a bit too fast.

"Where'd you get this?" Jo and Patty ask together, holding up the photo Keeley sent. I'd left it on the coffee table.

"From Keeley." Cass answers for me when she sees I've stuffed another honey glazed into my mouth. "See the return address? But where did Keeley get it?"

I take Keeley's note from the envelope. They take turns reading it. " 'Our family minus me,' " reads Patty, then she goes back to the picture.

"Your parents were so young, so good-looking," says Cass.

"Your grandparents." She nods. "And every one of us in the picture clueless about what the future held." Fagan picking her nose. Our mother, as if her entire life's ahead of her instead of just a few more months. Da so proud of his girls.

I pick up the phone, speed-dial Keeley's work number. She picks up, sounding elegant and efficient. "Thanks for that photograph, Keeley. It's beautiful." I tell her the twins and Cass are with me, looking at it. They holler their hellos.

"It's hard, so hard for me," Keeley says, and I turn away from the others.

"Why, Keel?"

"Because I'm not in the picture and never knew our mother. Because my birth caused it all."

"No, it didn't. Get that thought out of your head."

"Aidan's genealogy has really done a number on me."

"I hear you. That's why I've always hated ancient history, the blighted family tree."

"Honestly, I'd never thought much about our real mother dying a few hours after I was born. Flanna was my mother. And then, of course, she, too, was gone."

"Your mother? Perish the thought."

"No, I never knew our mother. Or Fagan. She was gone by the time I showed up. And when I think about Da, I only remember him bringing us treats, and spoiling me. You girls spoiled me too."

"Spoiled?" I hate that word. "We never ever spoiled you, Keeley. Spoiled means rotten and self-centered. You've never been either of those things."

"No, spoiled," she insists, "because I never understood anything. I don't remember anything bad. Everybody loved me. I lived in a fog."

"You weren't spoiled, baby, you were protected. What's wrong with that? You've turned out kind and thoughtful, Keeley. You've got a great husband, a successful career, two homes, and those beautiful dogs. My daughters love you." Probably more than me, I'm thinking, but I don't add this part. Cassandra grabs the phone.

"When were you born?" she asks, knowing darn well the answer. February 11, 1933.

"Well, then you are in the picture," says Cass. "It was taken in August 1932. You were there, right where you were supposed to be, in your mother's belly, gestating away." Leave it to Cassandra to do the math.

I grab the phone back. Keeley's making a funny sound, laughing or crying, I can't tell.

"Cassie's right, Keeley. You're in the picture. Our mother would have been three months pregnant. So all of us are there, together." The funny noises get louder.

"Thank God I've got a private office," she says.

"Oh, Keeley," I say, "I'll get some copies made."

The twins take the phone from me. I catch my breath, but then Cass pulls me down beside her on the couch.

"The memories you've recovered so far explain so much."

"Recovered memories? Explain so much?" I'm thinking, More of Cassandra's blah-blah, but then I realize with a pang she might be right: the recovered memories seem to be pushing out the false ones, me remembering things the way they didn't happen.

"You've finally found the courage to let them come up into the light," she says.

"Courage?" I say loud it enough that the others turn around. I didn't hear them hang up. "Courage has nothing to do with it."

"Does too," says Patty the potentate. "You had more than Daddy did."

"What do you mean?"

"Some men rise to the occasion, whatever the occasion is, and some men fall below it."

Jo nods. "Our father, who art in heaven, did not rise to the occasion."

"What occasion?" Cassandra interrupts.

"His life, our lives," I say, seeing the sad truth of it. "Our father fell below the occasion of his own life."

"Which doesn't mean we loved him any less." Jo.

"No, we didn't love him any less."

All four of us look at the photo, Cass running her French-manicured fingertip over the ancient image of Da's face. Next to him, untouched, our mother, a woman we never got a chance to know and not one of us remembers. Our mother, lost to us forever. Our father, Da, despite his best efforts, unable to be the father I'm sure he longed to be. Pulled too hard, in too many directions, as if on a rack of his own making, and right there in the village square for everyone to see.

Again it comes to me, that image of my da, unshaven, his eyes bloodshot, the crusted cut across one cheek. Fallen, *a beast upon all fours*, in that familiar place I can't quite recognize, one of earth and stones. When did I see him like that?

"Keeley says you saved her life." Jo.

"That's what she just said." Patty.

"When we ran away." Jo. "You saved her life."

That hot summer day, the six of us setting out barefoot, pillowcases holding our few belongings, then showing up at Nana Sheehan's, not far from the Fore River Bridge. Nana's house, with its smells of baking bread and flowers. It wasn't Keeley's but Alberta's life I was trying to save.

The four of us, plus the ghosts of Eden and Alberta, head out in Cassie's Bimmer, back through Quincy, onto Route 3A, to see where the old house used to be on 27 Sea Street. Taken by the Commonwealth of Massachusetts and demolished in the late 1950s or early '60s. No trace of the old neighborhood, just a big loop of asphalt three lanes across, marked with guardrails, reflectors, and tall steel poles for the mercury vapor lights. Even though bits and pieces of our journey have come back to me, I still want to see it, the tiny patch of earth on which our home had stood, and my departed sisters urge me on.

"Pull over," I order Cass when we reach the spot where I think our house might have been. There's a breakdown lane just wide enough for a car if she pulls up against the guardrail.

"It's dangerous."

"Pull over anyway." She does, putting on her emergency lights. I get out. My sisters, both dead and living, join me. Soon Cassandra does too, the four of us, or the six—depending upon how you count—staring over the guardrail into the valley of dead grass. Styrofoam cups, shreds of the *Globe* and the *Ledger*, beer cans, broken bottles, a sneaker, a Filene's bag, a CVS sales flyer, a golden crown from Burger King. Not one damned thing of us. History wiped out. I can't tell where anything would have been, not the house itself, not Flanna's gardens, the foundation, or even a trace of that old coal cellar. I'd hoped to get a glimpse of Fagan dancing in the kitchen, or Flanna by the burn can, but all I see is this bowl of grass, filled with litter, a million motor vehicles speeding past it night and day.

"Seen enough?" Cass asks, not meanly, just wondering. I nod. Not one of my other sisters speaks. For all we know, Flanna made out like a bandit, getting paid the house's full market value just to leave so they could bring in the wrecker's ball. Maybe Flanna went back to the old country with her satchel full of money, back to Cullyhanna, County Armagh. But I wouldn't know. Because even though 27 Sea Street was just one town over, only a few miles from Nana's, it might as well have been on the far side of the moon.

Nana herself never brought it up, except to mutter that Flanna took the house and all inside it. We never heard the other grown-ups talking. Not a word about our father, our stepmother, our little sister. After we ran away to Nana's house we started our lives over, just the way Nana had when she came to America. That's what she taught us, how to leave things behind, how to start again—how to look ahead, not back. A lesson that made life possible for me.

We get back into Cassandra's Bimmer, the traffic pushing us forward, everything outside the car a blur. Now Cassandra, directed by Patty, exits the highway near Quincy Point and drives along the narrow streets of double-deckers and small cottages, just a few blocks from the water, and when the wind is right, the residents get that fresh salty smell. But when the tide is out, the air is filled with another type of smell, nowhere near as invigorating.

Our old neighborhood is gone, but the adjacent neighborhood remains, crammed up against the highway. The streets twist and turn. Started out as cow paths, never intended for use by SUVs. The houses still huddle close together, the way they always have. All that's changed in the years since we grew up are the cars—lots more cars—and of course more power lines and satellite dishes on the rooftops. Many of the houses have added upper floors and roof decks to give them views of the water.

"The whole neighborhood used to be full of shipyard workers." Jo. "Riveters, lofts men, welders."

"I couldn't stand living like this, the houses so close together," Cass complains. "Everybody in your business."

"These houses were built back when people still needed one another," says Jo. "They didn't mind if your kids and pets ran through their yards. They didn't have cars, so they didn't need driveways or garages."

In Cassie's luxury sedan, comfy as could be, we make our way through the old streets, then turn back onto Route 3A. We see the same ugly stretch of road connecting Quincy to Weymouth, a mess of bars, boatyards, banks, dollar stores, nail salons, and fast-food joints. When we were growing up, there was hardly any traffic, and just a grocery and the bakery.

Now, just ahead, is the Fore River Bridge, a steel truss drawbridge. Almost brand-new the summer we ran away, one of the wonders of the world when we were growing up. Every ship built at the Quincy yard had to pass beneath it to make its way out to sea.

"Eden was terrified of the bridge," says Jo. "Afraid every step of the way that it was going to open." I feel her fluttering, jostling Alberta, glad that her fear is being remembered.

"I've always had dreams, no, nightmares, about that. Still do," says Patty. "The bridge opening, while we're walking across it. We're just about in the center when it swings open like a book, and the six of us go flying."

I see us hurrying on foot across the bridge, then plunging toward the water after the bridge opens to let a big ship through.

"I never see where we land."

Thirty-three

SWINGIN' ON A STAR

inutes later, less than four miles from where our old house used to be, we pull up in front of Nana's, or what once was Nana's, a bungalow a couple of blocks from the water. Part of a row, all with front porches and postage-stamp lawns. We park across the street.

"Craftsman cottages," says Cass. "Worth maybe four hundred thousand today if they've got the original woodwork."

"When Nana lived here, she had the most beautiful gardens," Jo says. "Her kitchen garden was right here on this busy street."

"Of course, it wasn't all that busy back then." Patty.

"A young family must be living there now." Jo points to a swing set and a little yellow playhouse.

We get out. It's just after noon and the street is quiet. Down the block, a mailman with a big leather sack walks from house to house. A mother pushes her baby in a stroller.

"I can't say that Nana was glad to see us," says Patty

"No, she didn't smile or hug us, but she opened her door and let us in." Jo.

"Maybe she expected us." Me.

That day we showed up on her doorstep, she brought us in and fed us soup and toast and butter, which we were glad to have despite the heat. She looked at Alberta's burn, swollen and bubbled, then sent me and Eden around the corner to the doctor's—the same doctor who'd set my broken wrist a lifetime before. Later that evening, he came to tend to Alberta, and to give her something for the pain. Afterward, Nana made each of us scrub our feet in a tub of water on the kitchen floor. She gave us ointment to put on our blisters, and a clean pair of socks for each of us to wear so our blisters wouldn't get infected. Then she sent us up to bed.

Nana, Annie Sheehan, widowed for as long as any of us could remember, was a tiny woman, with pure-white hair rolled into a knot. She had sharp blue eyes, cold and lovely, and thin lips that were almost always pressed tightly together. She had a clean, pressed housedress, flower-printed, for each day of the week, and a work apron hanging on a hook by the soapstone kitchen sink. Nana, with hardly any accent, because she'd struggled so hard to become American.

Nana couldn't waste time talking when she could be working. Hard work was how her family had survived the Hunger and made it to the USA, although they lost too many along the way. Hard work, along with expecting and accepting loss. That's how Nana lived. She never explained the world to us. She figured we'd get it on our own.

We shared two bedrooms, one in front and one in back, with chenille bedspreads in pretty designs, and green pull shades at the windows. These rooms seemed to be ready for us. Nana slept in a small room downstairs, and on the front porch during the summer. That night, for the first time in ages, I slept through the night, knowing nothing bad would happen.

Suddenly Patty rushes across the street, like she's being dragged or chased. Doesn't even bother to look both ways.

"What's gotten into you?" shouts Jo, chasing after her. Cass and I follow, running too.

We run straight down the driveway to the edge of the garage, where Nana's compost pile used to be. Scraggly grass. Dead leaves left over from the fall. A crocus or two pushing through, all that might be left from Nana's garden. We're trespassing, and I'm really hoping no one's home. I'd be so embarrassed.

"The night before Da died, I saw a banshee in the yard," announces Patty. "In this yard. Right here."

"A banshee?"

"A banshee with streaming white hair. She wailed in the most awful way. Jo woke up too."

Patty herself has gone white.

"Recovered memory," says Cass, taking out a notebook and a pen so she can get it down in writing.

"I heard the wailing," says Jo, "but I didn't see the banshee. By the time I got to the window, she was gone." The twins look at each other, identical expressions on their faces.

"We were so scared." Patty.

"What exactly is a banshee?" Cassandra asks.

"A female spirit." Patty.

"Whose wailing foretells a death in the family." Jo.

"We jumped back into bed and pulled the covers up." Patty.

"The wailing only lasted for a few minutes." Jo. "Then we both went back to sleep."

"And sure enough, the next day, Da was dead." Patty.

As we look around Nana's yard, Eden and Alberta press close, and I swear Fagan shows up too—fierce, feisty Fagan. The story of the banshee washes over me, and I see Da prostrate, his clothes filthy. In agony or maybe just drunk, in that place of earth and stones. Something hard ricochets in my chest. Da. *A beast upon all fours.*

"Take me home, please." Suddenly I'm out of gas, right there at the end of the driveway of what used to be Nana's house, a house that's hardly recognizable anymore.

"Take me home now." Cass gives me a look, like she's about to argue, but changes her mind. She puts away her pen and notebook, takes my arm, and walks me back across the street to the Bimmer. The others follow.

"Call me Greta Garbo," I say once we're all belted in. "I vant to be alone."

I feel full and empty at the same time, everything I'm learning, everything I'm remembering and thinking—memories, either false or recovered—are spinning, like a load of laundry on its final cycle.

Thirty-four

WE JUST COULDN'T
SAY GOODBYE

What I want more than anything right now is to sit by myself and think. Too much is happening, and too fast, after nothing at all for so many years. It's like that feeling I got when I went to Ruthie's, looking out the window, the train moving forward as it pulled out of the station, but everything around me seemed to be sliding in reverse. I pick up the phone, call Siobhan, leave a message, tell her that I want to see her soon. Oh, and that I love her, which is still easier to say into the machine than to her face. Then I call Ruth Ann, Celestine, and Delilah, just to say hello, trying not to feel my grudges, duct tape wound tightly around my heart. We exchange pleasantries, which we've never done before. What's doing, how's work, how are the kids, etc., and "I love you," before hanging up.

I'm still jittery from the phone calls, my sciatica in excruciating mode, when Duffy tap, tap, taps on my door. Who else would it be? So much for my downtime. So much for my chance to think.

"Mrs. Malloy, oh, Mrs. Malloy!" His voice is edgier than usual, some shard of pain in it.

"Mrs. Malloy?" he calls again, sharper, a question.

Suddenly I'm full of dread. We finally make whoopee and now he wants to dump me. Just my luck. I put out and get put in the trash. On my coffee table, within reach, is the photo of my family, my mother's hankie, the lock of Fagan's hair. I'd like to trash them, too.

"Mrs. Malloy," he says one more time, and then I hear the key turning in the lock. Himself is letting himself in. The nerve. Of course, or maybe curse, he's got the master key.

"I'm here, I'm here," I call, but I can't crank up the volume. My voice stuck on low. And furthermore, I'm stuck in the recliner, and I'll be damned if I'll let him see me hobbling around.

But once he starts walking toward me, I see the look on that old face—weathered like the masthead of an old ship, but looking better with age—and I read the worry and sorrow in his eyes, the fear that I wouldn't answer, or maybe that something bad had happened to me.

"I saw you come in," he says. "I knew you were here. When you didn't answer, I . . . I . . . I . . ."

He's at a loss for words. An old Irishman at a loss for words. That's got to be a first.

I move the recliner to its upright position. If only I had that kind where you pull the lever and it ejects you from the seat. Ed McMahon advertises them on TV.

"Duff. Oh, Duff."

"Mimi," he answers, and I'm stunned. Mimi. Such a beautiful little word. "You OK?"

I can tell by his dazzling eyes, focused so steadily on me, how much he wants me to be OK. So I tell him, sure, sure, I'm fine, even though I'm feeling like a nut case, strange feelings storming around inside my skull, my sciatica riled up, plus me loving him way too much.

He sits down at the edge of the couch without me asking him to. He's got something to say, but now I'm pretty sure he isn't going to dump me.

"I'll mix us a Manhattan," I say. Without thinking, I stand up and let out a yelp, cringing from the pain. If only the floor would open up to swallow me. Instead, Duffy grabs my arm.

"Poor Mimi," he murmurs, reseating me gently onto the couch

beside him, like I'm a combat vet, enfeebled by an old war wound. "Tell me where the whiskey is."

Duff gets up and goes into the kitchen. He's not exactly limping, just that list from his old wound, but he's moving slowly; stooped, maybe, from the weight of what he's said, or possibly from our roll in the hay. I watch him, thinking of the two of us together, of his son in that awful other place. I remember, vaguely, Cass and Delilah gabbing about the case when he went to trial, how terrible it was; this karate instructor, an Army veteran with a girlfriend, you couldn't trust anyone anymore. But I didn't pay much attention, and never made the connections. Minutes later, Duffy's back with our drinks, straight-up, in those glasses that are so hard to hold if your hand is shaking, even a little bit. I don't think mine is until I see the amber liquid slosh.

After a few swallows, my sciatica settles down. I sip my Manhattan, my hand less shaky now.

Duffy lights up, but I pass. No desire for a smoke. Instead, I make us breakfast for dinner, one of my favorites. Eggs, bacon, toast, and home fries.

"Do you like 'em straight-up or over-easy?" I ask from the kitchen, where I'm cracking eggs and stretching the strips of bacon neatly into the pan. Just enough to satisfy, but not enough to clog our arteries.

"Over-easy, Mrs. Malloy," Duffy says from the living room, his voice sweet and warm as syrup. "Over-easy every time." I'm glad he can't see me blush. He'd think I have a dirty mind.

The next day, Duffy and I run errands—the bank, post office, Stop & Shop. Each of us picks up a few things, coffee, English muffins, the usual. We don't talk much. No need. He's the type of guy who doesn't mind a little silence, which is exactly what I need right now, plus some Advil for the pain. Peace and quiet. He's what we used to call the strong, silent type. But whenever he looks at me now, ever since our trip to Bridgewater, plus our trip to, well, anyway . . . Since then, his eyes, the color of deep salt water—the color of the Atlantic—are fully lighted in a way that makes me glad. Gladness, a new feeling at my age.

When we're done with our errands, Duffy suggests the Squantum Diner for a quick bite. All morning I've felt Duffy's sorrow, plus the presence of his incarcerated son, Christopher, who's with us now, like all of my dearly departeds. A regular entourage. While I down a turkey club and he polishes off the Hungry Man Special—eggs and pancakes and hash browns and three types of grilled meat—Duffy gives me a lesson on wrongful convictions.

"Wrongful conviction?" It's still hard to believe everything that's happened to his son.

"Happens more often than you'd think," he tells me, "the main reasons being inadequate defense, prosecutorial misconduct, eyewitness misidentification, and false confessions."

"What about false memories?" I ask. "Isn't that a big reason?"

"Well, the false memories come under prosecutorial misconduct. In cases of alleged child abuse. Mostly because kids are easy to manipulate, easy to convince that something happened when it didn't."

I order coffee and sip it while he tells me that this advocacy organization, Justice for the Wrongfully Convicted, is convinced of Chris's innocence. With its help, and the help of law students from Boston University, his lawyer has been developing his appeal on the basis of prosecutorial misconduct, and he thinks they've got a better than even shot of winning.

"Wow," I say, considering that the original prosecutor is now our attorney general. *Good luck to them and the Red Sox*, I'm about to add, when I remember my commitment to believe in him. Still, I struggle to understand.

"From the start it was a bad case," he says. "No DNA. Nothing except the testimony of these kids, two of them sons of the cop whose wife Chris messed around with. They actually started off with six kids, but the others insisted Chris had never done anything inappropriate, and the prosecutors dropped them from the case."

"Dirty business," I say. Can't help it, but Duffy doesn't disagree.

"Chris was thirty at the time, still immature, still sowing his wild oats."

"Bad judgment."

"Terrible, the worst," says Duffy, nodding, agreeing, not angry at all. "But he doesn't deserve incarceration, or to have his name in the state's official registry of sex offenders for the rest of his life."

"An appeal based on prosecutorial misconduct," I say, just to try it out.

Then Duffy lists all the things that the prosecution had done wrong. He's memorized them: the missing first recordings of the so-called victim interviews; the trial transcripts demonstrating the children's identical testimony; the lack of any physical evidence—no injuries to the children, no signs that sexual abuse occurred—plus the results of the brain tests showing Chris's reaction to the pornography.

"Lastly," he says, "they'll subpoena the cop's wife. She'll have to testify under oath."

"A hot mess," I say.

"Doesn't get much hotter or much messier," he answers, "but I'm in it for the long haul. What else can I do?"

"We have to follow them, don't we, go to the places our children take us, even if we don't want to go there."

He nods and takes my hand, his eyes brighter, his cheeks pinker than before. And I realize looking at him that Duffy is a father who has risen to the occasion. He's stepped up for his son. What else can you ask for in a man?

We finish up in silence. Duffy lights up and offers one to me. I shake my head no. He raises his eyebrows.

"You quitting?"

"Trying. Doctor's orders."

"I quit for more than twenty years," says Duffy, taking a last deep drag, then stubbing out his half-smoked cigarette. "Then Chris got into this mess. Within a few days I was lighting up like I'd never stopped."

"Want to try again?"

He shrugs, like it's a no-brainer, no answer necessary.

"We'll try together."

"You bet."

Duffy pays the bill. As we get up to leave he asks, "Anything else you'd like to do, Mrs. Malloy? Your wish is my command." His eyes twinkle and a sweet smile tugs at his lips. He feels better now. He needed to talk and I needed to listen. "The rest of my day is yours."

"Bowling," I tell him. "Let's go bowling. I haven't been in ages."

So we head over to the Colonial Lanes, where the Angel Babies used to play. Waste the afternoon laughing at each other, a regular laugh riot. Turns out we get a senior discount for playing on a Tuesday afternoon. He ties my shoes, and I tie his, and we make the biggest deal picking out our balls. I have trouble finding one light enough for me to handle. Not that it matters. Most of my balls end up rolling into the gutter, and every time he's up, Duffy has to do a funny little hop to make up for his bad leg. I laugh, and he exaggerates a bit, just to entertain me. Duffy, with his bum leg and big heart.

"I've really lost my touch," I say whenever my ball rolls into the gutter. "I really held my own back when I was with the Angel Babies," I tell him, and he insists he never had one to begin with.

"Nope, bowling's never been my game," he says. "I prefer other indoor sports. I'm a little better at them."

I'm probably supposed to ask which indoor sports, but I don't. "I should hope so," I say instead, and he throws his head back, laughing. I don't bother to look at him. Instead I take another turn, and again, halfway down the lane, my ball slides into the gutter. Duffy applauds and I take a little bow. Pretty soon, we give up keeping score. No point. Instead, we keep slamming the big balls down that gleaming alley, clapping when we knock down a pin or two, laughing our heads off when we don't. Lucky for us, the place is almost empty. Otherwise we'd have gotten dirty looks.

Thirty-five

CALL ME
IRRESPONSIBLE

*N*obody has ever accused me of being deep—quite the opposite, in fact—and that's always been fine by me. Never claimed to be a deep thinker. I leave the profundities to Jack and my daughters. If it looks good, it probably is good, that's my philosophy, always has been. Celestine, my third, the copyeditor who lives in Philadelphia, once said I'm as deep as Formica. Me, Mimi, deep as Formica. I happen to love Formica, how durable it is, how easy it is to keep clean, plus all the pretty colors. I took it as a compliment until Ruthie clued me in. "A laminate. No depth, get it?"

This story always gets a big laugh from my daughters, and no doubt from their father, too. But Celestine was right: Mimi Malloy, with her strong and sturdy surface, is tough and made for wear. What you see is what you get. Who cares what's underneath?

But now, with all that's happened, I can't stay on the surface. A laminate won't do. Got to go deeper.

False memory. Recovered memory. The two of them colliding.

As a result of the first, an innocent man is punished. Years in jail, his reputation ruined, for a crime he did not commit. Without a whiff of mercy from his accusers, whose lives have now been ruined too, having been tricked into believing that a horrific thing had happened to them when it hadn't. As a result of the second, we now know who the guilty party is, the witch at the heart of all the trouble in my family, but it's way too late for punishment. That's been meted out to the survivors.

False memory, remembering things that didn't happen. Recovered memory, at last remembering things that did. A banshee in the yard the night before Da died. Cozy in my own bed, alone, holding the blue pendant, I poke around the edges of Patty's recollection, called back to it by the banshee's wail.

It had to have been July 3, 1937. Amelia Earhart, the beautiful, high-flying aviatrix, disappeared over the Pacific on July 2, but we didn't hear about it until the next day, News moved slower then.

AMELIA'S PLANE VANISHES!!! LADY LINDY LOST!

Amelia with her copilot, Fred Something, gone, just like that.

A mistake. We thought it was a terrible mistake. *Amelia Earhart loves to fly. Amelia Earhart will never die.* Keeley and the twins were too young to understand, but Eden, Alberta, and I stumbled around in shock, whispering our rhyme, looking at one another, trying to figure out how to feel.

PACIFIC CLAIMS AMELIA'S PLANE!!! LADY LINDY LOST!

That day was so hot and bright, and all of us had chores to do, no sloth in Nana's house. We made beds, swept floors, hand-washed laundry in Nana's black soapstone sink, then hung it outside on the line. Nana, in the kitchen, peeled potatoes and rolled out pie dough, the RCA Victor radio turned up loud so everyone could hear. And we did, we heard the news all through the house, over and over again while we worked, the harsh twang of the broadcaster's voice: *Amelia Earhart, beautiful and fearless, has disappeared over the Pacific.*

Nana kept two gardens, one for flowers, and one for vegetables. To the side of the flower garden was Nana's shrine to Mary, a statue of the

Virgin, tall enough that I saw eye to eye with her when I was four or five years old. The Virgin, chipped and weather-beaten, yes, but still with her shiny marble eyes, her gold crown and blue robe, the serpent arched beneath her sandaled foot. In Nana's garden, flowers bloomed near Mary from March until November. Crocuses, tulips, hyacinths, and daffodils in the early spring; then peonies, my favorites, and irises, roses, dahlias, gladioli, hydrangeas, and hollyhocks through summer, and at last, in fall, chrysanthemums and marigolds.

In a plot next to the flowers, in careful rows, grew Nana's peas, squash, potatoes, carrots, tomatoes, peppers, corn, and onions. Here I inhaled the smell of the earth, and of the root crops, which I loved pulling out of the ground. Nana counted on her vegetables to survive, but the flowers, the flowers gave her something else: peace, or maybe joy—something she did not, in her silence, get any other way.

Ages before, when he was still in school, Da had built his mother a wooden bench next to the shrine. Most afternoons, during good weather, Nana said her rosary there, her face porcelain, as unchanging as the Virgin's, her lips shaping the words of the Our Fathers, the Hail Marys, but no sound coming out. We knew enough not to interrupt her when she prayed.

When Nana said her daily rosary, we girls had our free time. We played canasta, did jigsaw puzzles, tried out new hairstyles, or sewed ourselves skirts and blouses. Now and then, I slipped outside to watch Nana pray. Her rosary beads were black wood—no frills—shiny as licorice lozenges. Nana kept them in the pocket of her housedress, where she'd finger them throughout the day. Whenever she moved, they clattered. That's how you could tell when Nana was nearby, the soft rattle of her rosary beads.

The day we heard about Amelia Earhart, Nana said her rosary, as usual. She sat on Da's bench, in front of the Virgin, amid the flowers— cosmos, daisies, and gladioli—her head bent, her hands pressed together, the shiny beads twined around her fingers. *Hail Mary, full of grace, the lord is with thee.*

Nana knew all the holy mysteries, the five each for the Joyful, the Glorious, and the Sorrowful, and she knew which set of holy mysteries was correct for each day of the year. Who knows which set was the right one for July 3, 1937, but in my mind, it had to be the Sorrowful, hands-down, and in particular the Agony in the Garden, which Nana prayed over and over again. I watched her for a long time, hanging close to the back door. From time to time, Nana stared up at the bright sky as if she hoped to see Amelia in her plane. But the sky was empty, not even any clouds. Nana prayed and prayed. It was like I was witnessing a transfiguration of some kind, something I couldn't, and didn't, try to explain to my sisters. The Agony in the Garden. But why was Nana crying for Amelia? That's what my nine-year-old mind couldn't figure out.

That night, the six of us went to bed exhausted. No trouble whatsoever falling asleep, despite the awful heat. The next morning we were going to the Independence Day parade, one of the greatest events of the year back then in Weymouth. We couldn't wait.

I fell into a deep, deep sleep. Dreamed Da was calling out to me, calling and calling, *Maire, Maire, Quite Contrary. How does your garden grow?* Deep into my dream. But at some point, loud angry voices, urgent cries, cut through it. I sat up shaking. Da was really there. Yes, he was there calling out to me, and my dreams had spun themselves around his voice. I tiptoed to the top of the stairs to see what was going on. Knew enough to hide.

On the front porch stood Da and Nana. My heart thumped when I saw him. Da, Daddy, he'd come for us. He'd come to take us home. It took everything I had not to run down to him and hug him. But their voices, tones I'd never heard before, held me back. Da and Nana fighting. I crept partway down the stairs to see them better. Crouched against the railing on the landing, out of sight.

I could see Da clearly under the front porch light. My handsome, handsome Da. Cheeks red, eyes bloodshot, an open cut beneath one eye. Hair matted like a bum's. Daddy, who'd always groomed himself to perfection. I wanted to run down the stairs and kiss his cut and tell him I'd make his hurt go away, the way he'd done for me when I was small. But I didn't. I hid on the stairs, my arms around the railings.

I've told you so many times, Joseph Daniel Sheehan, Nana cried, *you*

*want to see those girls, you show up sober. I'm not going to let you see them
when you're drunk.*

Not drunk, Da answered, but his slurred words told the truth. *Just
had a couple to settle my nerves.*

Settle your nerves? You think you're the only one with nerves?

Please, Ma. Please.

You stink, said Nana. *You need a bath and a shave. I won't let your
daughters see you like this. You should be ashamed. Now, get out of here.*

Maire, at least let me see Maire. I have to tell her something.

*Where's your self-respect? Your pride? You, Joey, you, the smartest and
best-looking of them all, and you've turned into a drunk.*

Da tried to push past his mother, but all four feet eleven inches of
Annie Sheehan stood firm in the doorway. Then she shoved him. He
lost his balance, stumbled backward down the steps, sprawled into the
grass. I couldn't tell if he was laughing or crying.

Come back when you're sober, Nana cried. *Then you can talk to her all
you want.* Nana slammed shut the door.

Shaking so hard I thought my joints might snap, I tiptoed through
the still heat of the upstairs, to the room where the younger ones were
sleeping. I looked out their window, hoping I'd see Da stumbling off
down the street. If I had, I might have jumped out the window and run
after him. But Da had disappeared. I got back into bed, hearing their
voices all over again, swirling and shrieking, Da and Nana fighting on
the porch.

Maybe I'd gone back to sleep by the time I heard something against
the window screen. I sat up, hearing it again, and realized it was a
stone.

I hurried to the window in the dark. There was Da, outside in the
yard, a finger by his lips, making a shushing sound.

Oh, Da, Da, I cried.

*You did the right thing, Maire. I'm betting you were the instigator, and
I want you to know you did the right thing, running away.* His hoarse half-
whisper cut through the still air. I started laughing. Couldn't help it.
Da whispering loud enough to wake the dead. Or at least his own
mother.

Sorry isn't good enough, but I'm sorry anyway, he said.

Now I wonder what he meant, what he was sorry for. At the time it didn't matter. Because he seemed to be so close to me, close enough that I could feel the warmth of his breath and smell the whiskey on it. Close enough for me to look into his eyes and see the kind of pain no man should ever have to feel.

Listen to me good, Maire, his whisper echoed through the night. *I'll come back for you and the other girls. OK? You wait. And be good. Not so contrary, huh? I'll be back. Soon as I can figure out how to take care of the bunch of you by myself. No more Flanna, OK? We're done with her.*

I love you, Da, so much. I was about to yell my love down to him, how I would always love him, no matter what, when Nana flew into the yard in her white nightgown, her white hair flowing down her back. *Get out of here, Joe Sheehan!* she shrieked, her words chased by a strange and awful sound, a banshee's wail. *You've already broken my heart. Don't break your daughters', too. Come back when you're clean and sober.*

I left the window, crawled back into bed. Couldn't bear to see them out there fighting in the yard, Da and Nana, near her shrine to the Virgin and the bench he'd built for her to pray on. But I only stayed in bed a minute. Nana's cry, a needle in the marrow, yanked me back to the window. When I looked out I saw Nana running around the yard, her arms outstretched like she'd gone mad. She wailed, reaching for the sky, her white hair streaming. Danced a wild dance, then fell to her knees before the statue of the Virgin. She prayed, her palms pressed hard together, then reaching up, up, up. Da, our father, was no more than a shape, a shadow prostrate by the compost heap, near the garden shed and Nana's plow. *A beast upon all fours.*

I got back into the bed with my sleeping sisters, Eden and Alberta. Didn't wake them. Didn't tell them what I'd seen. Put the pillow over my head, but still I heard the banshee's wail, Nana's cry.

Thirty-six

DIG DOWN
DEEP

esterday, I woke up thinking about Geraldo Rivera. That fool Geraldo, of all people, and all that hoopla a few years back, about the mystery of Al Capone's vault. There was all kinds of hype about this vault discovered under Al Capone's house in Chicago, locked up since Prohibition, and all the skeletons he must have hidden there. And Geraldo was going to open it, live on national TV.

We couldn't wait to see what was inside, my sisters and me. Of course, the bones of Al Capone's victims, those he'd had whacked, plus bags of cash and documents confirming ancient crimes. We gathered at Patty's place to watch, with her kids, and Jo's, and a couple of mine. She made popcorn, buckets of it to have enough to go around. But when Geraldo finally got the damned thing open, the only thing inside was an empty Four Roses bottle. Oh, and some dust bunnies. It doesn't get much funnier than that. We Sheehan sisters loved it. Laughed for days over that big-shot Geraldo, and Al Capone's empty vault.

So I woke up thinking about Geraldo, but saw, superimposed over Al Capone's vault, the furnace of our old house in Quincy. The image is black-and-white, blurred at the edges, exactly as the cellar used to be, unlighted, shadowy, cobwebs hanging everywhere; the coal bin and the big black furnace taking up most of the space; smells of soot and ash. Again, I see the bucket, the shovel, the poker, propped against the wall by the coal bin. Flanna opening the furnace door, flames exploding outward, enough to silence all of us. All of us except Fagan.

These images came to me after I dreamed of falling a great distance—falling precipitously, unexpectedly—the way my grandfather fell off the scaffolding on a ship oh so long ago, leaving Nana widowed and alone. A terrible fall, a fall of many stories, because some fool had left a coiled rope on the pathway to the riveters. A great fall that, for my grandfather, ended in his death.

After my grandfather's fall came my father's, right there in the street, at the July Fourth parade. Me, witnessing those falls, experiencing those falls, a sensation of falling and falling with no place to land.

I thought about Amelia falling from the sky, *Amelia Earhart loves to fly*. Lady Lindy Lost. A fall that captured the world's attention the way Flanna captured Da's and changed all of our lives.

Eden and Alberta, falling through their lives, forever stumbling and falling, picking themselves back up, but only for a while, never quite getting their footing. Then, too, Alberta's son, falling, dying alone on the sidewalk in Brockton, an event that brought Alberta down for good. That time when she fell she couldn't get back up.

Finally, those rebel angels, falling out of heaven, falling and falling from a place even higher than Amelia, falling and falling, stopping wherever they happened to be because God the Father stopped to think. Landing in Flanna's world where she could see them, hear them, believed she could outsmart them.

Our fear of falling, falling through the open drawbridge when we ran away. At last, my own falls, first down the stairs when I broke my wrist and Da helped me get it fixed; again when Flanna pushed me down into the cellar; and, last, a fall from grace, fast and straight down—*ashes, ashes, we all fall down*. A real memory pasted over with the false ones of Fagan Sent Away.

I woke up in my own sweet bed, in Duffy's arms, with all that falling on my mind and in my heart. But I also woke up with a feeling of elation, the hope that I, Mimi Malloy, might get another shot. The minute Duff went on his way, I called Siobhan, and I told her to do what she does best, brain that she is, and she told me that she would. ASAP. No questions asked. After that, I only had to wait.

Today, we're heading back to Weymouth in a little caravan, and this time I'm going to keep my act together. Maybe I'll come up empty, like Geraldo, looking like a fool, the way he did, not on national TV but in front of my sisters and my daughters. But I'm pretty sure I've solved the ancient mystery in the middle of our lives, what really happened before Fagan Sent Away, before Keeley showed up on our doorstep walking and talking like a Chatty Cathy doll. I won't know for sure until we get there. And it's worth the risk of looking like a fool.

I'm in the lead, me in my trusty Shadow with Siobhan beside me, the two of us in our pretty sweaters. Keeley follows in her Avalon, with the twins, Jo and Patty. I invited Ruthie, but she said no—too busy, too much to do to make the trip. But Cass and Del will join us in a few—in the Bimmer, natch. They'll meet us at the beach around the corner from Nana's house, what we used to call Nana's Beach. After that, we'll go back to the house, and I'll say everything I've got to say. Whatever that is. I'll know when we get there.

Over the bridge to Nana's house, like when we ran away, except everything is different now. The bridge is short and narrow, steep in the middle. The middle stretch is steel mesh, the water visible below. When you drive over it, this surface makes a high-pitched hum, a keening sound, like women wailing for the dead. The only time I ever walked it was the day we ran away. Once was enough. Today I put the pedal to the metal. Less time for those wailing women.

These days, the bridge hardly ever opens. No more big ships gliding out from the yard, only an occasional tanker down from Canada or other points north. Still, there's a bridge tender who gives plenty of warning, whistles and blinking red lights and such when the bridge is about to open. When it does, you're stuck there swaying on the open bridge for however long it takes for the ship to pass. To avoid that situation, you can check for scheduled openings in the newspaper or on the radio. I always do. None are scheduled for this morning.

Yes, today's gorgeous, a reminder that winter's over, spring is here, and summer's just around the corner. Like Nana's Beach is just around the corner from her house. Not much of a beach, really, compared to others nearby, developed beaches like Wessagusset, Wollaston, and Nantasket. It's small, well off the beaten path—down a winding gravel road, with no facilities, and used only by the few neighbors who live nearby. They're the only folks who know the beach is there. When we lived at Nana's, we would walk to it, and swim in old clothes because we didn't own bathing suits. Back then, during the war, it didn't matter because nobody else did either.

After I married Jack and we moved into our new house on the bluff just above it, we swam there again, but in bathing suits this time, Jack always wanting us to look our best, to show off our prosperity to the world. I took the girls down every day when the tide was in. We still called it Nana's Beach.

I park at the end of the little lane, careful not to go too far and get stuck in the sand or mud flats. Keeley pulls in next to us, and all of us get out. Nobody asks me what we're up to. For once, the Sheehan sisters and their nieces are silent. Mum's the word. We walk the few steps toward the water. It's blue and calm, the tide low, the water's edge clumped with debris, the high tide line a snake of seaweed, driftwood, Styrofoam packaging, tampon casings, beer cans. I have an urge to grab a bucket and start cleaning it up. If I had one, I would. From here, we can see, way across the water, the backside of the shipyard—a rusted hulk that ought to be torn down, all traces of it carted off.

Every spring, way back when, Jack organized the other men in the neighborhood and they spent a weekend or two cleaning up the beach, raking up the driftwood and sea glass and clumps of tar from the shipyard. Jack always got the town to carry the trash away and bring in a few truckloads of white sand for the water's edge. Our own, mostly private, white-sand beach. My girls loved playing in the sand, the water, the smelly mud flats when the tide was out. That's when we'd dig for clams and I'd make Jack a nice rich chowder for his dinner.

Now Jo and Patty point upward, toward the bluff. A wooden staircase, recently constructed, zigzags up the side of it not far from where we stand. Our old house sits on top, all those windows still shining out toward the water, just the way they used to.

"Your first house," they chime together. The house Jack built for me, I think, and me the maiden all forlorn. We laid the hardwood floors ourselves, Jack and I. We painted all the rooms. So happy then, building our own world.

Its cedar shingles have weathered to a lovely brownish gray. The windows are trimmed white, and the shutters are bright blue. A sweet New England cottage with a deck out back for looking at the water, and now the new staircase leading down to it. When we lived there, we had to walk around by way of an unpaved lane to reach the beach. Back then, we couldn't afford to build a staircase. We had to count every penny. Once we could, Jack decided to move.

"It's stood the test of time," I say, feeling a sharp pinprick, but no longer a stabbing pain, looking at this home no longer mine.

"Worth a fortune now," says Patty. "Waterfront and all."

"A small fortune!" yells Cassandra, walking toward us, Delilah following, the pair of them in tight jeans and high heels. Cassandra and Delilah, my oldest and my youngest, wobble toward us through the sand. I focus on Delilah, once my precious baby. She and Siobhan, the blond betrayers. Got to forgive her. Watching her walk toward us, I know that I got stuck on her flaws behind her pretty face, had trouble getting past them. But she's got her own strength and goodness, a sharp mind and a soft heart, even though I haven't always seen it. What I see now is her heart and it's in the right place, beating there inside her chest despite the damage I've done to it, and my promises to myself that I would never, ever hurt my children. We've forgiven each other, Siobhan and I, and now I must forgive Delilah, too, and hope that the forgiveness will be mutual.

Cassandra and Delilah join hands to give each other balance, laughing at themselves as they walk in their ridiculous shoes. I laugh too, can't help it. I laugh and that abiding anger lifts and floats away. Delilah, my baby. Codependent, I think, looking at the two of them holding each other up. Codependent, another of Cassandra's psycho-babble words, but so what? What else are sisters for?

"You're the expert," Patty says to Cassandra once they reach us. Back to real estate. Patty's being sarcastic, but Cass nods, accepting it as a compliment. Because she does consider herself the expert on fortunes, both large and small, and, in a way, she is.

"In the mid–six figures," she says.

"We built it for next to nothing." But my words float away.

The two of them, Cass and Del, look around, as if they've never been here before when, in fact, they spent endless happy hours here as babies and toddlers. Cass curls her lip, shaking her head at the sight of the bedraggled beach, just like she did at Gate of Heaven. I recall the comments she made after I left Jack and moved into my apartment. "You've really come down in the world," she said, my firstborn, who knew darned well what Jack had done with all our assets. "I can't be-lieve how far you've fallen."

"Everything looks so small now," says Siobhan. "Seemed huge when we were growing up."

"I can't believe we actually went into this water," says Delilah, em-phasis on "this." "Must be full of toxins."

"We never worried about any of that." Patty. "We loved it. Every high tide, we dove right in. Had a blast. Never hurt a one of us."

"I remember catching minnows," says Siobhan. "Beautiful little iridescent minnows. I trapped them in a jelly jar."

"When the tide was in on hot nights, Daddy took us down after he got home from work," says Cass. "He took us into the water and tossed us high up into the air. We took turns diving off his hands. We wouldn't stop until we wore him out." My daughters, adoring their fa-ther, just as I'd done mine.

"When you got back, we washed you girls down outside with the garden hose and Ivory soap." Me, seeing my little girls, all six of them, naked, slick with suds, giggling and twirling under the spraying water in the last light of the day.

"Mimi, remember how much Daddy loved you with a tan?" asks Cass. My face is scorched by a sudden sunburn.

"All those babies born in April and May," my sisters say.

"No, Jack couldn't keep his hands off you when you had a tan, could he?" adds Patty, and the three of them chuckle while my daughters look away. Cass just stands there, embarrassed into silence, though she's the one who started it.

"Ruined my skin." I hold out my hands so they can see the wrinkles and age spots on the back of them. "It was my skin, not my brain, that aged prematurely. I went to a dermatologist a few years back. She was horrified. Wanted me to have some kind of abrasion, a chemical peel I couldn't afford. It sounded like torture. I said the hell with it. Love the skin you're in."

Thirty-seven

ALL OR NOTHING
AT ALL

Soon, without any discussion, we begin the easy walk back around to Nana's house—seven of us: me, plus three of my sisters and three of my daughters. Eden and Alberta will catch up soon enough. I keep Siobhan close by me because she helps me feel calm. Siobhan, of all people, the daughter I ignored for many years. Looking at her lovely face, strange and familiar at the same time, I feel substantial. She's my kid, after all. I gave birth to her. She's got a strength and wisdom neither Jack nor I ever had. All those shy years of hers when she was growing up, she must have been thinking, paying attention, taking it all in. Her knowledge changed everything, a halogen light shined into in the blackest black spot in my brain, a light so bright it hurts. Yes, Siobhan was the first among us to imagine that our family's dark history might make some kind of sense. She didn't accept the conventional wisdom, that her mother was just a nut job, someone to put down or ignore. Someone to stash for the duration of her existence in an overpriced storage facility like Squantum River Living.

The bunch of us walk close together, the way we used to do when we were small, when we ran away, and again, when my girls were growing up.

Nana's house is painted yellow now with blue trim. No sign that anyone's home. We cross the street to the end of the driveway, tar macadam where Nana's garden used to be. The front porch where Nana slept on hot nights, and the steps where Da and Nana fought. Glassed-in now, and a big central air-conditioning unit in the ground next to it. At the end of the driveway, the new two-car garage is there in place of her garden shed and compost heap. *Da on his knees in a place of earth and stone.* I feel the ghosts of my dead sisters fluttering around me. Eden and Alberta, they've gotten here just in time.

We're close, ever so close now, standing at the end of the driveway, looking at the scraggly grass, the plastic playhouse, the swing set. My sisters and my daughters reach for me; Eden and Alberta, too. I'm aware, if only dimly, that we're no longer inconspicuous, the bunch of us—the glorious Sheehan girls, plus my daughters, standing in a drive-way where we have no right to be.

I look down the driveway toward the new garage, but instead I see Fagan, ages ago, tap-dancing in her new Mary Janes with the shiny buckles. Shuffle, hop, step; shuffle, hop, step. Then again in her little panties, hand-me-downs sagging in the bottom—droopy drawers, we teased—her flame-red hair cut off into spikes, tears spilling down her cheeks. Fagan, part of the one body in the one bed after our mother died, the sister who has haunted me, stepping out of my dreams, my nightmares. For most of my life, I didn't just confuse Keeley with Fagan. I hid Fagan behind Keeley, because I could not bear to see her. No loss to feel.

Eden, Alberta, and me. Just the three of us, the twins still sleeping in their own bed, but Fagan's place in it is empty. She's not in the closet; not under the bed, places she sometimes hides and where we sometimes find her. We stand, we three, in the dark upstairs hallway holding hands, so alike it's hard to tell where one of us stops and the other one begins. Brave together, nothing when we are apart. *Amelia Earhart loves to fly; Amelia Earhart will never die.*

Not Mammy. We hear Fagan's cry, from a distant planet. *Not Mammy.* We squeeze one another's hands. We've heard this cry so many times before. *Not Mammy.* It echoes and repeats. *Not Mammy.* We hear other things, not with our ears but with our bodies—unnamable things, painful even now. Why couldn't Fagan just go along with the program? I wonder for the umpteenth time. Still don't have an answer.

Ashes, ashes, we all fall down.

"What woke us up that night? Fagan crying? Or Flanna muttering her nonsense? . . ."

"What night?" somebody asks.

"The night before Fagan got sent away. Eden, Alberta, and I got up to look into the other bedroom, but Fagan wasn't there. You two were sound asleep." I point to Jo and Patty. "Da nowhere to be found."

"We hesitated in the upstairs hallway, then, through the registers, heard Flanna mumbling her incantations. And, beneath that, Fagan crying, *'Not Mammy.'* "

"You three went downstairs?" Cassandra prods.

"Only so far. We stopped. We stopped halfway down the cellar stairs. Eden whispered 'Amelia Earhart.' Our rhyme. *Amelia Earhart loves to fly. Amelia Earhart will never die.*"

"But she did, she disappeared without a trace," says Cassandra.

"Like Fagan." Delilah.

I prefer to leave the story there, on the cellar steps, but Eden and Alberta are with me now, the way it used to be; the three of us as one, feeling one another's feelings, knowing one another's thoughts. Plus Fagan, clutching at me with her death grip. She has finally reached me, our stolen child.

"I told Eden and Alberta that we had to save her. We thought we could overcome Flanna. Rescue Fagan. We tiptoed down, a few stairs at a time, holding hands." Siobhan reaches for me and hugs me close. "The smell was awful, something burning but not for heat. So many voices. We thought four or five people must have been down there."

"Faeries," says Siobhan. "The faeries in a pitched battle for Fagan's soul."

Fagan drags me with her. Eden and Alberta, too. This time, there's no way out. I'm triple-teamed, right up to the furnace.

"Flanna was there, in the shadows. The furnace door was open. She held Fagan close to its flaming mouth. Fagan kicked and screamed.

Not Mammy. Not Mammy. Flanna laughed and cried at the same time. Speaking in those tongues, or whatever it was she did at times like that."

Ashes, ashes, we all fall down.

Everything stops. Everyone is quiet, as if we've fallen out of time.

"Flanna killed her?" Cassandra breaks the silence.

"In the cellar. With fire," says Delilah. "Fagan was never sent away."

"What did you do, Mimi?" Cassandra, just a whisper.

"We ran back upstairs. Hid in our bed. Left Fagan there with Flanna." My own great fall, running back upstairs. Maire Sheehan Malloy's fall from grace.

A great uproar—that's what I expected after this revelation, my confession. Instead, moments of agonizing silence pass. Don't they believe me? That's what I begin to wonder. Then, all at once, they rush me, gasping and sobbing, and clasping me and one another. As for me, looking back, I didn't feel anything. I was empty. At eight or nine years old, what could I have felt? Short circuits everywhere. Only ages afterward did I realize that I, Maire Sheehan Malloy, better known as Mimi, was irredeemable, though I was no longer sure why.

"The next day or the day after, Da told us Fagan had been sent away. To Cullyhanna, County Armagh. What a relief!" I shake my head, laughing at the memory of it. "He'd rescued Fagan and sent her to where she would be safe. We didn't have to worry anymore."

"But why are we here?" Delilah points at Nana's house. "Why did you bring us here?"

"Fagan's buried here," Siobhan answers.

"How do you know?" Cass, annoyed that Siobhan knows more than she does.

Siobhan shrugs. "An educated guess."

"Very educated," Delilah digs.

"But she's right." I'm as sure as I've ever been of anything in my life. "Fagan's buried here." Da's place of earth and stone.

Then Siobhan tells us that, at my request, she called several U.S.

government agencies and checked all their available archives. She also made some calls to her colleagues and professors at Trinity College, Dublin, to check any records that might relate to Fagan's situation.

"No passport was ever issued for Fagan Marie Sheehan to leave the USA, nor any visa issued for her to stay in Ireland," she says. "No records exist of her ever having lived or died in Cullyhanna."

Important facts, yes, but irrelevant by now.

"We couldn't overpower Flanna."

"How old were you?" asks Delilah.

"Nine," answers Patty, the great historian. "She would have been nine, and Eden and Alberta, twelve and eleven."

The twins hold each other, weeping about what they did or didn't suspect or know, and why and how it happened. But I cannot imagine ever having been so young, or having known what I knew then, at an age when my own daughters worried only about pretty dresses, Brownies, learning to write cursive, and how to read and dance.

"How could she have gotten away with it?" Delilah, full of doubt. Like her sisters, she grew up in a world where more or less everything made sense.

"These days, giving your kid a well-earned smack on the bottom can get you into trouble," adds Cass, speaking from experience, I assume, given the proclivities of her ex.

"Away with it?" says Siobhan. "They weren't seen as doing anything wrong. They were fighting a mortal battle."

"Da must have carried Fagan to his mother's, maybe hoping Nana could save her." I say this, my theory, but I wonder how he did it, how he found her, and if he carried her—or whatever was left of her, Fagan having been silenced now at last—the way he'd carried me when I broke my arm, his chest heaving against her like a bellows.

"Too late," says Siobhan.

"Nana would have called a doctor," says Patty. "She did things by the book. She played by the rules."

"Not exactly," Jo argues. "She'd never have called the police." Nana, like most of the other immigrants, was terrified of the authorities. "But a doctor . . ."

"An Irish doctor," interrupts Siobhan, "one who understood the old ways."

"The one who treated Alberta's burn." Me. "Who set my wrist." Yes, a healer who understood the old ways, who kneeled in his own garden, near a statue of the Virgin and the vanquished serpent.

"Somebody who understood that such an accident, under certain circumstances, was possible, maybe even inevitable." Siobhan. "That Flanna was only trying to make the faeries let her go."

"So now we know where Fagan is." Cassandra.

"We know where Fagan is at last." Me, though I'd known, without knowing that I knew, this entire time. Almost sixty years.

Keeley and the twins bless themselves and start to pray. *Our Father who art in heaven . . . Hallowed be thy name . . .* and the rest of us join them, on the street in front of the house where we used to live together. Yes, Fagan's little bones, whatever was left of her, are buried under the detached garage, in Da's place of earth and stone. The rest, whatever else happened, is smoky wisps, but I'm pretty sure I've avoided Geraldo's fate, ridicule and laughter. My vault of memory, in spite of areas of atrophy, holds more than dust bunnies and an empty whiskey bottle.

Thirty-eight

SUMMER
WIND

When we get back to the beach, the tide is coming in. We see it, creeping up across the sand toward the last line of debris. Cassandra takes off her heels and strides across the sand, looking out toward the shipyard, heading toward the staircase to our first house. Delilah, barefoot too, follows. I'm afraid they'll climb it, bang on the back door, introduce themselves to the current owners. Instead, they sit together on the next-to-bottom step, and the twins join them there.

Keeley, Siobhan, and I walk over and sit below them, on the bottom step, our feet in the sand. All seven of us are scrunched here, where we have no right to be, looking at the water, like we're waiting for high tide in summer, so we can jump in and splash around.

We sit there, enjoying the sunlight, the promising spring breeze layered over our sorrow. I feel twenty years younger and at least twenty pounds lighter. Yes, me, Maire Sheehan Malloy, known to all—even to God Himself—as Mimi, has solved an ancient mystery. She stumbled around for ages before she discovered the correct path, stunned to realize it had been right in front of her the entire time. Along the way, she fell down, but got back up again. Scorched, scarred, damaged in a million different ways, but still with her warm heart intact. Her hungry heart, A-fib and all, now satisfied.

"Da lied," somebody says, and the rest of us murmur agreement. We lived a lie. We had to live a lie, but didn't understand it. An ancient betrayal, but one that's easier to forgive here in the bright light, looking out over the water toward the shipyard where he toiled year after year for us.

"May he rest in peace," says Jo. "And Fagan, too."

"May perpetual light shine upon them." Patty.

"And on Eden and Alberta." My old sweethearts, who bore witness to Fagan's death with me. I see their weaknesses and their failures in a new light, a perpetual light, the same one in which I see myself; the three of us running back upstairs, hiding in our bed, burying what we'd seen.

"Their lives never went anywhere but down," says Patty.

"No matter how hard we held on to them." Jo.

"I didn't hold on tight enough." Me.

"You held on as tight as you could, Mimi," says Cassandra of all people, defending me. "What else could you have done?"

Cassandra reaches for me, massages my shoulders, a technique she learned in one of her therapies. She reaches below several layers of crust, maybe to the real place, where the two of us, my firstborn and me, will forever be connected. I glance down, see that her bright acrylic talons are gone. In their place, the small pink, white-tipped nails she was born with. I touch her fingernails, my firstborn, the everlasting thorn in my side. Always there. Loyal as a puppy. Day after day she looks out for me. I squeeze her hand, realize I'm a lucky woman. Even though I've yet to say it out loud.

"Flanna . . . Flanna with her herbs and whiskey," says Jo.

"Her prayers and incantations." Patty.

"Her two faces, and her eyes for getting lost in." Me.

"A healer," says Keeley, her voice soft. "A *cailleach*. A wise woman with special powers from the countryside where the faeries lived."

"A *cailleach*," I repeat, the word sticking in my gullet.

"I thought she was my mother." Keeley, paler than I've ever seen her, and trembling like a leaf. "You saved me, Mimi. You saved us, all of us. You got us out of there."

But I never once thought of it that way. Ever. Couldn't see anything but shadows. Couldn't feel anything, not even pain.

"Your episodes," says Delilah. "Now I get it, Mimi. You weren't kidding. They were real."

"The source of them, all those repressed memories." Cassandra massages me some more, getting even closer.

"Well, next time you see your father, you might pass this info on to him. That he wasn't married to your ordinary nut job." Everybody laughs, because Jack will never be convinced.

Now my sisters, both living and dead, surround us, murmuring that there was nothing else we could have done, any of us, to save Fagan from Flanna's madness; her conviction that Fagan was a changeling, left behind by the faeries who kidnapped the real one. *Come away, O human child . . .* We had to save ourselves. A small breeze blows up off the water, then turns and gusts away. Forgiveness. Yes, we forgive our father, Joey Sheehan, forgive him his trespasses, his failures; forgive him for falling so hard and so far below the occasion of his own life. Da loved us, oh, he loved us all—he loved too much, but this love of his could not save us. Daddy. Da. Who knew how to work hard, and did work hard, but didn't know how to manage his feelings or his family. Poor old Da. No, a correction: just poor Da, who never got to be old like me. He did the best he could.

Forgive me, for I have sinned. Me, myself, and I, Mimi Malloy. *Yes, I, too, have sinned.* Fagan, in agony or joy, flies away. An ember in the wind, the soul's eternal life. Beside her are my sidekicks, Eden and Alberta, the top of the line. They're content, I feel it, all three of them together, at peace, at last.

Thirty-nine

ALL THIS AND
HEAVEN TOO

Siobhan drives me home, back over the Fore River Bridge, the water below clear and sparkling, the banks and bars and boat-yards just as ugly as before, gray and brown, grimed by the elements. We've traded places, my kid and I. She drives the Shadow while I settle down, thinking about all that's happened, the ancient lies and secrets, the tragedy of Fagan's death. Deep inside me, I feel a sense of resolution if not an absolution. Closure. Another word I hate, but I'll take it anyway. And at the last possible minute. Who'd a thunk it?

Instead of black spots, my mind is full of light and laughter, balloons and cotton candy, like Nantasket Beach at night, everybody having the time of their life. I make a mental note to call that snotty brain guy. Order more maps. And I'll bet my life that they'll be brighter this time, full of swirls of color, those areas of atrophy transformed.

I reach into my pocket for the blue pendant, take it out, look at it. As we drive back to Paul Revere, another memory spills out from its sparkle, one I'd buried along with the rest of the shame and sorrow surrounding my da's death and Fagan's disappearance. While Siobhan drives, I tell her about those awful empty days after Da died, the summer of 1937.

"Nana seemed hollowed out and shrunken, and she never did recover. Not unlike Alberta in the next generation, after losing Danny. Couldn't get over the loss of her begotten son.

"One afternoon Nana brought me outside and she sat me beside her on the wooden bench Da built for her. We sat there for a long time, looking at the flowers, the statue of the Virgin, and behind them, the potting shed, the compost heap. She would have known, though I did not, that that's where Fagan was buried. She pressed something into my hand.

" 'Your father wanted you to have this,' she said. I looked down and saw the bright-blue pendant, the color of Da's eyes. 'He brought this over, the night before he died, but he was in his cups, and I wouldn't let him see you.' I nodded, not letting on what I'd seen.

" 'You know, Maire, he started out the best of them, but life didn't go his way.' She wasn't looking at me, instead dropping the blue pendant into its little velvet pouch. She held my hand when she passed it to me. She held it for a long time, the closest she would ever get. She warned me not to tell my sisters, because Da didn't leave anything for them. 'He didn't have anything else to give.' "

When we get to Paul Revere, Siobhan parks in my space up front, and we get out to say good-bye so she can go to her own car. I take Siobhan's hand, the way Nana had taken mine. I press the blue pendant into it. She tries to give it back, but I won't take it.

"Get that scratch fixed, will you please?"

I see the pouch in my daughter's hand and feel it's found its home. She will be its guardian.

Siobhan doesn't speak. She kisses my cheek, then turns and hurries to her own car. I glimpse her heart before she turns. Hers, too, is right where it's supposed to be. Scarred perhaps, but beating strong, glowing, full of life. I watch her go, my brainy kid. She'll be the protector of our heirloom—singular, not plural—Da's wedding gift to Mam, water and paste, the best he could afford. Siobhan will be the keeper of our stories.

Forty

GOT THE WORLD
ON A STRING

I cannot wait to see Paul Newman, aka Dick Duffy. Of course I love my sisters and my daughters, but we're too much sometimes. Girls, girls, and more girls. *I enjoy being a girl* . . .

No, I can't wait to see Paul Newman, because I have so much to tell him, so much I want to share. Plus, I really do feel twenty pounds lighter and twenty years younger, and I wonder if he'll notice. Don't have long to wait. He shows up just after dusk, knocking, and calling through the door, Oh, Mrs. Malloy. We're back to Mrs. Malloy, which strikes me as funny. I laugh as I open the door.

"What happened?" he asks as soon as he lays eyes on me. "Something's different." His comment tickles me. I pull him inside, and as we heat up the leftovers, mostly Chow Mei Fun, I give the details of all that happened in Weymouth, how great it feels to at last have some closure. I even use that awful word. "Closure."

"Like this huge weight has been lifted, even though my sister's buried under the garage at my grandmother's old house. Even though our stepmother killed her."

We take our plates to my table by the window, turn on the TV: *Family Feud*, with Richard Dawson doing the Big Bucks Challenge.

"Isn't it great he's back?" I ask, nodding toward the TV. Richard Dawson, I mean.

"You bet. I couldn't stand that other one."

I continue with the saga of all that happened, not just in the past, but today. News to Duffy, all that faerie business, and he's engrossed by my story, just the way I want him to be. Now I know, or at least feel, that I won't be an awful burden to him if we keep our relationship together, dragging around my ancient baggage.

"Let's go over to Quincy City Hall tomorrow," says Duffy. "As long as everything's quiet here. And there aren't any emergencies."

"Why? For what?" Good Lord, I'm thinking, I hope not a marriage license. I'm not close to being ready. He chuckles in that way he has, as though he's able to read my thoughts. So embarrassing.

"Oh, Mrs. Malloy, the records room, what else?" He grins, the tease. "We'll go to the records room and find your sister's documents, her birth and death certificates, for that all-important genealogy."

"Too late. It's done, handed in for a C+," I say, but then look at him again, like he's some kind of genius. Of course we ought to gather all those records. "Why didn't I think of that? Documented family history, in archives just down the street."

"We can get them for your whole family, at least for anyone who was born or died in Quincy."

"No job is finished until the paperwork is done." That's what I taught my girls way back when, during toilet training.

"Nope, no job is finished until the paperwork is done." Duff laughs. "It will be nice to have those."

Duffy himself is an expert in documents, practically a lawyer after all the legal work he's done for Chris. Duffy, a widower, a combat vet with an old war wound, a man who rose to the occasion of his own life, even the terrible part about his son. And now he's fighting for his son's redemption, or at least the slim hope of redemption, having already earned his own. At least in my book, anyway. Duffy's earned his own.

"So we'll go look for the birth and death certificates?"

"'Primary documents,' my brainy kid Siobhan would call them."

Then I tell him there's another loose end I want to tie up. He raises an eyebrow while munching on the noodles.

"I want to talk to Malvina in the Bronx. I don't even know her sons."

He pauses, shrugs. "Go for it, Mimi, call her," he says. "Right now."

And so I do; I find her number in my book, and punch in the numbers, area code 718. It rings five times. This time the answering machine clicks on. A boy's voice—Rafael or Judah? I can't tell, wouldn't know who was who even if I saw them, because I've never seen or spoken to them, not since Rafael was a newborn.

"You've reached the Malloy-Sosa household," says a happy little voice. I swear to God, a trumpet and a clarinet are playing in the background. "You know what to do. We promise to get back to you."

You know what to do. . . .

"This is Mimi," I say, "Mimi Malloy, your grandmother. I just wanted to say hello." I leave my number, and hang up, trembling. Duffy hugs me, a nice strong hug. Doesn't say a thing.

"I hope they keep their promise," I say.

"Promise?"

"You know, to get back to me."

"They'll do what they'll do," he says. We reach for the fortune cookies we didn't eat the other night. I read mine, " 'A well-aimed sword is worth three.' "

" 'It takes more than good memory to have good memories,' " reads Duffy.

"For real?" I grab his paper strip. Sure enough—*It takes more than good memory to have good memories.* Our eyes meet and we laugh. *A well-aimed sword.* We laugh some more.

This is when, in the past—our supper finished, our bellies full—we'd light up. No more. I'm wearing a transdermal smoking cessation patch, and Duffy has one too. Per instructions, we've applied them to the "clean, dry, hairless skin" on the inside of our forearms.

"Hangin' in?" He nods toward my patch, which I'm rubbing, as if trying to squeeze out more nicotine.

"Hangin' in," I answer. He takes my hand, sending me some strength. "I keep thinking how happy my girls and my sisters will be when I tell them."

Then Duffy turns on the TV, to the Weather Channel. On the screen, a map of the USA, colors swirl with storm systems and high-pressure areas moving this way and that. North, east, south, and west. The map looks the way the inside of my head feels right now, the black spots shrunken up, beautiful colors swirling over them, a vast and gorgeous landscape ripe with possibility.

"Whoa, looky-looky." Duff gestures to the screen with the remote.

"'Looky-looky'?" I echo. "One bowl of Chow Mei Fun and you start to talk Chinese?" He laughs.

"No, check out the weather map. Tomorrow is going to be perfect for a boat ride."

Both of us watch the screen.

"Hey, Mrs. Malloy, what say we save City Hall for another day? Instead, tomorrow, we'll go over to the *Miss Nomer*. We'll get her ready for the water. Get you ready for your maiden voyage."

"An offer I can't refuse." I lean in close to him so I can feel his warmth.

"Have you thought about where you want to go? I mean, on your first boat ride? Wherever you'd like. Your wish is my command."

One of Duffy's favorite phrases, my wish being his command.

"Under the bridge. The Fore River. I want to ride on all that water under the bridge."

He cracks up. He gets me. As I get him. Then I see the two of us, on Duffy's gleaming Chris-Craft—his cabin cruiser, the *Miss Nomer*, gliding out across the sparkling water. We'll speed around the shipyard, to the basin, where we might glimpse Nana's house and, on the bluff, the sweet cottage Jack built for me a lifetime ago. We'll turn back around on that water under the bridge. After that, we'll head out to the open Atlantic. Who knows where we'll go from there.

ACKNOWLEDGMENTS

I gratefully acknowledge my editor, Elizabeth Bruce, such a gifted one, endowed with all the qualities writers long for in their editors: intelligence, warmth, perspicacity, generosity, and mad skills with the line edit. Thank you.

Also, my agent, Janet Rosen of Sheree Bykofsky Associates, Inc., a woman of wit and passion, a lover of great sentences and stories, a tireless advocate for those whose work she believes in. (A very special thank-you, too, to Sheree for finding me at that writers' conference!)

Last, *mil gracias* to the Geraldine R. Dodge Foundation for funding a residency at the Virginia Center for the Creative Arts, where a first draft of *Mimi* was completed.